A SURVEY OF COUNSELING METHODS

THE DORSEY SERIES IN PSYCHOLOGY
Advisory Editors
Wendell E. Jeffrey
University of California, Los Angeles
Salvatore R. Maddi
The University of Chicago

A survey of counseling methods

SAMUEL H. OSIPOW
W. BRUCE WALSH
DONALD J. TOSI

all of The Ohio State University

1980 THE DORSEY PRESS
Homewood, Illinois 60430
Irwin-Dorsey Limited
Georgetown, Ontario L7G 4B3

ISBN 0-256-02189-9
Library of Congress Catalog Card No. 79–54418

Printed in the United States of America

1 2 3 4 5 6 7 8 9 0 ML 7 6 5 4 3 2 1

Preface

Our basic purpose in writing this text was to bring together in an understandable and interesting style a general survey of the counseling field. Such a purpose obviously had implication not only for content but also for writing style. We did our best to communicate in an understandable and interesting style, but you the reader must be the judge of our success.

In terms of the content of the book, we initially discuss the history and background of counseling, what counselors do and the nature of their professional work environments, the theories of counseling, and the counseling relationship. A second phase of the book focuses on diagnosis and assessment in counseling with some emphasis on the role of psychological inventories and tests in counseling and planned behavioral change. A third phase of the text is concerned with the use of counseling in a group situation, for educational or vocational development, and in a variety of other special applications (sex, marital, family, substance abuse, crisis intervention, and rehabilitation counseling). The fourth and final phase of the text takes a good look at the outcomes of counseling and psychotherapy and discusses the issues, ethics, and future trends of counseling.

A word is due about the heterogeneous orientations of the authors. Not only do we possess divergent theoretical orientations, but also different value systems, especially in terms of the "therapeutic" aspects of counseling. We tried to write about topics of concern to professional counselors. Sometimes the language describing these concerns seems more "therapeutic" (translate: clinical) than some of us prefer. Nevertheless, we bowed to common usage, although with misgivings.

We owe thanks to many people and many authors and remain convinced that our thoughts and writing have been much influenced by them. Our families are pleased, as we are, that the task is completed. Our sincere thanks are due Sally Wilcox for her careful attention to the preparation of the manuscript.

We sincerely hope that this text will assist and be of value to potential counselors, counselors in training, and practicing professional helpers and contribute to a more intelligent understanding of the counseling field.

December 1979   Samuel H. Osipow
                                                  W. Bruce Walsh
                                                  Donald J. Tosi

Contents

070874

Counseling: Major psychological disorders. Psychotic behavior. Psychotic behavior: An instance of a counselor interacting with a person exhibiting acute paranoid schizophrenic symptoms. Statistical approaches to the diagnosis of psychotic behavior. Counseling strategies for psychotic reactions. Psychoneurotic behavior. Neurotic behavior: An example of a counselor with a person exhibiting obsessive-compulsive symptoms. Counseling strategies for the neuroses. Psychophysiological disorders. Counseling approaches to psychophysiological disorders. Transient situational disorders. Counseling strategies for transient situational disorders. Limitations of diagnostic classifications. Family, marital, and sex counseling. Marital counseling. Sex counseling. Sex counseling and programming. Family counseling. Substance abuse counseling. Classifying alcohol problems. Criteria for the diagnosis of alcoholism. Drug dependence. Counseling approaches. Community resources. Rehabilitation counseling. Characteristics of rehabilitation counselors. Crises intervention counseling.

Is counseling effective? Problems in outcome research. Conflicts of interest. Counseling in social institutions. Kinds of counselors. Professionalism. Licenses and certification. Standards. Training and credentialing. Private practice. Continuing education for professionals. New roles and settings for counselors. The counselor as a consultant. Career counseling. The counselor in the medical setting. Counseling in legal settings. Counselors' role in social policy development. Family and marriage counseling. Human resource needs for counselors. Problems in counseling. Relations with other professions.

Introduction

It is generally agreed that modern-day life in Western industrialized countries is stressful in ways that were unknown to our forebears. We know that people in earlier days had problems. However, it is reasonable to assume that the nature of our grandparents' problems, and the resources available to them to deal with those problems, were sufficiently distinctive to expect that a comparison of their stresses and ours would reflect qualitative as well as quantitative differences. During recent years, society has developed a variety of institutions to help individuals cope effectively with their more complicated lives. The mental health professions represent one of these helping institutions, and counseling psychology is one aspect of and an integral part of them.

Modern Western society is complex. Being composed of a conglomerate of social subunits living uneasily with one another, numerous social and psychological problems, stresses, and strains on the individual are apparent. Our forebears, too, had problems of psychological and physical survival, perhaps no worse than or different from ours.

One of their means of dealing with personal and environmental stress included the real possibility of escape to the "frontier," with its fresh start and social as well as geographic distance from others. Such "second chances" are much harder to generate in late 20th-century America than they were a century earlier.

One result of the complexity of our society is that people are faced with a multitude of decisions. While the availability of the options underlying decisions is desirable, in that it represents freedom and the opportunity for self-actualization, the freedom of choice is in itself a burden (Fromm, 1941).

Choices and decisions create discomforts. What to choose, how to predict the outcome, how to deal with the anxiety associated with the possibility of undesirable outcomes of choice, and how to implement choices once made, are but some examples of stresses produced by the availability of options in a mobile society. People are required to make decisions about friendships, school subjects, value systems, schools to attend, careers to prepare for, jobs to aspire to or to accept or reject, potential mates, geographic locations, and many other issues. Toffler (1970) believes that since an excess of options may place a heavy burden upon the individual, some people simply choose to ignore or to blot out many of the options open to them, thereby reducing the array of choices to manageable proportions.

Another issue distinguishing our culture from those of an earlier time has to do with the consequences of geographic mobility. The most obvious result of geographic mobility in the United States is social and personal alienation and isolation. Many people come and go almost unnoticed; friendships are initiated quickly and superficially, and are soon forgotten after one party moves on. Many people, therefore, have questioned the value of being human and the authenticity of interpersonal relationships. Because meaningful interaction with significant others are often absent, people do not understand each other and find it hard to predict the behavior of their contemporaries. Who is honest and who is a scoundrel? Who is reliable and who is not? Who is sensitive and understanding and who is brutish?

An even more tragic consequence of geographic mobility is the physical, and often psychological, isolation from one's family. Children and grandparents remain strangers, cousins never meet, and siblings drift apart. All this contributes further to a lack of identity, a failure to know one's roots and feel confident in them.

Paradoxically, at the same time we seem to be strangers to one another, the communications networks of television, radio, and the printed word would seem to bring a sense of greater intimacy with each other. This media-produced intimacy may be more apparent than real.

For what the communication media do is allow us to observe social, economic, political, and personal events in the lives of others without a sense of personal involvement. Among other things, until we are not shocked by it, we may be brutalized through an overexposure to the human race's cruelty to itself, a point made in connection with the nightly news viewing of the Vietnam war during the 1960s.

The media graphically depict various lifestyles that differ greatly from one another and from our own, thus opening up new lifestyle options and further decisions to individuals already overloaded with decisional options. However, the media may further encourage a superficial and detached style of interpersonal relations, one in which the observer may feel closer to the person seen on television who is really 6,000 miles away than to the individual who lives in the adjacent apartment; in fact, the observer may not have significant interpersonal relations with either individual.

As a result of the greater exposure of the world to individuals because of the communications media, people are more clearly aware of the relative basis of morality and the existence of numerous and often divergent moral and value systems than formerly. Religion is not interpreted as in earlier times: its principles guide people in looser and redefined ways; existential philosophies orient people to gaining their satisfactions in the present rather than in an ill-defined future, which, in the nuclear age, has romantically and vaguely been assumed to be "tentative" at best. While some individuals cope with the decisions, the anxieties, and the questions of values and morals by denial, that is, by ignoring the issues as best they can, others are increasingly concerned with self-exploration and self-awareness, in hopes that, by somehow plunging into studying their feelings and emotions, they will develop a self-understanding that will both help them to make consistent and integrated decisions as well as to understand and relate to other individuals in improved ways.

In brief, one of the most articulated complaints to result from the stressful and complex social conditions just described—that is, the complexity of life, its decisions, the physical strains, the worries about the future, questions about morality, interpersonal inhumanity and degradation, crowding, and the apparent unpredictability and strangeness of others—is a sense of alienation from society and from other individuals. This translates itself into such statements as "I can't get it all together" or "I feel out of touch."

Lack of identity is the term sometimes used to describe the feeling some people experience when they are confused and anxious. People then search to find meaning in life, to be "secure" in some way in what is essentially an insecure existence and to relate in satisfying ways to others, to have a sense of their goals, and to possess a feeling that in one's strivings to have meaningful relationships and to understand ourselves and others we may potentially defeat ourselves. The actualization of one's potentials is by no means easy.

The picture portrayed is overdrawn for illustration, but may, in fact, approximate the situation faced by many in our society. While large numbers of people do not give full expression to their feelings, and while the intensity of concerns and feelings vary from individual to individual and from time to time within the same individual, the resulting difficulties represent a significant aspect of life in late 20th-century Western society.

A significant social response to help deal with these feelings and concerns are the many "helping professions" that have grown up since the 1930s. These include counseling and clinical psychology, social work, psychiatry, rehabilitation, school counseling, and school psychology—to name a few. These specialities generally try to deal with some of the stresses of life by applying scientifically based expertise to human behavior. Formerly, many of these social services were provided informally by family members, friends, and business associates. Professionals enter the scene mainly because methods have become sophisticated, people have less access to sympathetic family members and friends, and the stresses themselves are becoming more pervasive and intense, thus affecting more people more severely.

Why know about counseling?

The preceding discussion contains a number of clues about the usefulness of knowledge about the work of counselors. Most obvious is that nearly everyone is likely to need or desire the services of a counselor personally, or for a family member *or friend* at some time. In fact, it is very likely that the professional services of a counselor will be sought more than once by most people, particularly in times of transition across life stages and roles. For instance, when an individual moves from high school to college, from college to a job, from being single to married, into becoming a parent for the first time, or moving into retirement, counseling services can be especially helpful. In these instances one is often forced to either exhibit new behaviors and attitudes or to use old ones in new situations in ways that may not be easy to perform. At such times, the help of a behavioral specialist is useful, if not critical, to a person's well-being.

Counseling functions are already available in our culture and are becoming more accessible. What may pose a potential problem to the naive consumer of psychological services is the inability to differentiate from among the many types of services offered. It is of great importance that the consumer be able to assess and evaluate psychological services in terms of their usefulness, so that harmful efforts to obtain service do not persist. Thus, the more an individual knows about counseling—its philosophical, theoretical, and empirical bases, its goals, the various methods associated with them, the qualifications of its practitioners, and the appropriate criteria to be used in its evaluation—the more likely that individual will be able to select services well and at appropriate times.

A second context within which an individual might want to become more systematically knowledgeable about counseling is when working in a professional field which, at times, appropriately requires making referrals to counseling services. A faculty member might develop close relationships with students, and, as a result, at times be in a position to make useful referrals of some students to counselors; legal officials find that it is more appropriate at times to help individuals find counseling help than to proceed with formal legal action. At such times sophisticated knowledge about counseling is more than just helpful.

A third and somewhat related reason for having familiarity with the counseling profession is to permit sophisticated consultation with counselors and counseling agencies to improve one's own professional effectiveness with people. For instance, someone in the clergy might wish to discuss a parishoner with a counselor to decide whether counseling by the clergy is appropriate, whether that parishoner should be referred, or how the cleric's own behavior might be changed to be more useful to the parishoner. Or, a supervisor might consult a counseling specialist to get some suggestions about the ways available to improve and interact with a particular subordinate whose response to one leadership style is not positive. Another example might include a manager considering organizational redesign who might want to take interpersonal relationships into account in reshaping the structure of work in the organization. In these examples, society recognizes the complexity of life and the notion that professional knowledge may be required to understand and to deal effectively with that phenomena. The professional counselor may work directly with an individual or indirectly through a significant third party who is in a position to influence another individual in important ways.

Finally, a fourth reason for wanting to know more about counseling is that increasing numbers of individuals are themselves considering the possibility of becoming professional counselors. The counseling profession has many facets; the term *counselor* is confusing in that it often refers to activities of such diverse workers as the attorney, the social worker, the psychologist, the stockbroker, the camp leader, and school guidance personnel.

No group has territorial rights over the term *counselor;* it can be useful to restrict the title "counselor" to a behavioral specialist trained to apply psychological principles to the analysis and understanding of human behavior and the means to modify it. Such a focus emphasizes the psychological counselor, whose work overlaps to some extent with the clincial psychologist on the one hand and with the school guidance worker on the other. The student considering a career in counseling should, after some exposure to the concepts, methods, and examples of counseling described in this volume, be in an informed position about the work that counselors perform.

What is counseling and what do counselors do?

The previous discussion stressed the contexts in which counseling occurs. In addition, to understand what underlies various counseling procedures and how they work, it is necessary to know the most important and influential theories of counseling, the concepts which form a part of those theories, the techniques associated with the theories and concepts, and general counseling methods. Moreover, you need to know who counsels, where it is done, what the various types of counseling are like, the circumstances under which a particular type is appropriate, and on what basis and how to evaluate counseling outcomes.

What counselors do. Counseling activities are usually categorized into five basic functions: individual counseling, assessment of individuals and their environment, program development and consultation, research and training, and supervision.

Individual counseling. Individual counseling is considered the heart of the counseling function. This role is perhaps the most visible aspect of the counselor's work and what most people think of when they imagine a counselor at work. Individual counseling involves a one-to-one interaction between a counselor and a client, where the object is to either aid the client to solve some problem, to find ways to use personal qualities more effectively, or to make an important life decision.

Individual counseling is frequently divided into three subtypes: personal adjustment counseling, educational counseling, and career counseling. Recognize at the outset that these three types of counseling are not independent of one another. Human concerns rarely separate themselves into neat compartments. Individual counseling that emphasizes personal concerns very often has a substantial vocational or educational component, and vocational counseling frequently must deal with significant personal concerns.

Personal adjustment counseling emphasizes individual emotional responses to emotionally laden situations. Here, the counselor is concerned with helping the individual to identify behaviors toward other people that do not achieve their objective. Sometimes the counselor strives to identify troublesome interpersonal stimuli in the client's environment, so that the client can either try to avoid them or deal directly with them more satisfactorily.

Verbal methods are usually used in personal adjustment counseling. The counselor and the client meet in an interview setting in which the client airs concerns, and the counselor helps to identify the key elements and a series of ways to deal with the client's problems. The main procedures used involve the client and counselor discussing the things that are bothering the client.

Educational counseling typically refers to either of two sets of concerns. One set deals with improving a student's efficiency and adequacy in scholastic achievement. Here we consider learning difficulties, reading problems, difficulties in concentration, learning skills, such as listening in lectures, time management, note-taking, and the consideration of motivational barriers to learning. Also, sometimes educational counseling can help increase the learning efficiency of a student who is already achieving satisfactorily but who has the potential to perform even better than at present.

The second aspect of educational counseling deals with matters of choice and planning. What courses to study, where to go to school, and what programs of study to pursue fall into this category.

Career counseling overlaps somewhat with educational counseling. Career counseling concerns issues dealing mainly with choices: curriculum as it relates to occupational outcomes; choice of career area following an educational specification; or possibly, help in narrowing a set of position choices down to one when entering the labor market for the first time. Career counselors also help people to deal with mid-career changes, career adjustments resulting from physical or psychological trauma that interferes with one's primary work, and adjustment to retirement, to name a few examples. To a lesser extent, career counseling can help people identify gratifying career pathways and objectives, and the behaviors necessary to implement them. These activities parallel the work of the educational counselor who assists individuals to use their talents to achieve higher results in school. The career counselor attempts to encourage a client to use talents more efficiently and directly in attaining stated occupational goals.

Naturally, although the previous discussion refers to "the career counselor," "the educational counselor," or "the personal adjustment counselor," all three counselors are usually combined in one person. This professional must have skills and knowledge in all three areas to function effectively in working with clients. The particular emphasis is frequently determined by the setting within which the counselor works and the nature of client problems the setting attracts.

Counselors spend much of their professional time in individual consultation with clients. These consultations may be for any or all of the purposes implied in personal, educational, or career counseling described above. The nature of the individual interaction in counseling is different from ordinary social intercourse in some very important ways. In nonprofessional interpersonal relations there is typically a balance between the parties. The personal needs of both parties are considered, and to some extent met, in ordinary social relations. Each party makes an effort to relate with interest to the other person's affairs and concerns. At any given moment, the balance might vary; but over the long run, both parties have their needs met or the relationship terminates if it is unsatisfactory.

In the professional individual relationship typical in counseling, however, certain significant differences exist from those found in the ordinary social interchange between two people. In counseling, one party is seen to have some knowledge or expertise that is potentially useful to the other. Also, one party is "using" the other (in the best sense of the term "use"), to help deal with a set of problems or concerns. Thus, the personal and psychological need satisfaction available in the relationship tends to be "one way" rather than reciprocal. Among the results of the one-way nature of the relationship is that it has structure in terms of when and where the parties meet, the duration of their meetings, the content of the discussions during their meetings, the ratio of talk of each party (usually the client talks more than the counselor), and certain ground rules about matters such as who is responsible for what in the interview and about privacy of communication.

Several important counselor skills for individual counseling exist. The counselor needs to possess skill in interpersonal communication; in particular, counselors need to present the appearance of "expertness" and "trustworthiness" (Schmidt & Strong, 1970; Strong & Schmidt, 1970a, 1970b) as well as to display what Truax and Carkhuff (1967) have called "congruence, empathy, and positive regard" for clients.

The counselor must also possess skills in paying attention to client behavior: sifting the significant from the less significant and behaving in a manner encouraging the client to display increasing amounts of those behaviors deemed to be significant (e.g., Ivey, 1971).

Moreover, the counselor must be well acquainted with a body of knowledge that permits data-based conclusions to be made about human behavior. These conclusions must be relevant to client problems and concerns and to ways in which the counselor can help clients function more effectively *in their own* terms as well as in those of the counselor.

In sum, the counselor needs to be skillful in listening and communicating, as well as understanding and acceptance as a result of that listening. In addition, certain knowledge about human behavior is necessary to interpret the information gathered from listening in order to better understand the meaning of the client's behavior and the significant events controlling it.

Assessment of the individual and the environment. Individual counseling is change oriented. Considerable behavioral information is gained about the client through individual interaction. A major role of the applied psychologist has traditionally been individual assessment. Recently, individual assessment has taken several new forms; besides the well-established procedure of administering, scoring, and interpreting standardized tests of ability, and personality and interest inventories, the behavioral approach to counseling has reintroduced observational methods. These observational methods derive from the principle that the overt behaviors that clients engage in are of great significance not only in understanding the client but also in connection with verifying the frequency, intensity, duration, and pervasiveness of client behaviors (Kanfer & Saslow, 1965; 1969; Osipow & Walsh, 1970).

Both trait-oriented measures and behavioral inventories assume that people will and can respond truthfully and accurately. If the client's responses do not meet this assumption, then, of course, the data generated will be worse than useless; they may be misleading. However, steps can be taken to increase client ability to observe and report behaviors accurately, and these steps form yet another aspect of the counselor's role in the assessment function. The counselor should be prepared to teach clients how to observe critical events in their environment along with the frequency and qualitative aspects of these events and their responses to them.

A corollary of the new methods of individual observation is environmental assessment, a legitimate task for the counselor. Environmental assessment is typically conducted along dimensions that correspond to those of individual assessment. This permits the counselor to make inferences about those situational events that may be reinforcing certain client behaviors, as well as to make inferences about responses by the individual that may be elicited by the environment. Such information may be highly important to the counselor in identifying situational components that may be significantly and undesirably affecting a client. Thus, the counselor may decide to try to alter the environmental impact to improve a client's responses, rather than to try to change the client's behavior in an unhealthy environment. The counselor needs to know several kinds of information about assessment and have certain skills to be well qualified, such as:

1. Knowledge of the criteria for evaluating the technical adequacy of a test or inventory.
2. Skill in observing behavior and identifying important personal elements and environmental influences.
3. Skill in putting clients at ease during testing.

Program development and consultation. The role of environmental assessment leads to the third major counselor function, program development and consultation. Counselors do more than meet with individuals to discuss significant life events, feelings, and behavior. A recent and increasing emphasis has been in connection with the counselor's interaction with the design of institutions and programs. It is possible to think of the work of counselors in terms of three dimensions: the correction of deficiencies and problems in the behavior of individuals (remediation); helping people find ways to avoid developing ineffective behavior (prevention); and devising methods to enhance the ability of individuals to fully apply their special attributes (facilitation). The three —remediation, prevention, and facilitation—will be discussed more fully later; for now, it is important to note that the impact of the counselor's intervention increases in its effects as the ladder from remediation to facilitation is climbed. Individual counseling tends to emphasize remediation, though it can include aspects of prevention and facilitation. Program development tends to emphasize prevention and facilitation, though, of course, it can include remediation.

The principle behind the counselor as a program developer is based on the assumption that the lives of numerous individuals are often negatively affected by the institutions within which they live. Sometimes the redesign of these institutions would be more likely to produce desirable individual changes than would continued individual counseling, which is aimed at helping the individual function slightly better in an institutional setting that elicits maladaptive responses by its very structure (Sanford, 1955).

For example, if a counselor observed that nearly all ninth-grade students were seeking counseling to correct inappropriate decisions about their school curriculum, the counselor might hypothesize that something systematic was occurring in the institutional environment that was interfering with the stability of student program choice. Since the problem appears widespread, the likelihood that the source of the problem lies outside the individual seems tenable. Upon analysis it might be found that students are required to choose from among 25 curricular options during the latter part of the eighth grade. Either the timing of these choices (eighth grade) or the number of options could be the culprit: 14-year-old students may not be capable of making highly stable choices of program from among a list of highly discrete curricula. It may be that both the timing and range of program choice would have to be changed. Perhaps students can successfully discriminate among 8 very different choices of program, but not 25; perhaps students are not mature enough to choose and must wait until they are 16 years old rather than 14. Perhaps some combination of both remedies should be considered. Such program planning might replace the counselor's attention to many individual curricular corrections. If successful, the counselor would use the resulting free time to work with students on truly individual concerns. Through such programmatic impact, the counselor's potential effect on clientele is both strengthened in intensity and expanded in scope.

A second kind of very important programmatic counseling activity involves the counselor as a group leader. The principle underlying such intervention is that clients have many concerns and experiences in common. Approaches to the solution of these difficulties in the company of similar clients with the same concerns can add a qualitative dimension to counseling services that is absent when the counselor is the only person available to the client. In other words, in discussing problems in the transition between high school and college in a counseling group of peers, a client might extend the notion of what is normative and get new ideas about how to deal with concerns from solutions others have tried and found helpful. Also, the client might provide the same service to others, an activity that can be reinforcing in itself and add to the client's own sense of self-worth, an important side benefit.

While many group counseling interventions were initially conceived to maximize the cost efficiency of counselor-client contacts (it is obviously cheaper for a counselor to see a group of six clients in two hours than one or two clients in the same two hours), and while the increase in counselor productivity can be significant through group work, the qualitative benefits of group counseling in certain circumstances are the most convincing arguments in its behalf.

Many variations on group approaches to counseling exist. Groups can be topic-centered or loosely structured; closed (one set of people from start to finish) or open (people coming and going) in terms of membership; or sequential, in terms of meeting a limited number of sessions to accomplish a particular goal or goals. The range of possible group activities is continually expanding.

A final aspect of programmatic activity for counselors is consultation with other professionals. Here, the counselor's role is a combination of educator, sounding board, information source, and methodologist. The counselor's role in this activity is based on the premise that extensive knowledge about human behavior can be helpful when applied either to individual personnel actions (for example, a manager who may be trying to solve a supervisor coordination problem), policy decisions (e.g., when should a school administrator engage in disciplinary action against a student and when should a referral for counseling be made), or program design (e.g., what are individual development considerations that should be taken into account in planning a curriculum). Frequently, the counselor is usually the most knowledgeable person, in terms of personnel psychology and human behavior, conveniently available for consultation, and also is often the individual with the best data base concerning the behavior of the people in the system that is based on personal, firsthand observation.

To work effectively as a program consultant, the counselor must know something about group process, policy making and power structures, organizational development, interpersonal influence, and effective methods of feedback to individuals about sensitive issues. The skills of the effective individual counselor are very basic to program consulting. Program consultants are usually very experienced counselors.

Research. A fourth function engaged in by counselors (usually counseling psychologists) is research and training. Traditionally, most psychologists have been extensively trained in the skills associated with empirical research. This research training emphasis is one of the particular aspects of preparation in psychology which has distinguished the professional applied psychologist from colleagues in the related professional fields, such as social work and psychiatry. The latter professions tend to train their students to deliver services, although some minimal research training may be provided to permit the practitioner to keep abreast of professional developments. It is psychology, however, that emphasizes the development of skills in research design, data analysis, and the interpretation of empirical results.

As a result of a research orientation in psychological training programs, counseling psychologists and counselors with extensive backgrounds in psychology who work in interdisciplinary applied settings, such as schools and hospitals, often find themselves cast in the leadership role in research and evaluation of services. The training they have clearly indicates greater competence in problems of research concerning the evaluation of services than their colleagues in other helping fields.

Another reason for a research emphasis in counseling psychology exists. Frequently, the only source of relevant data about the effects of counseling interventions is at the grass roots level of the practitioner. If the skillful and precise application of principles of human behavior to counseling situations is to become more sophisticated and effective, then counselors in applied settings must use their research skills to systematically examine the effects of their counseling interventions under various conditions. In this way, the research training provided to students of counseling psychology can contribute to the eventual accumulation of a set of data on which to base counseling plans.

The necessary research skills for the counselor involve knowledge of research design, statistics, instrument development, and data processing.

Supervision. Finally, counselors, as part of their obligation to the advancement of their profession, owe a certain portion of their professional time to the supervision and training of others less experienced than they. Once again, for the advanced student, there is no substitute for experience in counseling under the direct supervision of a master counselor who feeds back evaluative information about the novice counselor's behavior. Furthermore, the experience of working in the setting of a service agency can give the trainee significant understandings about the life and work of the counselor that cannot be gained through classroom methods. The combination of classroom and experiential aspects of training is essential to produce a skillful and well-rounded counselor. The classroom can provide the setting for the former; the service agency for the latter, through the provision of observational opportunities, practicum facilities, and internships. Thus, eventually many counselors are likely to find themselves in a role including training.

The supervisory role of the counselor is also commonly found in the job description. Many counselors eventually find themselves as agency directors, or as coordinators of sectional services. In these jobs, supervision and in-service training is usually expected. Moreover, with the increasing advent of paraprofessionals in mental health agencies, the counselor is further called upon to provide supervision, since a basic assumption underlying the use of paraprofessionals in the helping professions is that they are well supervised by more highly trained workers.

To be a good supervisor one must be familiar with counseling and personality theory, interviewing methods, effective use of tests and inventories, and above all, how to communicate this knowledge to the novice counselor in a supportive and unthreatening manner.

Counselors: Work settings, characteristics, and behaviors

What motivates people to become counselors or therapists? What kinds of needs do they satisfy? Why would someone want to function as a "change agent"? Some insight into these questions can be gained from the results of a study by Henry, Sims, and Spray (1971). These investigators asked psychologists, psychiatrists, and social workers about the reasons behind the selection of a general field and of a professional specialty. The most common reasons psychologists gave for selecting psychology as a field were to understand people, to help people, and to understand and help themselves. Psychiatrists said they chose their field to gain an identity, to gain professional status, and to meet practical pressures. Social workers reported their career choice was motivated by the desire to help people, to achieve affiliation with others, and to understand people and to help themselves, while psychologists reported a greater desire to gain professional status.

In another effort to understand the motivations of "helpers," Milk and Abeler (1965) hypothesized that to be helpful, a counselor must experience a need to help as well as a need to be with other people. In a study to test the hypothesis, Milk and Abeler (1971) found a positive association between liking clients and the nurturance need (wanting to help people) and the affiliation need (enjoying working with others) with beginning students. However, these findings did not hold for advanced graduate students or trained counselors and therapists. The results suggest that, with experience, motives to help and develop close relations with others may diminish in counselors. One possible reason for this may be the tendency for counselors to function in a variety of work settings requiring many different activities. In other words, as counselors develop professionally, they tend to move into occupational environments that may only be indirectly related to the counseling task. In the following section, counselor work environments and professional positions will be discussed more elaborately.

Work environments and professional positions

As noted in the introduction, counselors work in a variety of settings with many different types of persons. The many agencies and institutions have been grouped into five broad occupational environments by Thompson and Super (1964). Educational settings (colleges and universities, private and public schools) employ the largest number of counselors and counseling psychologists, 64 percent. Of this 64 percent, about nine out of every ten are in college and university environments. Second to educational settings are industry and government, which employ 13 percent of counseling personnel. An additional 11 percent of counselors are found in health-related settings (hospitals, rehabilitation agencies, and mental health clinics). Private practice and community counseling agencies each employ about five percent of counselors. Table 1–1 summarizes the occupational environments in which counselors and counseling psychologists work.

TABLE 1–1
Occupational environments in which counselors and counseling psychologists work

Occupational environment	Percent employed
Educational environments	64
Industry and governments environments	13
Health-related environments	11
Community counseling centers	5
Private practice	5
Other	2

Another way to get a picture of the people who practice a profession is to ask what they do (see Table 1–2). The tasks in which counseling psychologists participate most frequently are counseling, consulting, administration, teaching, and research (Jordaan, 1968). However, for the most part they participate in more than one of these activities. Thus, a counselor may teach and do research in addition to counseling students; be involved in counseling, administration, and teaching; be involved in research and consulting. In any event, about 70 percent of all counselors devote at least some time to counseling.

TABLE 1–2
What counselors do

Position held	Percent
Mainly service	38
Mainly teaching	32
Mainly service administration	23
Other	7

Most (38 percent) counselors are employed primarily in service work (counseling and consulting) (Thompson & Super, 1964). For example, the counselor in a college counseling center may teach some courses and hold academic rank, but the primary job function is service (to counsel); most of the work involves counseling students.

Approximately another 32 percent of counselors are employed in academic positions and work primarily in teaching and research. Thus, the professor of counseling psychology will teach, advise students, serve on committees, study, write, and conduct research. Research efforts are likely to deal with such areas as vocational psychology, behavior modification, interpersonal influence, the outcomes of counseling, and group counseling.

An additional 23 percent of counselors are primarily involved in administering a service agency. These counselors direct counseling centers, psychological clinics, community health centers, and student personnel services. Their primary task is administration; but they may also get involved in research, teaching, and consulting.

The final 7 percent of counselors hold a variety of positions and engage in mostly administrative tasks. These people hold such positions as dean of a college, president or vice president of a college, a research position in industry, and so on.

In general, the occupational environment in which counselors work seems to determine the professional role (Thompson & Super, 1964). Although certain competencies, functions, and interests are for the most part common to most counselors, there is great variation in what they do and how they do it. The occupational environment of the counselor determines the people with whom the counselor interacts, as well as the function, tasks, and goals of the interaction. To paraphrase B. F. Skinner, behavior is a function of the professional environment. For example, the primary behavioral task of a counselor in a college counseling center is counseling students. The counselor devotes the day to counseling college students and other individuals who are served by the center. The clients are students with problems associated with college-major choice, social life, shyness, poor grades, loneliness, depression, lack of self-identity, and inadequate self-concept. In addition to the counseling role, the counselor may teach courses and hold academic rank, but the primary function is to counsel students.

A professor of counseling psychology in an academic environment assumes a different role. Different behaviors are expected in this environment since the primary function is to train counselors. The professor will advise students, teach, serve on committees, consult, study, do research, and write. Also, it is important to keep up to date in the practice of counseling by doing some counseling, by supervising the work of counselor trainees, and through teaching and research.

A school counselor is likely to spend much time in planning schedules, advising about post-high school plans, helping students with social-interpersonal troubles, placing students in jobs, making referrals, and consulting with parents, school officials, and teachers.

The environment entered by a counseling psychologist depends upon the desired rewards and the valued personal and professional satisfaction. The ideal value held up to psychologists in training is that they should attempt to be scientists as well as practitioners.

Personality characteristics of counselors

The results of research over the years suggest there is great variability in counselor personality characteristics and behavior. However, in spite of this variability, there seem to be some counselor characteristics that cut across most theoretical models of counseling. A few of the descriptive research studies focusing on counselor personality characteristics are discussed here.

The beliefs about human nature held by counseling, clinical, and rehabilitation faculty and students were explored by Dole and Nottingham (1969). Graduate directors, faculty, and students responded to the Philosophies of Human Nature Scale. In general, the findings suggest that students across the three groups (counseling, clinical, and rehabilitation) tend to exhibit a slightly favorable attitude toward other persons. Graduate program directors wanted students to believe that human nature is neither favorable nor unfavorable. Both students and faculty agreed that human behavior is complex and hard to understand, but they did not agree on variability. The students tended to endorse behavioral variability and individual differences.

Roe (1969) reviewed the literature on differential personality characteristics of counselors. She noted that counselors tend to score high on the MF scale of the MMPI, Minnesota Multiphasic Personality Inventory, (tend to become feminine), have relatively little interest in mathematics, considerable interest in persons, and have higher aesthetic and theoretical values than comparable groups in related disciplines. Other results (Kazienko & Neidt, 1962) suggest that counselors and therapists value the qualities of empathy, dependability, interest, sincerity, and respect.

Another way of looking at counselor personality characteristics is by comparing various professional groups. Donnan and Harlon (1968) compared the personality characteristics of persons committed to careers in counseling and administration using the Sixteen Personality Factor Questionnaire. The results indicate that compared to administrators, the counselors are calm, casual, sensitive, trusting, adaptable, and natural. Administrators are seen to be emotional, conscientious, realistic, suspicious, opinionated, and calculating.

A few other studies have attempted to identify various counselor personality characteristics associated with counselor interview behavior. Asa (1967), using the Edwards Personal Preference Schedule with 15 male graduate students in a guidance and counseling program, found the need for Dominance to be positively associated ($r = .67$) with the use of probing responses, but negatively associated ($r = -.56$) with the use of acceptance responses. Other findings showed the need for Aggression to be positively related ($r = .58$) to the use of diagnostic responses, but negatively related ($r = -.74$) to the use of interpretation responses. Another study explored the relationship between personality and counselor responses made to reduce ambiguity in the counseling situation. Counselors who are intolerant of ambiguity show evidence of dominant, achievement-oriented, and aggressive-need patterns. These counselors also report a need for female companionship and a need to be the center of attention.

In general, the research results reveal a picture of a counselor personality emphasizing affiliation and sensitivity. Sensitive people with strong affiliation needs are attracted to counseling as a profession. However, there is no way—yet—to relate counselor personality to counseling effectiveness or client benefit. The next section focuses on counselor qualities that cut across theoretical models which are related to client behavior.

Counselor personality and client change

Although much of the research focusing on counselor personality has yet to be related to client change or to client benefit, counselor qualities seem to be fundamentally related to the task of changing the client for the better. Effective implementation of counseling and therapeutic techniques and ultimate client benefit seem to be associated with counselor personal qualities. In general, the findings of a number of research studies (more than 60) suggest at least three counselor variables or characteristics that seem to be associated with client benefit. These three personality qualities are counselor empathy, warmth, and genuineness. The evidence indicates that these three variables are significantly related to client benefit acoss a wide variety of counselors and therapists, regardless of training and theoretical orientation. Also, data indicate that the personality variables are associated with client benefit for a wide variety of clients in individual and in group counseling. In terms of causation, evidence indicates that it is the counselor who determines the level of empathy, warmth, and genuineness in the counseling relationship. Clients whose counselors make frequent empathic, warm, and genuine responses tend to benefit more and to show more positive change than clients whose counselors engage in fewer empathic, warm, and genuine behaviors.

All three of the qualities are related, and therefore in some ways are difficult to define independently. The first counselor personality variable, empathy (understanding), has been defined in different ways. Tyler (1969) defines empathy as the process of the counselor experiencing what the client is experiencing. Stated another way, empathy involves grasping the meaning the client wants to convey with great clarity. However, keep in mind that probably no human being completely understands another person. Some authors have suggested that accurate empathic understanding involves the ability to perceive and to communicate accurately and with sensitivity both the feelings and experiences of another person and their meaning and significance. The counselor should step into the client's shoes (so to speak) and assume a world view from the client's emotional and perceptual vantage point.

Our definition of empathy is similar yet different in an important way. To us, empathy (perhaps better called "social intelligence") is the ability to understand and to accurately communicate the meanings of the client's cognitive and affective responses (instrumental and mediational) about his or her self and the environment. Instrumental responses (Osipow & Walsh, 1970) tend to have an immediate effect upon the environment. Mediational responses are thinking responses and cannot be labeled meaningful behavioral data until verbalized. Much of the task of the counselor is aimed at eliciting the mediational responses to make them accessible to outside observation and possible change. Thus, to empathize is to understand the meaning the client is attempting to deliver. An empathic counselor response conveys this understanding to the client.

The second personality variable has some different but meaningful labels, such as *unconditional positive regard* (Rogers, 1957), *acceptance* (Tyler, 1969), and *nonpossessive warmth* (Truax & Carkhuff, 1967; Bergin & Garfield, 1971). To Rogers, unconditional positive regard means the complete acceptance of all of the client's characteristics and behaviors. This acceptance is to be without reservations. Tyler defines acceptance as a willingness to allow individuals to be different from one another in many ways. Acceptance further involves the realization that the experience of each person is a complex pattern of thinking and feeling. An accepting attitude is the opposite of contempt, and does not involve either approval or disapproval of client personality characteristics or behavior. Bergin and Garfield (1971) suggest that the purpose of nonpossessive warmth is to preserve the client's self-respect as a person and to provide a trusting atmosphere in which to feel safe to interact. The responses (nonpossessive warmth) themselves reflect a nondominating attitude. The attitude seems to involve an acceptance of what is, rather than a demand for what ought or should be. In sum, unconditional positive regard, acceptance, and nonpossessive warmth responses reflect a nondominating attitude and an acceptance of what is. Such responses stimulate client trust and client recognition of the fact that one can be "liked" in spite of unlikeable characteristics.

The third counselor quality, genuineness, also has varying labels and descriptions. Rogers (1957) first called it "congruence"; he defined it as consistency between the individual's actual behavior and self-concept. In other words, congruence is consistency between what a counselor says and does and the counselor's real self. Tyler (1969) refers to this same quality as sincerity. Operationally, it means that the counselor is "together," and is a person who knows his or her status and objectives. Truax and Carkhuff (1967) and Bergin and Garfield (1971) have also called this personality quality "genuineness." Truax and Carkhuff, looking at the opposite side of the coin, suggest that it is the absence of phoniness that is important and related to client benefit, rather than the presence of genuineness. These authors suggest that being phony or acting a part stands in the way of effective counseling. To Bergin and Garfield, being genuine is basic to an effective human relationship and ultimately contributes to an open and trusting relationship.

To sum up, the counselor personality variable called genuineness tends to reflect an ability to be open, honest, and nondefensive. In many ways the counselor serves as a model in helping the client be honest and to talk about undesirable characteristics and behaviors. It is unreasonable to expect a client to be open, trusting, and honest if the counselor does not show these qualities. It is therefore important that the counselor not be phony and not act a role.

The research results clearly suggest that counselors/therapists who are accurately empathic, nonpossessively warm in attitude, and genuine are effective. Some of the more significant research is discussed below.

The classic study of outcome and of therapist personality was carried out by Whitehorn and Betz (1954) at Johns Hopkins University. They compared seven psychiatrists who demonstrated an improvement rate of 75 percent in their schizophrenic patients with a group of seven psychiatrists who had an improvement rate of only 27 percent. The findings showed that the more successful psychiatrists tended to be more warm and understanding while the less successful psychiatrists tended to respond to the patient in a more impersonal manner.

Rogers, Grendlin, Kiesler, and Truax (1967) conducted a four-year study with 16 hospitalized schizophrenics, which produced a number of relevant findings. One finding indicated that patients whose counselors/therapists exhibited high levels of nonpossessive warmth, genuineness, and accurate empathy showed a significant personality change on a number of different criteria. However, patients whose counselors/therapists offered low levels of warmth, genuineness, and empathy during therapy demonstrated deterioration in personality and behavior functioning.

Another study (Truax, 1963) compared 14 schizophrenics receiving individual treatment and 14 matched control patients. The findings of this work revealed a significant difference in psychological functioning among patients receiving high conditions (high levels of warmth, genuineness, and empathy), patients receiving low conditions, and control patients. The findings further showed that patients receiving high conditions in counseling/therapy spent significantly more time out of the hospital than the patients receiving low conditions in counseling/therapy and the control patients.

Truax, Carkhuff, and Kodman (1965) studied 40 hospitalized patients who were given group therapy sessions over a three-month period. The Minnesota Multiphasic Personality Inventory was administered pre- and post-therapy. The findings indicated that the patients who offered high levels of empathy showed improvement equal to, or better than, that of patients receiving relatively low levels of empathy on all of the subscales of the MMPI.

Working with a group of juvenile delinquents, Truax, Wargo, and Silber (1966) found that the delinquents receiving high levels of warmth, genuineness, and empathy in group therapy showed significant improvement when compared to the control or no treatment group. The findings showed that the delinquents receiving high conditions in group therapy spent significantly more time out of the hospital when compared to the control delinquents that received no treatment.

In the research just cited, the concepts of nonpossessive warmth, genuineness, and empathy have been explored. Some related and current research trends have investigated the counseling process by focusing on counselor credibility, counselor attractiveness, and counselor nonverbal behavior.

The social influence factors of counselor credibility (perceived expertness and trustworthiness) and attractiveness were defined by Strong (1968) and drawn from social psychological research. (For additional information see the social psychological theory of counseling discussed in Chapter 2.) Beutler, Johnson, Neville, Elkins, and Jobe (1975) have shown that client perception of counselor credibility is a very important determinant of counseling outcome. Counselor experience, prestige, and verbal and nonverbal behavior tend to communicate this perception. Other evidence (Strong, 1968; Heppner & Pew, 1977) suggests that a prestigious introduction, diplomas, and awards tend to influence client perception of counselor competence. More recently, and based on this kind of information, Krumboltz, Becker-Haven, and Burnett (1979) indicate that counselors who wish to be viewed as expert and trustworthy should obtain a Ph.D. degree, display their awards and license, and behave in a prepared, confident, and relaxed manner.

On the atttractiveness factor, LaCrosse (1977) has shown that counselors who are perceived as attractive are also viewed as genuine, warm, and empathic. Client ratings of counselor facilitativeness were highly related to ratings of attraction and expertness. For purposes of practice, this indicates that counselors who are perceived to be attractive tend to be empathic, warm, and active (Krumboltz, Becker-Haven, & Burnett, 1979).

Strong, Taylor, Bratton, and Loper (1971) suggest that frequency of movement is a significant characteristic in person perception. The results show that active counselors are perceived by clients as being more casual, warm, friendly, and carefree. Active counselors were defined as ones who gesture, smile, and change postural position more frequently. LaCrosse (1975) found that affiliative, nonverbal behaviors are judged by clients to be warmer and more atttractive. Affiliative, nonverbal behaviors were smiles, head nods, hand gestures, eye contact, and a slight forward body lean. In general, these findings indicate that certain counselor nonverbal behaviors tend to be associated with perceived counselor empathy and warmth. In other words, clients are aware of counselor nonverbal behaviors and use these responses to interpret the counselor's empathy and warmth.

An additional research fragment suggests that other personal qualities of counselors may be associated with positive client benefit. For example, Zarski, Sweeney, and Barchihowski (1977), using eight experienced counselors and 93 students, explored the relationship between counselor social interest and counseling effectiveness. They found that the counselor's level of social interest was positively correlated with the client's satisfaction with counseling and with measured client self-acceptance and sociability. A tentative interpretation of the results is that counselors with higher social interest may facilitate the development of social interest (self-confidence and self-acceptance) in others by being effective models (Dowling & Frantz, 1975).

Tinsley and Tinsley (1977) investigated the needs, interests, and abilities of effective and ineffective counselor trainees. The students were judged as relatively effective ($n = 32$), relatively ineffective ($n = 30$), or indeterminant ($n = 12$) on the basis of their practicum supervisor's evaluation. Compared to the effective trainees, the relatively ineffective trainees had stronger needs to make use of their abilities, to get a feeling of accomplishment, to tell others what to do, to get paid well in comparison to other workers, to do things for other people, and to have good working conditions.

The studies just noted imply that counselor behavior, probably influenced by counselor personality, does have a systematic impact on clients. As the folklore suggests, counselor personality is likely to be a major tool to be applied in counseling.

SUMMARY

This chapter has reviewed the counseling profession. Counseling is one of several mental health professions that has grown to help people and institutions cope with the demands of an increasingly stressful world lacking available and traditional helping sources because of shifts in social organization. The professional antecedents of counseling are primarily the mental hygiene movement, stemming from the work of the psychoanalyst through that of humanistic psychotherapists, such as Carl Rogers, and the educational-vocational guidance movement, stemming from the work of Frank Parsons, public school guidance workers, and industrial psychology and sociology.

The work of the counselor essentially includes some of all of the following: individual counseling, assessment of people and their environments, program development and consultation, research and training, and supervision of mental health services. The nature of the interventions made by counselors usually are aimed at some combination of personal, educational, and career issues. The overall objectives of counselors tend to be toward the higher-order goal of helping people develop in the most positive way possible under some of the constraints of individual traits and environments. Counseling also includes efforts to help people avoid developing difficulties and to remedy problems already in existence.

Research suggests that counselors who exhibit high levels of nonpossessive warmth, genuineness, and empathy tend to be more effective and helpful to clients. Furthermore, these results tend to be obtained by a variety of counselors and therapists irrespective of theoretical background or training. These findings seem to apply to a wide variety of clients and patients.

Counselors are likely to be individuals who value interpersonal relations, aesthetic activities, and are trusting, calm, and interpersonally sensitive. While it is not clearly demonstrated that such traits enhance counseling effectiveness, it has been speculated that these traits *may* be related to the ability to display nonpossessive warmth, genuineness, and empathy.

Theories of counseling

Scientists have given us many definitions of theory. Theory has been defined as a provisional systemization of events enabling us to see relationships among facts (McCabe, 1958). Another definition views a theory as a human convention for keeping data in order (Pepper, 1961). Pepinsky and Pepinsky (1954) view theory as a possible world that can be checked against the real world. All views of theory reflect our needs to organize information and make sense out of life.

Formal theory in the behavioral sciences has certain defined characteristics that have their roots in the more sophisticated physical sciences. First, theory is nested in a set of unproven assumptions that define the field the theory is investigating. The assumptions should be verifiable, open to development, and suggest observable data. A theory to be scientific must admit to testing and development (Eysenck, 1952). Second, concepts are operationally defined to permit data collection through empirical means. The stated assumptions and operationally defined concepts should allow the development of testable hypotheses. Theory should organize and permit the interpretation of existing knowledge in a meaningful frame of reference as well as to predict events.

This chapter is designed to show how theory may be useful in counseling and to review the highlights of several major counseling-oriented theories.

How is a theory useful?

What advantages exist for a counselor using an integrated theoretical point of view? It is possible to identify at least four ways in which counseling theory may be helpful and useful in a counseling situation (Osipow & Walsh, 1970). First, theory assists the counselor to plan a strategy or treatment plan. Second, theory contributes to the understanding of human behavior or, more specifically, of client behavior. Third, theory suggests certain counseling techniques. Fourth, theory identifies goals and objectives to be pursued for client benefit and for evaluation.

Theory assists in the development of a treatment plan by suggesting a way in which the counselor may think about the person. Each theory has a view of human behavior—be it rational, emotional, cognitive, historical, or behavioral. Furthermore, theory defines for the counselor the cognitive and behavioral roles to be used in bringing about positive client benefit. Knowledge of these roles make the counselor's efforts in the client's behalf more consistent and predictable. Applying different theories leads the counselor to vary the process of effecting client benefit to fit client characteristics and need.

Theory also provides the counselor with a framework that assists in organizing understandings about client behavior in a meaningful way. Theory tends to suggest hypotheses concerning client behaviors to be tested. Behavioral data collection, hypothesis development, and hypothesis testing within a theoretical framework usually improve counselor ability to reach a valid and useful "diagnosis."

The techniques used by the counselor vary, depending upon the theoretical framework adopted. A counselor whose theory focuses on the cognitive aspects of human behavior will use logical, rational, and directive techniques. A counselor whose theory emphasizes the affective aspects of human behavior will use feeling-oriented responses, such as the reflection of feeling. In general the techniques associated with a given theory are mainly used to implement the concepts of that theory.

Finally, theory can focus on short- or long-term goals, or both, for counseling. These goals, and the process by which they are pursued, are likely to vary with the theoretical viewpoint being used. For example, rational approaches to counseling suggest the "curing" of unreason with reason. The counselor helps the client order and discipline thinking. The orthodox psychoanalytic view has the goal of restructuring the client's personality by making unconscious material conscious. The perceptual phenomenological approaches are primarily designed to help individual self-actualization. Thus, direction about which attitudes, emotions or behaviors (or both) are to be changed, and how to do so, stem from theory.

The question of the effectiveness of one counseling theory compared to another is difficult to answer. What evidence does exist tentatively suggests that different counseling theories lead to procedures differentially effective with clients reporting different problems. Patterson (1973) has categorized counseling theories into five major groups according to their primary theme: perceptual, existential, analytic, rational, and behavioral. Following is an overview of major theoretical points of view in the Patterson framework.

PERCEPTUAL PHENOMENOLOGICAL APPROACHES

Perceptual phenomenological theoretical approaches to counseling focus on reality, or, stated another way, on the environment as it is perceived and reported by the individual. Reality becomes a matter of each individual's perception. The judge of reality is the individual. Therefore, subjective and personal data are considered valid sources of information.

A number of perceptual phenomenological theories to counseling have been developed, e.g., Kelly's (1955) psychology of personal constructs, Grinker's (1961) transactional approach, Perls's (1969) Gestalt therapy, Carkhuff's (1970) eclectic approach, and Rogers's (1942, 1951, & 1961) person-centered approach. Of these theories, Rogers's person-centered approach has probably had the most profound impact on the counseling community.

At a time when Freudian psychoanalysis was the zeitgeist, Rogers introduced a theoretical viewpoint suggesting that the person is basically good and trustworthy. His theory emphasized the positive features of the individual. Such a view of the individual is not compatible with the Freudian notion that the individual is dominated by the sexual and aggressive drives of the id with a primary drive for pleasure.

The person-centered approach (C. R. Rogers)

Concept of the person. Rogers's conception of the person seems to be based on a belief in the Protestant ethic. Rogers holds basic a belief in the democratic ideal—a belief in the dignity and worth of each individual. He believes that individuals have the right to their own opinions and that each should be in control of their own destiny. Rogers also believed that the world is as the individual perceives it to be, since each individual lives in a private, personal, subjective world. The individual's primary motivating force is the tendency to self-actualize. Self-actualization is the tendency of the person to develop all capacities and to grow and to develop all potentialities. Finally, contrary to the Freudian view, Rogers believes the individual to be basically good, trustworthy, and rational.

Theory of personality. Rogers's theory of personality is based on a phenomenological approach to human experience. The phenomenological approach deals with the world as a person sees it. The personal, phenomenological world includes the individual's concept of self. During counseling, both the counselor and the client become aware of the client's self-concept. When counseling is successful, it is the client's self-concept that changes.

Rogers's theory of personality is basically composed of three central ideas: the organism, the phenomenal field, and the self-concept. The organism is the total individual. The phenomenal field consists of all the individual's experiences as perceived by that person. The self-concept is the person's picture of self and the self-evaluation of this picture. Experiences perceived to be incongruent (inconsistent) with the self-concept will lead to tension, feelings of being threatened, and, possibly, confusion. Because incongruent experiences tend to threaten the individual's self-image, people attempt to deny or may distort their perception of these experiences to reduce the threat to the self-concept. Thus, according to Rogers, psychological maladjustment (incongruence) exists when the individual denies or inaccurately perceives experiences. Congruence (psychological adjustment) implies a matching of awareness, experience, and communication.

How and why does incongruence occur? As noted earlier, when an individual interacts with the environment and learns about self, a self-concept (a picture of self) gradually develops. This awareness of self is associated with a need for positive regard from others and positive self-regard. People want to be liked and cared for by other people; and at the same time, people strive for self-esteem. Because of the need for positive regard and positive self-regard, the individual develops what are called "conditions of worth," or "standards of behavior." Conditions of worth are standards of thought and behavior that permit the person to like himself or herself and to be liked by other people. However, experiences that are perceived to be incongruent with the condition of being worthy are viewed as threats; consequently, such experiences may be distorted and not integrated into the self-concept. To change this threatening process, the self-concept must become more congruent with the individual's experiences. Rogers's theory of counseling describes the conditions that make this possible.

Theory of counseling. The central hypothesis of Rogers's approach is that the growth potential of any individual will be realized in a relationship in which the helping person communicates acceptance, genuineness, and understanding (Meador & Rogers, 1973). According to Rogers, certain conditions tend to facilitate the release of growth potential and contribute to positive client benefit.

These conditions exist on a continuum; the more of each condition displayed, the better the counseling outcome. Rogers suggests that the counseling process will be effective to the extent that: (1) the client and the counselor are in psychological contact with one another; (2) the client is in a state of incongruence, being vulnerable or anxious; (3) the counselor is congruent in the relationship; (4) the counselor experiences unconditional positive regard toward the client. (Unconditional positive regard means that the counselor is able to accept the client in spite of the client's unlikable characteristics.); (5) the counselor experiences empathic understanding of the client's internal frame of reference; (6) the client perceives, at least to a minimal degree, the counselor's unconditional positive regard and the counselor's empathic understanding of his or her internal frame of reference.

According to Rogers, if these environmental conditions exist, a counseling process will develop. In this supportive, nonpunitive situation the client becomes freer in exploring and expressing thoughts and feelings. Because of the reduced threat resulting from the counselor's acceptance, the client is able to become more aware of experiences that have been denied or distorted. The client becomes aware of the incongruence between certain experiences and his or her picture of self. During the counseling process the client's self-concept gradually changes to include experiences that were previously distorted in awareness. The client again begins to develop self-esteem (positive self-regard). Rogers's desired outcome is that the client will be more congruent, more open to experience, and less defensive. Theoretically, according to Rogers, the client-centered approach may be used in any relationship where the persons want to understand each other (Meador & Rogers, 1973).

Technique. The techniques used by Rogers and his colleagues vary, depending on which of these time periods were used to examine Rogers's work: the nondirective period (1940–50), the reflective period (1950–57), and the experiential period (1957 to present). During the nondirective period, counselors used responses characterized by a minimal degree of lead (simple acceptance, clarification responses, and restatement responses). The counselor made little attempt to go beyond the client's self-understanding or insight.

In the reflective period (1950–57), the counselor focused on the reflection of client feelings. Reflection refers to attempts to mirror the client's emotions. It involves focusing on the emotional theme expressed by the client and not on the content of what was said. This reflective technique, often thought to be a naive and innocuous technique by the beginning counselor, has some very powerful characteristics that contribute to its effectiveness. These characteristics are reinforcement (the client is rewarded for talking about emotions and feelings) and interpretation (going beyond the client's insight).

The third period in the development of Rogers's work is characterized by the use of a wide range of techniques and responses used to help clients experience and reorganize their self-concept. The watchword might well be: To experience is to be aware. Techniques emphasized during this period are leads, approval, open-ended questions, personal experiences, and interpretations.

Research. The client-centered approach is probably one of the most thoroughly studied methods of counseling in existence (Meador & Rogers, 1973). The primary reason for this empirical base reflects Rogers's need to look at the facts (Rogers, 1960). Rogers and his colleagues over the years made a concerted effort to look at and understand the raw data of counseling and psychotherapy. An up-to-date review of the research on the client-centered approach has been carried out by Shlien and Zimring (1970). In general, the research evidence suggests that positive client benefits tend to be associated with counselors or therapists who are empathic (understanding), genuine (honest), and accepting. Rogers's notion that certain counselor conditions (characteristics, responses) tend to facilitate client growth and positive client benefit is generally supported by research findings.

Carkhuff's extension of person-centered counseling

Another perceptual phenomenological approach, which is an extension of Rogers's person-centered theory with an existential and behavioristic emphasis, has been developed by Robert Carkhuff (1969a, 1969b), at times in collaboration with Charles Truax (Truax & Carkhuff, 1967) and with Bernard Berenson (Carkhuff & Berenson, 1967). The basic notion of Carkhuff's eclectic approach is that individuals have the greatest opportunity for personal movement and growth at crisis points—times of physical or psychological life and death urgency.

Concept of the person.   In a way similar to Rogers, Carkhuff views the individual's optimum goal in life as self-actualization or, in Carkhuff's language (1969a, 1969b), "to become whole." The attributes of "wholeness" are honesty, creativity, and internal consistency. The process of becoming whole (growing and self-actualizing) involves a constant effort at self-definition. However, society as it exists tends to work against this growth process in individuals since growth threatens the continuance of established values and myths (Carkhuff, 1969a, 1969b).

Theory of personality.   Carkhuff (1969a, 1969b) does not seem to have an explicit theory of personality. However, his thoughts about the individual and behavior seem to be based on a few related assumptions (Carkhuff, 1969a, 1969b). First, individuals have the greatest opportunity for personal movement (in either a positive or negative direction) at crisis points, times of physical or psychological life and death urgency. The principle is that people in crisis are in need of and particularly vulnerable to the influence of significant others in the social environment. A second series of assumptions focus on the theme that people in crisis may be influenced by means of a human relationship. According to Carkhuff (1969a, 1969b) human relationships have attributes that make them more or less helpful to others and powerful in influencing behavior change. Any significant human relationship is constantly in the process of deepening or deteriorating. The interpersonal intimacy possible in any relationship depends on the "wholeness" of the individuals in the relationship. Thus, intimacy depends on the honesty, the creativity, and the internal consistency of the individuals in the relationship. It is important to note that how an individual approaches other people reflects attitudes toward self and self-understanding.

Theory of counseling.   The basic assumption of Carkhuff's theory of counseling is that helping relationships may be either facilitative or retarding, depending on the counselor's own level of functioning (Carkhuff, 1969a, 1969b). Carkhuff, in a way similar to Rogers, proposes the existence of certain core conditions that facilitate client growth and development and contribute to positive client benefit. Carkhuff suggests that a counselor's effectiveness during crisis periods will depend upon the counselor's level of functioning on the core conditions. The seven core conditions suggested by Carkhuff (1969a, 1969b) may be defined as follows:

1.   Empathy (understanding) involves a striving to understand another's feelings while suspending one's own judgments.

2. Respect (acceptance) may be defined as positive regard for the other person and for oneself.
3. Concreteness (specificity) is defined as the direct and complete expression of content personally relevant to the client.
4. Genuineness (honesty) is defined as openness and honesty with oneself and others.
5. Self-disclosure (risk-taking) involves the counselor freely volunteering personal ideas, attitudes, and experiences that reveal him or her to the client as a unique individual.
6. Confrontation (intervention) occurs when the counselor communicates to the client his or her experience of a discrepancy in the client's communication or behavior.
7. Immediacy (here and now) involves the counselor responding to discrepant client thoughts or behaviors in the immediate situation.

Empathy is the key ingredient of the helping relationship. According to Carkhuff, nothing useful in counseling can happen without counselor empathy. Empathy and the three qualities that follow (respect, concreteness, and genuineness) are basically the postulates that Rogers originally observed and identified in his client-centered approach. Carkhuff (1969a, 1969b) labels empathy and respect as facilitative core conditions; concreteness, genuineness, and self-disclosure as action-oriented conditions; and confrontation and immediacy as both facilitative and action-oriented conditions. The facilitative conditions are primarily used to support client self-exploration. Facilitative conditions are seen to be necessary and the most important conditions in counseling, but they are not sufficient, taken alone, for client growth. The action-oriented conditions tend to be behaviorally oriented and lead to constructive behaviors.

What characterizes the counseling process? The counseling process in Carkhuff's (1969a, 1969b) eclectic approach consists of two phases: downward and upward. The downward phase focuses on client self-exploration and client self-discovery of feelings and experiences. The counselor supports and reinforces client self-exploration by engaging in the facilitative responses of empathy and respect. This phase of counseling emphasizes not only client self-exploration but the need for the counselor to learn about the client's internal frame of reference.

After the client has engaged in self-exploration, the helping relationship enters into a second phase—the upward phase or the phase of emergent directionality. Here the client experiences a need to change self-defeating behaviors and acquire more productive behaviors and an acceptable lifestyle. The counselor supports this change process by engaging mainly in the action-oriented behaviors associated with concreteness, genuineness, and self-disclosure. The counselor's orientation is one of action, with a focus on client behavior change. The desired counseling outcome is that the client will acquire a new lifestyle that is more constructive (Carkhuff, 1969a, 1969b).

Technique. A listing of preferred techniques is theoretically unlimited since Carkhuff (1969a, 1969b) suggests that what techniques work are good. However, Carkhuff poses two conditions: First, what are the unique contributions of a given orientation or technique over and above those contributions accounted for by the core conditions of an effective helping relationship? Second, where and under what conditions is this orientation or technique applicable? The more treatment possibilities a counselor has the skill to use, the greater the probability of matching a treatment with the client's desired behavioral change. It must be reemphasized, however, that Carkhuff sees the relationship, not the technique, as the critical component of counseling.

Research. Extensive data exist relating the core conditions to a number of different process and outcome criteria (Carkhuff, 1969a, 1969b; Carkhuff & Berenson, 1967; Truax & Carkhuff, 1967; Truax & Mitchell, 1971). Carkhuff's (1969a, 1969b) review of existing research suggests that the presence of high levels of the core conditions tend to be related to positive client benefit in individual and group psychotherapy with a wide variety of clients—including juvenile delinquents, hospitalized schizophrenics, college clients, mild to severe outpatient neurotics, situationally distressed clients, and a variety of hospitalized clients. Truax and Mitchell (1971) reviewed studies that used the core research scales of accurate empathy, nonpossessive warmth, and genuineness. These studies indicate that client benefit is strongly related to high levels of the core dimensions, whereas low levels of the core conditions tend to be associated with client deterioration.

There are contradictory findings and opinions. Garfield and Bergin (1971) investigated the relationship of the core dimensions (empathy, nonpossessive warmth, and genuineness) to a variety of outcome measures using a sample of counselors and therapists primarily non-client-centered. The findings failed to show a relationship between any of the three therapeutic conditions and any outcome variable. These data suggest that it may be difficult to generalize about the importance of core conditions beyond client-centered counselors. In a review of data presented by Truax and Carkhuff (1967), Shapiro (1969) found that while contradictory findings do exist, the general trend favors concluding that there is a relationship between high core conditions and positive client outcome. Similarly, it has been pointed out that, although the conclusions made by Carkhuff and his colleagues often tend to be more supportive of their hypotheses than the data may warrant, the general trend of the findings seems to be supportive.

EXISTENTIAL APPROACHES

Existential approaches to counseling are concerned with understanding the person in the framework of the individual's world, his or her commitment to life, and self-awareness and the immediate present. In counseling and psychotherapy the existential effort is represented by a number of different approaches (Boss, 1963; Frankl, 1962; Kaam, 1967; May, 1967; Sartre, 1956). While these approaches certainly are different, it is possible to identify certain common aspects across the existential approaches.

First, most existential approaches to counseling suggest that people are conscious of themselves, are able to make decisions, and therefore are responsible for their personal actions. What an individual achieves reflects personal choice. External influences (heredity, environment, upbringing) are limiting but not determining.

A second common element is that people tend to live in three worlds simultaneously: the biological world (without self-awareness), the world of interrelationships (or the psychological world), and the world of self-identity (the spiritual world). In general, from an existential perspective, it is important that one attempt to integrate these worlds to enhance "awareness."

Third, people are not static, but rather are in a constant state of "emerging, becoming and self creation." However, the individual also knows that at some future time he or she will not exist. "Being" implies "nonbeing"—not developing or nothingness. The existential approaches hold that this fact of nonbeing (death) gives life meaning and, in addition, is the source of normal anxiety, hostility, and aggression. Anxiety is identified as a normal condition of existence because the threat of nonbeing is always present for all individuals.

The fourth commonality is a shared diversity of methods. Existential philosophy does not necessarily dictate method. Some of the techniques used in existential counseling are free association, interpretation, suggestion, reasoning, convincing, persuasion, and teaching.

A fifth commonality is the existential emphasis on the present moment, and the human conditions of loneliness, isolation, depersonalization, and detachment.

Finally, the aim of the existential approaches is to help people increase their commitment to life, to self-awareness, and to an authentic existence. In becoming aware of self and potentialities, individuals are more able to control the influences on their lives. The existential point of view concerning the counseling task is illustrated in Frankl's logotherapy (1962) and is discussed next.

Concept of the person. According to Frankl (Patterson, 1973) the individual has three dimensions: the biological (or physical), the mental (or psychological), and the spiritual. Logotherapy emphasizes the spiritual dimension, which Frankl suggests most distinguishes humans from animals. Freedom is still another distinctive human characteristic. People are free to make decisions in spite of the influence of instincts, inherited disposition, and environment. Responsibility is also an important human attribute. The person is responsible to self, to conscience, and to one's God. After the individual is aware of "responsibilities," a decision must be made regarding to whom and for what one is responsible.

Theory of personality. According to Frankl (1962), the primary motivator is the "will to meaning" that most deeply inspires the individual. A common complaint reported by clients is that their lives are meaningless. People lament that they don't know what to do, what they want to do, and are not aware of a meaning worth living for. Frankl (1962) asserts that this concern over the worthwhileness of life is a spiritual problem but not a mental disease. The search for meaning in life may lead to tension as the individual becomes aware of the gap between what one is and what one should become (Frankl, 1962).

Theory of counseling. Logotherapy is concerned with making people conscious of their responsibilities. Responsibility suggests meaning, because responsibility implies obligation, and obligation, according to Frankl, can only be understood in terms of the meaning of life. Logotherapy, thus, is concerned with problems of a philosophical or spiritual nature and problems involving meaning: the meaning of life, the meaning of death, the meaning of suffering, the meaning of work, and the meaning of love. The goal is to help the client achieve meaning in life. This is accomplished by helping the person understand and accept responsibility for self-decisions, and for responses to the environment (Patterson, 1973).

The significant aspect of the counseling process of logotherapy is the relationship between the client and the counselor. The relationship is more important than any method or technique. Within the framework of the relationship, spiritual or philosophical problems are discussed rationally, with a focus on client attitudes toward various symptoms. The aim of logotherapy is to make the person consciously accept responsibility for self and actions. This approach is primarily concerned with clients troubled by problems of values and goals, the meaning of existence, and questions about freedom and responsibility.

Technique.   In Frankl's logotherapy the discussion of technique is not elaborate. In general, the techniques used by existential counselors tend to be as varied as the number of counselors following the existential approach (Osipow & Walsh, 1970). However, Frankl does describe two specific techniques frequently used in logotherapy, i.e., paradoxical intention and de-reflection. Paradoxical intention focuses on symptoms. This technique encourages and urges clients to expose themselves to a feared situation, but without the expected fear responses actually occurring (Patterson, 1973). The approach to the feared situation is carried out in as humorous a setting as possible in an attempt to change the client's attitude and reduce or eliminate the fear responses. This technique seems to be similar, in principle, to the technique of desensitization used in behavior modification counseling. An example of paradoxical intension follows:

Client: Everytime I think about asking Linda to go out with me, I feel as if I will faint.

Counselor: Oh? I'd like to see how that works. Think about Linda, about asking her to go to dinner with you.

Client: I can't—it makes me light-headed.

Counselor: Does it?—Show me how you will faint. Are you thinking about it?

Client: I can't—I am . . .

Counselor: But you're not fainting! I'm disappointed . . .

Client: No, I'm not . . .

Counselor: See, you do have some control over your reactions after all.

De-reflection is a technique used to treat excessive self-observation or self-attention. In using this technique, the client is encouraged to ignore the problem (Patterson, 1973). The client is urged to direct awareness toward something favorable and pleasant. The client focuses attention away from self. This technique (de-reflection) seems to be a form of counter-conditioning, which will be discussed under the behavior modification approaches.

Research.   The research exploring the existential approaches, and specifically logotherapy, is limited. However, Gendlin (1969, 1973) and his associates (Klein, Mathieu, Kiesler, & Gendlin, 1970) over the past decade have developed a technique with a tape recorder that may be used to explore the therapy process. Their findings indicate that the level of experiencing tends to be associated with positive client benefit. The results show that clients are able to increase their level of "felt experience" as a function of the therapy process and treatment.

PSYCHOANALYTIC APPROACHES

Orthodox psychoanalysis as derived from Sigmund Freud is primarily concerned with making the unconscious become conscious. Psychoanalysis was the first approach to study the role of feelings and emotions in the psychological experience (Patterson, 1973). However, as a method of counseling and therapy, psychoanalytic approaches are primarily verbal in nature. "Reason" is used as the method for exploring and coping with emotional problems and situations.

In counseling and psychotherapy, psychoanalytic orientations are represented by a variety of approaches (Adler, 1927; Alexander, 1963; Horney, 1950; Jung, 1954; Rank, 1947; Sullivan, 1953). Although these approaches are certainly different in important ways, there are some areas of commonality worth discussing.

First, most of the psychoanalytic approaches during treatment are primarily concerned with making unconscious material conscious. The treatment attempts to help the client verbalize experiences or thoughts that have not been previously verbalized. Psychoanalytic theory suggests that the treatment process increases "the action of the ego" (the ego being the rational arm of the personality). The ego, as it becomes aware of unconscious thoughts, is able to integrate these thoughts with more conscious material. Second, the bringing forth of unconscious material is accomplished mainly by three techniques: (1) the counselor's/therapist's objective and nonevaluative attitude; (2) the interpretation of material emitted during free association; and (3) the transference relationship or the client's emotional interpersonal experience in the therapeutic situation. A transference relationship occurs when the client perceives the therapist in the same way as some significant other is perceived in the environment. Third, psychoanalytic theories suggest that sooner or later clients direct their disturbed attitude toward the counselor through the transference relationship. Thus, the disturbance of the client, which is probably based on early childhood experiences, is transformed into an artificial transference disturbance. The working through or the resolution of these transferred thoughts and feelings becomes the goal of the psychoanalytic treatment. However, during this process the client exhibits resistance. The client wants help but at the same time resists it because the treatment is painful. Overcoming client resistance is an inherent problem that must be dealt with in psychoanalytic treatment.

Transference is illustrated in the following exchange:

Patient: (extended silence)

Therapist: You've very quiet today.

Patient: I'm not going to talk to you today. (sulking)

Therapist: Oh?

Patient: (more silence)

Therapist: (waits)

Patient: You think you can outlast me—I know your tricks. You think you know everything; you think I have to do everything you say. (petulently)

In the above exchange the patient related to the counselor in a manner similar to a small child challenging the patient authority of a parent.

Bordin's (1955) psychoanalytic counseling, which tends to be eclectic in orientation, is the one approach in general counseling that implements psychoanalytic theory and technique (Pattrson, 1973). For the reason mentioned, this eclectic point of view developed by Bordin (1955) is discussed next.

Concept of the person. Bordin's approach views the person as being caught and tormented in a struggle between sexual and aggressive hedonistic impulses on the one hand, and socially based responses on the other (Osipow & Walsh, 1970). Basic sexual and aggressive drives (id impulses) conflict with society's expectations of the person. Ideally, people will find socially acceptable ways to channel their impulses. However, frequently these socially unaccepted impulses are repressed to the unconscious level and emerge in the form of psychological complaints (Osipow & Walsh, 1970). The task of the psychoanalytically oriented counselor (Bordin, 1968) is to focus on the causes of the conflict by interpreting the meaning of client behavior with the aim of making unconscious material conscious.

Theory of personality. The personality theory underlying Bordin's psychological counseling is based on certain assumptions. First, that behavior is related to attitudes, emotions, and impulses. Therefore, a change in behavior probably should involve a change in attitudes, emotions, and impulses.

Second, it is important to understand the individual's basic impulses, drives, and satisfactions. Bordin thinks that it is probably most reasonable to attempt to understand the individual within a psychoanalytic framework, because this theory seems to offer more of a basis for explaining human behavior. Thus, while diagnostic categories are not significant, it is important to understand the individual in terms of a personality theory—primarily psychoanalysis.

A third assumption is that there are certain dimensions of growth that tend to be associated with personal development. These dimensions are: basic trust-mistrust, autonomy-shame and doubt, initiative-guilt, industry-inferiority, identity-role diffusion, intimacy-isolation, generativity-stagnation, and integrity-despair (Erikson, 1950). Ideally, the individual should function successfully on these dimensions or stages of development.

Fourth, Bordin assumes a basic conflict between independence and dependence. People want attention and desire to be liked, but they also at times prefer to be on their own and behave as they want.

The fifth and final assumption is that psychological counseling assumes the existence of resistance and transference. Transference occurs when the client begins to perceive the counselor as a significant other in the environment and projects onto the counselor many of the positive or negative feelings experienced toward some other person in the past. Resistance is displayed by the client when threatened. Threat is aroused when the client becomes increasingly aware of previously unconscious and unacceptable impulses (e.g., sex, hostility). According to Bordin, resistance and transference are always present to some degree in the counseling relationship.

Theory of counseling. Bordin's theory of counseling is based on specific dimensions of the counseling relationship, i.e., the ambiguity dimension, the cognitive and conative dimensions, personal dimensions, and the warmth dimension (Patterson, 1973). Ambiguity is a lack of structure or incompleteness. A vague or incomplete situation stimulates anxiety to some degree in people. Manipulating ambiguity to elicit varying levels of anxiety can be useful to the counselor as a motivator for client change.

The aim of the counselor is to maintain an optimum level of ambiguity for the following reasons. First, the vagueness of counseling expectations helps the client bring conflicts into the counseling situation. Ambiguity helps the client make responses that are personally unique. Second, ambiguity facilitates the transference relationship and enables the counselor to better understand the client's motives, impulses, and satisfactions. Third, ambiguity (vagueness or incompleteness) in the counseling situation tends to contribute to the effectiveness of interpretation (going beyond the client's self-insight or understanding).

According to Bordin, all behavior in counseling falls on two dimensions: the cognitive and the conative. Cognitive (thinking) behavior is purposeful and goal directed. Conative (emotional) behavior refers to feelings and emotions. In psychoanalytic theory, cognitive behavior corresponds to the superego and ego and the conative behavior corresponds to the id. Counseling tends to be cognitively oriented in nature primarily because the client's problems are relatively less severe than in most clinical situations. However, Bordin is quick to point out that cognitive and conative understanding are both important.

The personal dimensions suggest that the emotional tone of the relationship is influenced by the counselor's personality and natural style of interacting with others. According to Bordin, the counselor must be involved and must actively participate in the relationship. Who the counselor is, plays an important role in determining the quality of the counseling relationship.

Warmth is defined in terms of acceptance and being genuine and human. More specific characteristics of the warmth dimension are commitment, effort to understand, and spontaneity. Both the counselor and the client must make commitments. The counselor commits time, energy, and skill. The client must attend appointments, pay fees, and work toward the agreed-upon goal. The counselor must also make an effort to understand the client. Counseling is based on the counselor understanding another person. The counselor's commitments and efforts to understand the client tend to cognitively and effectively communicate a sense of warmth to the client. Spontaneous behavior tends to be human, free, expressive, but directed. If the counselor's commitment and effort to understand are spontaneous, they are likely to be warm and personal.

The counseling process of Bordin's psychological counseling seems vaguely described. The process involves a relationship in which the client, with the help of the counselor, is able to anlayze problems, reach solutions, and, when necessary, understand and modify personality characteristics (Patterson, 1973). Counseling, compared to psychotherapy, tends to be less ambiguous, more cognitive, and less feeling-oriented. The counselors, in fact, discourage long-term intense relationships. The psychoanalytically oriented counselor attempts to make conscious causes or aspects of conflicts that are already close to awareness and not threatening to the ego. The ultimate goal is to help the client develop more acceptable social ways of coping with tensions created by the conflicts.

Technique. In medically oriented therapy, the techniques frequently used are free association, interpretation, transference, and counter-transference (Osipow & Walsh, 1970). In counseling situations where clients tend to be less disturbed, the methods include acceptance, understanding, and the interpretation of the client's defenses, because these defenses serve the interests of the ego. Bordin (1968) suggests the use of three different types of interpretation (clarification, comparison, and wish-defense), which have been defined by Colby (1951). Clarification interpretations attempt to crystallize the client's thoughts and pick out a theme. Comparison interpretations place two thoughts, emotions, or behaviors side by side—to demonstrate similarity or differences. Wish-defense interpretations refer to the approach-avoidance components of a conflict. A person may wish or desire something, but this wish, thought, or behavior may produce anxiety. Last, since clients in counseling settings often report vocational problems, the use of tests in diagnosis and in the interviews occurs frequently in psychological counseling. Tests may be used to help a client review self-perceptions of abilities, interests, and personality traits. The fact that Bordin's psychological counseling focuses on vocational counseling and the use of tests is a major value of the approach (Patterson, 1973).

Research. The available research specifically focusing on Bordin's psychological counseling is limited. The following brief review looks at outcome research on psychoanalysis in general.

Cartwright (1966) conducted one of the few adequately controlled comparative-outcome studies in the literature using psychoanalysis as one of the treatments. She compared the outcomes of psychoanalytic treatment with client-centered treatment. Her findings suggest that it is very difficult to say that one type of treatment is more effective than another, or that one type of treatment produces client changes that are different from another treatment. However, Cartwright (1966) did find that certain changes associated with positive client benefit seemed to occur during the process of psychoanalysis. Her results indicate that in the course of psychoanalysis clients tend to increase their level of experience and self-observation. Increased level of experiencing means that the clients are more able to feel deeply, and they are more aware of this feeling.

A review of comparative treatment studies by Luborsky, Chandler, Auerback, Cohen, and Bachrach (1971) showed that no one counseling therapeutic treatment may be established as superior to another.

Research on the transference concept, thought to be the core of change in effective psychoanalytic treatment, is practically nonexistent (Luborsky & Spence, 1971). For a comprehensive review of the research on psychoanalytic therapy, see Luborsky and Spence (1971).

RATIONAL APPROACHES

The rational theories of counseling reflect an intellectual approach to client problem solving. The rational counseling process is an active-directive one primarily concerned with curing "unreason" with reason. The rational approach is represented by the approaches of Ellis (1962, 1971, 1973a, 1973b), Tosi (1974), Thorne (1961), and Williamson (1950). All three present the counselor mainly as a teacher-collaborator who administers a rational, logical, problem solving process in a cognitive teaching relationship (Patterson, 1973). The interchange, primarily cognitive in nature, focuses on the identification of intellectual problem solving responses, as contrasted to emotional feeling-oriented responses (Osipow & Walsh, 1970). Currently the most popular and representative of the rational approaches is Albert Ellis's Rational Emotive Therapy (RET).

Concept of the person.   As do all theorists, Ellis (1973a) makes certain assumptions about the nature of the person and about the origin of unhappiness. Ellis suggests that people can be uniquely rational, as well as irrational. When people are thinking and behaving rationally, they are happier and more productive than when they are irrational. Emotional disturbance or unhappiness is a function of irrational and illogical thinking. This irrational thinking is frequently first fostered by the family group during childhood, a time when one is most vulnerable to outside influences. Children are more suggestible than adults and therefore are more subject to social pressures. Ellis suggests that people tend to maintain the irrational beliefs and behaviors they learned when young by means of the things they say to themselves.

Theory of personality.   The basic tenet of Rational Emotive Treatment is that emotional upsets are caused by the individual's irrational beliefs (Ellis, 1973a, 1973b). These beliefs are irrational in their insistence that some event, behavior, or attitude of another person should, ought, or must be different from the way it is. People demand that events happen for the best in life; when things go badly, they condemn themselves and others. People tend to be disturbed not by things, events, or other people, but by the views or perceptions that they themselves take of things, events, or other people.

Ellis organized and defined this basic tenet of RET, using what he called the ABC theory of personality. A (Activating Event) is defined as a fact, an event, that is associated with some emotional upset. C (Consequence) is the individual's response (emotional upset or unhappiness) that is presumed to follow directly from A, the Activating Event. However, it is not A that is the cause of C, but B (rational or irrational Belief). The emotional upset (C) is not determined by the stimulus (A), but by the individual's belief (B), perception, or appraisal of it. For example, if something noxious happens to an individual (Activating Event) that causes emotional upset (Consequence), the individual probably will think (Belief) in one of two ways—rationally or irrationally. If the person thinks rationally about the Activating Event, the following self-talk probably occurs: "I don't like this event! It is inconvenient and I wish it did not exist! But this is the way it is!" If a person were able to stick with this rational belief, no emotional upset would be felt. However, if a person thinks irrationally about the Activating Event, the self-talk is likely to sound like this: "Isn't it horrible and awful! It should not exist! I am a terrible person for letting this happen!" This irrational belief leads to unpleasant consequences, such as depression, anxiety, and feelings of worthlessness. Furthermore, these unpleasant feelings interfere with attempts to change the Activating Event.

Theory of counseling. The general assumption of the theory of counseling is that thought and emotion overlap and that, therefore, disordered emotions can often be improved by changing one's thinking. A rational emotive counselor attempts to induce clients to organize and discipline their thinking, to be tolerant of self and others, and to reduce "demandingness." In RET these goals are accomplished through a rational restructuring of those irrational ideas that produce negative emotions and maladaptive behavior (Ellis, 1973a, 1973b). The counselor directly and authoritatively attempts to show the client how to accept reality, even when rather bleak. The counselor actually tries to show or demonstrate how the client would be better off accepting himself or herself unconditionally, rather than demanding such acceptance and approval from others. Behaviorally, the counselor gives the client homework assignments that augment the counseling (e.g., assertive behavior, bibliotherapy).

The counseling process itself involves the following steps (Ellis, 1973a, 1973b):

1. Identification of client irrational beliefs associated with the disturbed behavior.
2. The counselor asks the client to validate those beliefs.
3. The counselor shows the client that these beliefs cannot be logically and empirically validated. The counselor shows the client that these irrational beliefs cannot work and will lead to more self-defeat.
4. The counselor gets clients to change their thinking by replacing irrational beliefs with rational ones.
5. The counselor teaches clients how to think logically and empirically.

The major goal of rational emotive counseling is the reduction of the client's self-defeating view and the acceptance of a more realistic, tolerant, rational philosophy of life. According to Ellis (1973b), individuals with mild or serious emotional disturbances may be treated with RET, except those who are out of contact with reality (Ellis, 1973a,

1973b). Ellis does not claim that his approach is effective with all kinds of clients and problems.

Technique.   The primary counseling method of a rational emotive counselor is active, directive, and persuasive (Ellis, 1973a, 1973b). The counselor, in an active-directive style, gives insight; there is no need to wait for the client to get insight independently. The counselor uses a variety of techniques, such as logic, reason, suggestion, confrontation, commands, indoctrination, prescription of behavior, role playing, assertive training, desensitization, humor, support, and even homework. Furthermore, the counselor encourages and persuades the client to engage in some behavior in a real-life setting that will provide experience to serve as counter propaganda regarding irrational beliefs held. The counselor does not devote much time to the client's personal history. Nor does the counselor make much use of other psychoanalytically oriented techniques, such as free association and dream analysis.

Research.   In general, the research evidence (Dua, 1970; Rimm & Litvak, 1969; Tosi & Carlson, 1970; Velten, 1968; Tosi & Eshbaugh, 1975; Tosi & Reardon, 1976; Reardon & Tosi, 1976; Moleski & Tosi, 1975) shows that emotional difficulties tend to be associated with specific irrational ideas. For example, the irrational belief that one is only worthwhile if completely and nearly perfect in all that is attempted, stimulates emotional upset and leads to self-defeating behavor. Also, the research findings (Folkins, 1970; Geer, Davison, & Gatchel, 1970; Jordan & Kempler, 1970; Steffy, Meichenbaum, & Best, 1970; Valins, 1970) exploring the ABC theory of personality are generally supportive. In other words, the notion that emotional upsets (C) tend to be related to irrational beliefs (B) rather than activating events (A) has received some statistical support. Finally, RET seems to more effectively cope with client "demandingness" and absoluteness than do other counseling approaches (Ellis, 1971, 1973). For a more comprehensive listing of the research, see Ellis (1973a, 1973b).

Reality counseling

Another common-sense approach to counseling is Glasser's reality counseling (1965). This approach associates mental disturbance with irresponsible behavior. Glasser suggests that irresponsible behavior is self-defeating behavior and involves hurting self and others. Thus, his theory emphasizes the notion that people are rational beings, personally responsible for their own behavior.

Concept of person.   Reality counseling views the individual as having a basic, socially derived need for an identity. This need is intrinsic, inherited, and is viewed as the driving force for all behavior. The identity need is seen in the desire each of us has to be a different, separate, and unique person. We all want to believe that there is no other individual quite like ourself on the face of the earth. According to Glasser (Glasser & Zunin, 1973), to change our identity we must change our behavior.

Theory of personality. As noted, reality counseling is based on the premise that each individual has a need for an identity (self-image). Glasser defines two kinds of identity: success and failure. These identities (Glasser & Zunin, 1973) begin to develop early in life (during the first six years). People with a positive or successful self-image believe that there is at least one other person in the world who cares about them and about whom they care. Most of the time these positive people think they are worthwhile. Glasser suggests that there is a tendency for people with positive self-images to associate with other people having positive or success identities.

People unable to develop a success identity tend to form an unsuccessful self-image or a failure identity. Most of the time such individuals have problems caring about other people and do not perceive of themselves as worthwhile. People with failure identity engage in behavior characterized by the withdrawal from and the denial of reality. According to Glasser, denial, withdrawal, and ignoring lead to failure identities, mental problems, and loneliness. Failure identities tend to be perpetuated by irresponsible self-defeating behavior that involves hurting the self and others.

Theory of counseling. The general assumption of Glasser's counseling theory is that "we are what we do"; if we want to change "what we are" (identity), we must change "what we do" (behavior). Change in identity follows change in behavior (Glasser & Zunin, 1973). Thus, the focus in counseling is on the identification and alteration of the client's self-defeating, irresponsible behavior. Behavior change must precede identity change.

The counseling process involves the following principles (Glasser, 1965; Glasser & Zunin, 1973):

1. The counselor communicates warmth, understanding, and concern to the client.
2. The focus is on behavior.
3. The focus is on the present. The past cannot be changed.
4. The client must make a judgment and identify self-defeating, irresponsible behavior before being open to counseling help.
5. The counselor assists the client in developing a plan to change behavior. It is important that this plan be in writing.

6. The counselor helps the client make a commitment to carry out the plan.
7. The counselor makes it clear to the client that excuses for not carrying out the plan are unacceptable.
8. The counselor does not punish the client for failure.

The main goal of reality counseling is the reduction of irresponsible self-defeating behavior and the development of a positive self-image. It is through the making and carrying out of a plan that the client is able to experience responsible behavioral success and begin to gain some sense of self-worth. The client is judged to be making progress when responsibility for personal behavior is assumed, and when attempts to meet personal needs without hurting self or others are evident.

Technique. The reality counselor believes that most forms of mental disturbance are based on irresponsible behavior. Regardless of the behavioral symptoms, it is the self-defeating nature of the client's behavior that is troublesome. The counselor's task is to help the client identify the self-defeating characteristics. The counselor thus focuses on behavior, the client-counselor relationship, and the present. According to Glasser (Glasser & Zunin, 1973), a successful identity cannot be acquired without being aware of one's present behavior. Also, Glasser believes that clients have more control over their overt behavior than their thinking or feeling responses. In the counseling relationship, the counselor communicates warmth, understanding, and concern. Counselors present themselves as genuine people who care. The focus on the present is based on the notion that the past is not changeable. When the past is discussed, an attempt is made to relate it to present behavior. Diagnosis and a variety of other techniques (confrontation, free association, silence, nondirective techniques, and the like) are not used.

Research. Glasser and Zunin (1973) report that there has been no long-term research on the effectiveness of reality counseling with outpatients. However, follow-up work at the Ventura School for Girls shows that the use of reality counseling in their treatment program has significantly reduced the recidivism rate for that environment (Glasser & Zunin, 1973). Other research (English, 1970; Hawer, 1971) has focused on use of reality counseling in various school environments. English (1970) has shown that reality counseling is an effective treatment for reducing disciplinary problems, increasing school achievement, and improving teacher-teacher and teacher-student interactions. Hawer (1971) studied the impact of a reality counseling program on 340 black students from the third and sixth grades of two schools over a period of 16 weeks. In general, the findings revealed that the students showed more involvement in school activities, more frequenly sought information, were more sociable, and were less compliant. The above very limited research lends some support to the notion that reality counseling is helpful. Clearly, however, additional research is needed to substantiate the validity and usefulness of the concepts and principles of reality counseling.

BEHAVIOR MODIFICATION APPROACHES

There are many behavioral modification approaches (e.g., Wolpe, 1958, 1969; Dollard & Miller, 1950; Phillips & Wiener, 1966; Rotter, 1954; Bandura, 1969; Stampfl & Levis, 1967; Krumboltz, 1966; Krumboltz & Thoresen, 1969; Lazarus, 1968; Ullmann & Krasner, 1965). These approaches share the fact that they are based on principles of human learning. The aim of the behavioral approach is to help people either acquire adaptive behavioral responses or eliminate maladaptive responses so that either more effective or less self-defeating behavior, or both, will result. The behavioral views generally have in common a focus on overt behavior, rather than the subjective responses of clients (Osipow & Walsh, 1970). Because of this focus, behavioral approaches usually attend to changing client overt behavior (instrumental responses). Goals emphasize symptom removal; sometimes it is assumed that changes in overt behavior will generalize and affect thinking responses, but many behavioral counselors do not even think about client subjective behavior. Symptom removal refers to the elimination of the client's behavioral problem.

Behavioral approaches use various techniques to effect behavioral change, most of which are supported by empirical findings. In fact, the behavior modification view is the only counseling view in which empirical observation preceded theoretical formulations. Although a number of different behavioral modification views exist, the one developed by Wolpe (1958) is probably most representative.

Concept of the person. Behavior modification approaches make one assumption about the nature of the person; this assumption is based on the concept of determinism. Behavior is viewed to be a function of (or is determined by) antecedent conditions (past experiences or past behavior, or both). Thus, a person is viewed as possessing a collection of previously reinforced responses that can be and are generalized to new situations. The concept of free will is inconsistent with behavior modification approaches in the sense that people behave in ways which are contingent upon antecedent conditions. For a behavioral counselor, the truism that "the best predictor of future behavior is past behavior" holds.

Theory of personality. Limited attention has been given to a theory of personality by the behavior modification approaches (Goldstein, 1973). One potential reason for the dearth of attention may be the emphasis by behavioral models on empirical observation, rather than on theoretical assumption. In any event, little work has been done in the area of individual differences as they relate to the impact of treatment (Goldstein, 1973), with the possible exception of Eysenck's work (1967; Eysenck & Beech, 1971; Eysenck & Eysenck, 1969).

Theory of counseling. Wolpe's reciprocal inhibition counseling is primarily concerned with changing maladaptive behavior. It is necessary that the counselor determine which behaviors are not adaptive, and under what conditions these responses occur. Most maladaptive behavior in one way or another has anxiety at its core. Fear or anxiety is a learned emotional response to originally neutral stimuli that were presented a number of times with a painful stimulus. Wolpe's reciprocal inhibition counseling focuses on eliminating or weakening anxiety responses by introducing a competing response. The principle of reciprocal inhibition asserts that, if a response antgonistic to the anxiety response can be made to occur in the presence of the stimulus producing anxiety, this will tend to weaken the stimulus-anxiety response bond. Wolpe usually uses one of three compatible responses, i.e., relaxation, assertive and sexual responses. The relaxation responses are used most frequently. Figure 2–1 schematizes the rationale. Antagonistic responses are introduced to weaken the stimulus-anxiety response bond.

FIGURE 2–1

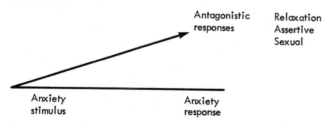

Antagonistic responses — Relaxation, Assertive, Sexual

Anxiety stimulus — Anxiety response

The counseling process involves these steps (Osipow & Walsh, 1970; Patterson, 1973):

1. Identification of stimulus areas associated with anxiety responses and consequent maladaptive behavior.
2. The client is taught muscular relaxation and is encouraged to practice the relaxation procedure outside the interview situation. The

relaxation response is being used to interface and weaken the stimulus-anxiety response bond.

3. In a relaxed state the counselor has the client imagine a graded series of scenes associated with the anxiety response.
4. Progress along this hierarchy of scenes is halted when the client experiences anxiety.
5. Eventually the client will be able to control the anxiety response by countering it with the acquired relaxation, assertive, or sexual responses.

This technique has been shown to be effective in a variety of anxiety-producing situations, including interpersonal ones (Wolpe, 1958).

Technique. The reciprocal inhibition principle is based on two behavior modification techniques, i.e., adaptation (or desensitization) and counter-conditioning. The technique of desensitization involves the presentation of the anxiety stimulus at very weak strengths, so that it will not be strong enough to elicit the anxiety response. The strength of the anxiety stimulus is gradually increased until the presentation of the feared stimulus at full strength does not stimulate the anxiety response. The technique of counter-conditioning involves the presentation of the anxiety stimulus in sufficient strength to elicit the anxiety response when the person is making a response that is incompatible with the anxiety response. The reciprocal inhibition principle couples these two techniques by gradually presenting the anxiety stimulus (desensitization) when the client is making a response (relaxation, assertive, or sexual) that is incompatible with the anxiety response (counter-conditioning). Graded anxiety-producing stimuli are paired with a relaxation, assertive, or sexual response until the connection between those stimuli and the anxiety response is reduced or eliminated. Since the technique relies upon imagined situations, it is easier to use and is more convenient than real-life situation procedures.

Research. Behavior modification strategies are in the unique position of being based on empirical observation, rather than on theoretical assumption. Evidence shows that Wolpe's procedure has been used effectively (successfully) in a number of clinical and laboratory settings (Paul, 1967; Rachman, 1967; Wolpe & Lazarus, 1966). It is a technique that may be easily learned by a counselor, and is effective as a method of treatment. A review of the literature (Paul, 1969) on controlled analogue studies showed systematic desensitization to be more effective than no treatment and insight-oriented treatment. Follow-up studies (Paul, 1967, 1968) show that the effects of systematic desentization can be maintained two years after treatment. However, Murray and Jacobson (1971) suggest that systematic desensitization may also be viewed as a method of modifying beliefs by the use of social influence. This view is based on the fact that the evidence on the nature of systematic desensitization is not conclusive. In fact, some evidence suggests that muscular relaxation (Cooke, 1968), a progressive hierarchy (Cohen, 1969; Wolpin & Rainer, 1966), and imaginal rehearsal (Folkins, Lawson, Opton, & Lazarus, 1968; Zeisset, 1968) are not essential for successful desensitization.

SOCIAL PSYCHOLOGICAL APPROACH

A very contemporary view of counseling is the social psychological approach, which focuses on counseling as a social influence process. From this perspective, counseling is viewed as an environment for interpersonal influence. One person (the counselor) influences another (the client) to improve the client's effectiveness in social behavior.

In his book, *Persuasion and Healing* (1963), Jerome Frank, a student of Kurt Lewin, introduced to counselors the notion that counseling is aptly viewed to be a social influence process. Following Frank's rather profound book, others began to apply social psychological concepts to counseling (Bergin, 1962; Goldstein, Heller, & Sechrest, 1966; Strong, 1968). Strong (1968, 1970, 1971), Kilty (1970), and Goldstein (1971) have been leaders in extending social psychological concepts to the counseling process.

Concept of the person.   The social psychological approach to counseling views the person as determined by the environment, but to some extent capable of controlling the environment (Strong, 1979). As in the behavioral tradition, the person is viewed as shaped by antecedent conditions, past experiences, and the environment. It is by this means (environmental impact) that the counselor is able to influence the client. At the same time, the environment is seen as operating on people, people are seen as capable of environmental control. Improved environmental control by the individual should lead to more self-control and, thus, more effective social behavior (Strong, 1975).

Theory of personality.   The social psychological approach attempts to understand human behavior in terms of the individual functioning as a control agent (Bergin, 1972; Strong, 1979). It is assumed that people are responsible for and capable of controlling their behavior. In the social influence framework, the purpose of counseling is to help the person become a more effective self-regulator. The individual is assisted in regulating affect, cognition, and actions by means of self-control. Counseling in sharpening the individual's self-control behavior permits the emission of more effective social behavior. Strong (1979) suggests that ideally the healthy person is one very much in control of the here-and-now environment, and capable of additional self-regulation.

Theory of counseling. The general assumption made by social influence theorists is that, if we want to improve the individual's self-regulation, we must sharpen the traits associated with self-control. Strong (1979) suggests that this process involves three phases:

1. The counselor helps the client reduce perceptual distortion of events or people.
2. The counselor helps the client associate or attribute behavior to a cause that is more controllable.
3. The client must be motivated to action, to trying out new behavior.

Strong (1968) indicates that the counselor, by managing perceived credibility and attractiveness, is able to change client behavior and to facilitate client self-control. The counselor's ability to influence the client is then based on these two sources of perceived power—credibility and attraction (Strong, 1979). Credibility comes from the client's perception of the counselor as possessing knowledge and skills needed by the client to solve problems. Notice that the social influence potential is managed not by the actual existence of counselor resources but by the client's perception of the counselor's resources. The attraction power base arises from the client's need for psychological congruence, the client's need to be liked, and the counselor's physical attractiveness (Strong, 1979). The client identifies perceived similarities between himself or herself and the counselor.

Motivation for change in counseling comes from the client's desire for congruence. During the counseling process the counselor's task is to identify psychological inconsistencies for the client. Cognitive and behavior change occurs when a client confronts believable information that is inconsistent with the perceived self-concept. Such information helps clients identify causes of their problems which, in turn, facilitate self-control and more effective social behavior.

Technique. In the social psychological approach, the counselor attempts to introduce credible and inconsistent information (inconsistent with the client's thinking) that will bring about client change and eventual client psychological congruence. Within this framework the counselor introduces two kinds of information (Strong, 1979). First, the counselor identifies psychological inconsistencies for the client. This information may have been previously distorted, denied, or ignored. Second, the counselor introduces different standards for evaluating perceived experiences and behavior to help the client process information and attribute behavior to causes which are more controllable. Both kinds of information stimulate client psychological incongruence and eventual change.

How is psychological incongruence brought about? At least four methods have been identified that attempt to introduce credible and inconsistent information to the client (Strong, 1979):

1. In the attribution method, the counselor communicates acceptance of the client as a worthy person. The counselor attributes to the client the qualities of worth and dignity.
2. The perspective method introduces new standards against which old and new experiences may be evaluated.
3. The methods of interpretation, empathy, and instruction go beyond the client's current insight (understanding) and consequently stimulate client psychological incongruence.
4. The counter-attitudinal/forced-compliance method attempts to get the client to act in some way that is antagonistic to the self-defeating behavior.

Social psychological counselors believe that information presented to the client must be discrepant and credible to produce change and facilitate more effective self-control. Of course, diagnosis is a meaningful method in the counseling process. Diagnosis of the perceived cause of the initial psychological imbalance is necessary to determine the desired controlling behaviors and to restore psychological congruence.

Research.   In general, the research evidence provided mostly by counseling analogue studies (Tinsley & Harris, 1976; Spiegel, 1976; Strong, Taylor, Bratton, & Loper, 1971; Peoples & Dell, 1975; Strong & Schmidt, 1970; Kaul & Schmidt, 1971) suggests that a relationship between perceived counselor credibility and client change may indeed exist. For example, Spiegel (1976) found that interviewers introduced with expert credentials were rated more expert and competent when compared to interviewers introduced with inexpert credentials. Other research (Strong, Taylor, Bratton, & Loper, 1971; Peoples & Dell, 1975) shows that counselors responding in a relaxed style in the interview situation tend to be perceived as competent, expert, and helpful. Research reports by Strong and Schmidt (1970) and Kaul and Schmidt (1971) have found that such counselor responses as breaking confidences and dishonest comments tend to lower students' rating of trustworthiness.

The evidence on the attractiveness variable as a source of counselor power for social influence is more ambiguous. Cash, Begley, McCown, and Weise (1975), using videotapes, asked college students to rate physically unattractive and attractive counselors. The physically attractive counselors (compared to the unattractive ones) were perceived to be more competent, friendly, trustworthy, and likely to produce a favorable counseling outcome. Counselors introduced as warm as compared to cold were perceived by college students as more attractive, persuasive, and influential (Goldstein, 1971). Other research has not been as supportive of the attractiveness variable (Goldstein, 1971; Cheney, 1975; Schmidt & Strong, 1971; Strong & Dixon, 1971)—tentatively suggesting that, for counselors lower on perceived credibility or expertness, attractiveness may serve as a more important influence agent (Strong, 1979).

It should be noted that a great deal of the social influence research in counseling has not been conducted in real-life counseling situations with real clients and counselors. Instead, most is *analogue* research, which has the limitation that we can't be sure how closely our observations would match real-life situations. This imposes a serious limitation on the degree to which we can generalize about the research results to real-life counseling.

SUMMARY

This chapter has presented a general review of the five major theoretical approaches to counseling. This is not a complete and thorough treatment of existing counseling theory. For additional information on theoretical approaches, reference to other books is recommended (e.g., Patterson, 1973). This book and others are listed in the reference section.

Five major groups of counseling theories have been reviewed: perceptual, existential, analytical, rational, and behavioral. The perceptual approaches to counseling focus on the environment as it is perceived and self-reported by the individual. Thus, it is the individual's self-concept (perceived image of self) that is of primary importance in these approaches. The existential approaches are concerned with understanding the individual in the context of the person's world and the individual's commitment to self-awareness. Psychoanalytic approaches emphasize the role of unconscious forces underlying behavior and are, in the main, concerned with making unconscious material conscious. The rational theories to counseling reflect a cognitive approach to client problem solving. The counseling process is an active-directive one concerned with curing unreason with reason. The behavioral approaches have in common a focus on overt behavior. Thus, these last approaches are oriented toward the acquisition of adaptive behavioral responses or the elimination of maladaptive responses that will contribute to more effective behavior.

The counseling relationship: Structure and process

In chapter 2, theory, we saw that nearly all theoretical approaches stress the importance of the counselor-client relationship. In this chapter we will review the ingredients necessary for the establishment of a good relationship in counseling, how the counselor must behave to create the necessary ingredients at the beginning of the relationship and, as the counseling process develops, how to set goals, assess their accomplishment, and appropriately terminate counseling.

The viewpoints of diverse theoretical positions have been synthesized to portray a general perspective of counseling. As a result, the material presented in this chapter should provide sufficient flexibility for the potential counselor to use a variety of counseling methods.

The counseling relationship

One of the major influences in counseling is the quality of the relationship the counselor has with the client. As noted earlier, outcomes of research conducted from many theoretical positions have shown that the counselor-client relationship lies at the heart of the counseling process. If positive outcome is to take place in counseling, a good interpersonal relationship between client and counselor must be established and maintained. Evidence for this abounds.

Parloff (1956) found significant associations between the quality of the counselor-client relationships, defined as counselor closeness and understanding, and the reduction of psychological symptoms expressed by the client. Heine (1950) found that the most helpful counselors were perceived by their clients as trustworthy, understanding, and accepting, whether they were Adlerian, psychoanalytic, or client-centered in orientation. Barrett-Lennard (1962) and Truax (1962) found that the clients of counselors who were empathic, accepting, genuine, and experienced reported more therapeutic gains. More recently, positive relationships have been demonstrated between the counselors' expression of genuineness, confrontation, empathy, concreteness, and respect and the level of client self-exploration (Alexik & Carkhuff, 1967; Piaget, Berenson, & Carkhuff, 1967; Mullen & Abeles, 1972).

A number of early studies on the counselor-client relationship and its impact on client self-exploration and outcomes reveal the importance of the relationship in initial sessions. Grater (1964) found that clients focus more on personal problems when they perceive the counselor as being warm, friendly, and accepting. Similar findings have been reported by Wagstaff, Rice, and Butler (1960). Findings of more recent studies replicate these earlier findings (Friel, Kratochvil, & Carkhuff, 1968; Tosi, 1970; Vitalo, 1971).

How to promote a good relationship

The counselor-client relationship should not be construed as a magical phenomenon that produces or affects changes in persons in mysterious ways. There are definite characteristics of the relationship that make it helpful to the client. But even though the counselor may possess many of these relationship qualities, such as empathy, genuineness, openness, and acceptance, these qualities need to be perceived by the client. Client perception of these counselor qualities in a positive way increases the attraction to the counseling process. Moreover, these perceptions are related to decreased interpersonal anxiety, increased self-exploration, and commitment to counseling (Truax, 1962; Van Deer Veen, 1970). Some of the most basic conditions for an effective counseling relationship are discussed next.

Empathy

Empathy refers to one's ability to be able to understand another's thoughts, feelings, and behavior in a way that is accurately communicated to the other person (Rogers, 1961). An empathic response is not merely a mirror reflection of the content of what another is saying. It is more of an accurate appraisal or inference about the underlying meaning of the words or nonverbal gestures derived from careful observation of the client's behavior, i.e., anxiety may be inferred if the client breaks into a sweat when discussing a heterosexual relationship.

Suppose a client is describing with a great deal of objectivity and little emotion a recent breakup of a relationship with a woman. A counselor responding to what is inferred to be the emotional content of the client's statement might say, "You seem to be able to talk about your situation, but at the same time you seem to feel very much alone. That must be frightening at times." If the counselor's response is accurate, the client would be more likely to focus on his loneliness and fear. The counselor would encourage a deeper exploration of the significance of loneliness and anxiety. The self-enhancing as well as the self-defeating aspects of these emotions would be explored.

Counselor responses that do not convey understanding and accurate empathy may erect barriers to effective communication and thus close off possibilities for client self-exploration. A low level of empathic counselor response is exemplified as follows:

> **Client:** I feel like I am being used by my friends. But I can't bring myself to say anything to them. I just go along with them.
>
> **Counselor:** Yes, I know. What kind of friends do you have? Why can't you pick better friends?

A more empathic or understanding counselor response could be:

> **Counselor:** You seem upset because you can't tell your friends you're bothered by how they treat you.

Acceptance

A counselor may intellectually grasp a client's innermost feelings and behavioral dispositions—and profess to understand these. But the question arises: Can a counselor accept the client's ideas, values, feelings, and behavior, especially if these differ from the counselor's? Acceptance implies a nonrating or evaluation of the total person in light of his or her acceptable or unacceptable tendencies. Acceptance need not imply that a counselor must agree with, or reinforce, every attitude, value, and behavior of the client. But it does suggest an acknowledgment that self-defeating behavior may be as natural as self-enhancing behavior, and that human beings are uniquely capable of both.

Client: I feel so impotent, so—no good. I can't seem to succeed at anything. I feel like a total failure in relationships with women, at work —just a total failure. Am I a worthless person?

Counselor: It's hard for me to conceive of you as a worthless person. But you have negative ideas about yourself that you may want to question or challenge.

Unfortunately, a counselor also may easily reinforce the self-defeating thoughts, feelings, and behavior of a client by indiscriminate, naive, and pseudo-accepting responses. If a counselor has strong needs for approval and acceptance from others, unconscious approval of client behavior may occur to obtain client approval. Nongenuine positiveness, which plays down or does not acknowledge the client's negative or self-defeating tendencies, may encourage an unrealistic view of self and environment and reinforce an avoidance of genuine personal difficulties. Of course, if the counselor focuses mainly on the client's negative attributes, the client may ignore constructive possibilities, and come away from counseling feeling the situation is hopeless.

Openness

Openness to experience assumes in the counselor an attitude of affirming and acknowledging the reality of the client's personal orientation to life. Openness assumes an awareness of human processes, whether these be of a rational or irrational nature—a willingness to attend to oneself and others with a minimum of distortion, defensiveness, and avoidance and denial (Rogers, 1961).

Client: I believe that most men, if not all, are sexist in their attitudes toward women. Maybe that includes you, too.

Counselor: Your experiences with men have apparently been poor. I can understand how you might distrust me, too, at least until you get to know me.

Counselors often ignore problem areas expressed by their clients, simply because they themselves are afraid of the same areas. A counselor may hide behind theoretical assumptions and techniques, and thus avoid a genuine human encounter with another person. Counselors often feel very anxious over emotionally charged topics, such as homosexuality, rape, abortion, feminism, and sex. If any emotion is likely to render a counselor ineffective, it is anxiety. Anxiety serves to cue defensive patterns of behavior, whereby the counselor may resort to avoiding significant problem areas by simply ignoring or not responding to those areas. An example of an inappropriate counselor response follows:

Client: When having sexual relationships with my husband, I image about being beaten by him. That fantasy really turns me on.

Counselor: You ought to stop thinking that kind of nonsense. What does that have to do with sex? What would your husband think of you if he knew that?

A better response would be:

Counselor: Does this concern you?

Counselor characteristics, such as attractiveness, trustworthiness, and expertness, influence counseling outcomes as do those of empathy, openness, and acceptance. However, these attitudes are by no means sufficient conditions for desirable counseling outcomes. Counselors sometimes also behave in an active-directive-authoritative way, wherein they apply techniques and methods aimed at educating, facilitating, and reinforcing the client's growth in personal, social, and career areas. Through the counseling process, people are guided to become more self-aware, to increase self-exploration, to make constructive behavioral commitments, to implement action, and to ultimately internalize healthy behavioral patterns (Tosi & Marzella, 1975).

The counseling process (initiating)

In all forms of counseling, the counselor functions to facilitate client self-awareness and behavior change largely through providing a relationship in which the counselee explores and possibly practices new and more productive ways of thinking, feeling, and acting. As the relationship climate develops, the counselor employs strategies or techniques and selectively reinforces healthy behavioral patterns.

To some extent every counselor operates from a set of assumptions about the laws governing human behavior. As we have already seen, the counselor formulates hypotheses related to client behavior and chooses appropriate behavioral modifying techniques to foster a desirable change in the client. In spite of all the counselor may do in the way of forming ideas and assumptions about the client's psychological world and applying counseling procedures, significant benefit will occur only if the client participates experientially in every phase of the counseling process. This section describes some of the most basic elements of the counseling process.

The initial interview. In the initial phases of counseling, it becomes essential that the client develops realistic and meaningful expectations and understandings of counseling. It is therefore of considerable import that the counselor sets forth the ground rules of a structure that will make clear to the client what is reasonably expected. In the first counseling session, it is generally a good idea to ask the client what knowledge, expectations, and previous counseling experiences he or she has possessed. The counselor can provide some general information about counseling in the first session—about the meaning of counseling, expectations, confidentiality, and the like. The confidential nature of the relationship should be clearly stressed.

The beginning counselor is often preoccupied with fears and misconceptions about the counseling relationship. A special concern or preoccupation of neophyte counselors has to do with the impact they will have on the client, and whether the client will be motivated to work. As a result, beginning counselors may adopt a very rigid approach during the initial session. When the initial interview is handled in a flexible and relaxing manner, the stage can be set for a good working alliance between the counselor and client. Many poorly motivated clients can benefit from counseling if the counselor maintains flexibility and is careful to explain to the client what is to be expected (Lazarus, 1971).

The counselor's personal flexibility is a key factor in the initial interview, and is necessary for the perception and response to what the client requires in the way of help. Lazarus (1971) asserts that the structure and the material presented by the client in the initial interview depend largely on the client's perceptions of counseling, intellectual functioning, psychological adjustment, and socioeconomic background. Moreover, Lazarus contends that with greater experience, a counselor's behavior will vary considerably in an initial interview, ranging from degrees of activity (challenging, confronting) to passivity (being silent, reflecting, listening). The attitudes of acceptance, warmth, friendliness, and understanding need to undergird whatever techniques the counselor uses to create a comfortable interpersonal environment that will facilitate counselor-client interaction. To achieve effectiveness the counselor needs to maximize personal attractiveness, trustworthiness, and expertise as a helper.

The counselor's manner of presentation may be a very potent technique. The influence of the counselor on a client largely depends on the way the counselor is perceived by his client. Truax (1962) and

Rogers (1961) have shown that when clients perceive the counselor as accepting and empathic, they will tend to feel less anxious about revealing significant problem areas. That is, clients tend to be more open to the demands of the counseling situation under proper conditions.

Structuring the counseling relationship. Structuring in counseling refers to defining and specifying the limits of the counseling transaction. However, imposing limits on a client is likely to be a delicate matter. Structures that are too rigid or too permissive could have negative effects on the relationship. It is helpful for the counselor to be familiar with a set of structural guidelines that may be applied with flexibility to each unique counseling situation. Structuring is continuous throughout the entire counseling relationship, because there are times when the client may deviate from some of the mutual expectations defined in early sessions (e.g., being late and missing appointments, physically acting out).

Structuring in counseling revolves around five key areas where limits are often placed. These areas involve placing limits on the *relationship, time,* counselor-client *behavior,* counselor *competence,* and counselor *role.*

The relationship. Relationship structuring or limits require that the counselor clearly communicates to the client the characteristics of the counseling or helping relationship. Sometimes, the client may be encouraged to become familiar with the counselor's point of view through outside readings. Counseling techniques, goals, and outside-of-counseling experiences need to be clearly understood by the client. A most important aspect of relationship structuring is for the counselor to make very clear to the client that their relationship is a professional one and that the content is confidential. Relationship limits are reviewed periodically and occur throughout the counseling process.

Time. During the initial interview, some general agreement needs to be reached regarding the frequency and duration of the counseling sessions. Counseling sessions range generally from 30 to 50 minutes. When counseling is of a time-limited and problem-solving nature, the counselor and client can easily reach an agreement on the number of sessions needed to accomplish specific goals. In more long-term, reconstructive counseling, the number of sessions needed to accomplish goals may not be as easily specified.

Counselor-client behavior. The counselor can explicitly instruct the client to express the full range of significant thoughts, emotions, and behavior. However, there are some limitations about acting in ways that may bring personal harm to the counselor or the client. The counselor can inform the client that, while emotional expression is a very important part of counseling, physical outbursts that may endanger self, others, and property should not occur. Generally, the counselor may need to refrain from using emotionally and physically evocative techniques that may provoke the client into self-destructive, hostile, or aggressive acts during the counseling session (e.g., physical and verbal abuse and harassment).

Counselor competence. Counselors are ethically bound to function professionally within the sphere of their skills and competence. Counselors not skilled in diagnosis or psychotherapy should not give clients the impression of possessing such skills. Moreover, counselors should not use techniques with which they have had little or no training.

Counselor role. In certain instances a counselor may play dual roles, serving as teacher-counselor, minister-counselor, or administrator-counselor. When moving from one role to another, the counselor has an obligation to clarify and separate appropriate expectations about the various roles. This is particularly recommended when the dual roles involve one that is of a judgmental nature, e.g., a teacher who must evaluate a student's academic performance who is also the student's guidance counselor.

Example of structure in the initial interview

Client: Hello, I'm Bill Smith.

Counselor: Hi. I am Mr. Don Jones—glad to meet you, Bill.

Client: I've never been to see a counselor before.

Counselor: This is your first time?

Client: Yes.

Counselor: How can I help you?

Client: I have heard that you help people with problems—personal problems and educational problems.

Counselor: Yes.

Client: Well, I'm not sure, but I think I am having some personal problems.

Counselor: Personal problems. How is that?

Client: Yes, I feel unmotivated. I thought I was physically ill and went to a doctor. He couldn't find anything physically wrong. One of my friends said I have an emotional problem. Do I?

Counselor: Well, I don't know that for sure at this moment—but that is something we could explore together.

Client: How do I find out?

Counselor: You need to tell me a bit about yourself . . . how you feel . . . so I can know you better.

Client: I've been pretty unhappy lately.

Counselor: Most people have times in their life when they're not so happy and need to talk to someone. Bill, could you tell me when you started to feel this way?

Client: Yes, about two months ago. I broke up with my girl friend. I was going with her for three years. She dumped me for another guy. We were living together for about a year. I didn't mind at first, but I do know I still love her.

Counselor: I see.

Client: About two weeks after we broke up I got into drugs pretty heavily and copped out.

Counselor: Un-huh. I guess you should tell me about how things went from then on.

Bill relates a story of moderate drug use, anxiety, depression, and eventually academic failure. The counselor elicits Bill's feelings of hopelessness. Bill asks, "What can I do?"

Counselor: Okay, Bill. Before we move on, let me say a few things about how I work. I can't tell you how long it will take for you to feel better. We will know more about that later. At this time, it is important that we get some of the main issues clarified and specify some goals that we want to achieve. Once that is accomplished, we can discuss some procedures that we might implement to help achieve those goals. I also need to know a lot more about you.

Client: Yeah, okay.

Counselor: Another thing, Bill. You seem to have some idea already about what counselors do. Let's see if I can clarify that a bit and emphasize a few important points. We'll sit down together and try to come up with some understandings and solutions to your concerns. We'll get together frequently at first. Then, after we decide what we want to achieve and agree on how to proceed, we'll see how often to get together. We take as long as we need. Our sessions will be here at the counseling center. I want you to know that what is said in these sessions is private, just between us. What is said in this room will go no further. Do you have any questions?

Client: Well, I think I understand.

Counselor: Okay. Let's get back to the business that concerns you most.

At this point the counselor can seek more clarification of the problem.

Counselor: Let's see if I have an idea of what you seem to be concerned about...

Toward the end of the session it is usually a good idea for the counselor to summarize the session and to make arrangements for the next counseling session.

Behavioral consequences of over- and under-structuring

If the counseling relationship is rigidly defined, wherein goals, objectives, and procedures are too narrowly specified, important opportunities for self-exploration may be denied the client. On the other hand, a loosely structured ambiguous situation may be too anxiety-provoking for the client.Given both extremes of over- and under-structuring, some similar as well as different behavioral consequences are likely. Both extremes should be avoided. These extreme conditions similarly could reinforce client dependency needs and defensiveness. Moreover, the extreme conditions may lead to an untimely termination of counseling.

Over-structuring can lead to an intellectualization of the counseling process, whereby the experiential or emotional aspects of the process are played down. If the relationship is under-structured or too ambiguous, the client may focus on irrelevancies, fail to develop a meaningful framework for self-understanding, become excessively anxious, and fail to engage in problem solving activity.

Some of the behavioral consequences of over and under structuring are presented in Figure 3–1.

FIGURE 3–1
Behavioral consequences of structuring errors

Over-structuring	Under-structuring
Counselor may mislead client by raising false hopes for success.	Client may experience excessive confusion and anxiety due to the lack of certainty.
Client may feel restricted and become frustrated, defensive, and resistive.	Client may feel he or she is not deriving any psychological benefits.
Client may terminate counseling because the counselor may be perceived as too rigid or the process as too demanding.	Client may focus less on problem solving and more on irrelevant aspects of his or her behavior.
Counselor's flexibility may be inhibited.	Client may not develop a meaningful system for understanding personal behavior.
Client may intellectualize the process.	Client may terminate sessions because of lack of structure.
Counselor may reinforce client's dependency needs by assuming too much control in the relationship.	Client dependency may be increased.
Counselor and client may become overly committed to counseling and fail to terminate the relationship at a reasonable time.	Client may show strong resistance.

Seating and room arrangements

Sullivan (1954) recommends that the counselor's and client's chairs be placed at about 90-degree angles. He feels that using such an arrangement makes the client less likely to see the desk as a barrier to communication. Some counselors, however, prefer to sit in face-to-face proximity to their clients, without any physical barriers. Whatever seating arrangement a counselor prefers, the client's emotional comfort should be considered. The seating arrangement should imply an atmosphere conducive to openness.

Room arrangements for counseling should be comfortable, free of outside distraction, and soundproof. Since counselors have different decorative tastes, they will have to be the judge of how they want their counseling rooms arranged. The client will feel more comfortable talking about personal matters knowing that others outside the room cannot listen (see Gelso, 1974, for a discussion of the effects of recording on clients). Outside interruptions often break one's train of thought, and therefore should be minimized.

Some general tips on the initial interview

When initiating the first interview, sometimes the counselor may want to begin with information already acquired about the client (e.g., "I sensed that when you called me you were feeling somewhat upset. Could you tell me more about that?") As the session continues the counselor listens with a sensitive ear to the emotional content of the client's statements. The counselor can encourage the client to disclose personal matters through active listening or simply by reflecting the emotional meaning of the client's verbalizations (e.g., "You seem to be saying that you are afraid.").

Behavioral assessment and the formulation of hypotheses about the client start in the first session. Questions that the counselor may raise during the session are: Is this person anxious or depressed, or both? Is he or she socially assertive or reticent? What is the client trying to say about himself or herself? What does he or she want or expect from me? What are my personal feelings about the client? How frequent and intense is the client's distress? What information and facts do I need to understand this person better? What are the client's strengths and weaknesses? Is he or she trying to tell me something through nonverbal gestures (e.g., Kanfer & Saslow, 1969; Osipow & Walsh, 1970).

In the later phase of the initial interview, it is well for the counselor to summarize the content of the session. In doing so, the counselor can also provide some perspective on the client's concerns, goals, treatment approaches, and further sessions. Any formulations or hypotheses about the client at this stage of the relationship need to be tentative and subject to later modification. If the counselor prefers to use homework assignments or extra counseling tasks, such as reading books about counseling, the later phase of the initial interview is a good time to give these assignments.

Tyler (1968) emphasizes three objectives for the initial interview: (1) set the stage for a sound counselor-client relationship, (2) encourage the client to express significant areas of concern, and (3) define and structure the counseling relationship. A fourth objective might be added, having to do with discussing, considering, and setting some tentative counseling goals. During the first few initial sessions a client may realize there is the potential for a more effective life. For many, a source of hope is generated anew. The work of the counselor and the client is beginning.

Some initial interview behavior characteristics of counselors and clients are summarized in Figure 3–2.

FIGURE 3–2
Counselor-client initial interview behavior

Counselor	*Client*
1. Introduces self.	1. Introduces self.
2. Asks client why counseling is sought.	2. Presents and articulates concerns.
3. Asks client about counseling expectations.	3. Asks questions about counseling.
4. Is warm and attentive.	4. Minimizes anxiety.
5. Listens to concerns of client.	5. Engages in some self-exploration.
6. Provides clarification and structure.	6. Sets some goals.
7. Reinforces client expression of concerns.	7. Agrees to return for second session.
8. Clarifies and reflects client's thoughts, feelings, and behavior.	
9. Observes client's verbal and nonverbal behavior.	
10. Encourages goal setting.	
11. Summarizes session.	
12. Discusses further sessions.	

Major techniques for building and enhancing the working relationship (facilitating)

Regardless of their theoretical orientations, counselors employ techniques designed to enhance the working relationship with the client to facilitate client progress. Counseling techniques designed for relationship building are reflection, clarification, confrontation, interpretation, cognitive restructuring, and reinforcement.

Reflection of feeling. One of Carl Rogers's (1951) significant contributions to counseling and psychotherapy process was his emphasis on the use of reflection of feeling as a means of communicating empathy. Rogers observed that the reflection technique focuses on the client's internal frame of reference—on how the client perceives the world and the feelings associated with the perception. The counselor reflects back to the client the emotional content of the client's words, even though the client may not be fully aware of the meaning of the statement. Thus, the reflection may go beyond the client's immediate insight or self-awareness. Reflection encourages the client toward self-exploration. Brammer and Shostrom (1978) define reflection of feeling as the attempt a counselor makes to express the client's most meaningful ideas and feelings about self in words understandable to the client. Reflection fosters the expression of emotions and the thoughts that produce them. Reflection of feeling also includes the thoughts or ideas associated with a feeling, as well as the physiological and behavioral manifestations.

An example of *reflection of feeling:*

Client: My wife keeps accusing me of having affairs. I try to convince her that she's nuts. That I am not having affairs. She really pushes me.

Counselor: You become frustrated over her accusations and you just boil inside.

Client: Yeah, I don't know what to do. Sometimes I'd like to shout at her.

Counselor: You'd like to blow off your steam by striking back at her.

Client: My stomach churns and burns. I get upset. I want to vomit at times.

Counselor: Yes—there's also a physical aspect to that whole sequence. You feel physically nauseated, and probably feel like a fool. (Here the counselor goes slightly beyond what the client stated and responded to how the client seems to be judging himself in that situation.)

Reflection of feeling, when accurate, may convey to the client a sense of being understood by the counselor, and thus increases the likelihood of the client talking freely. Reflection is a powerful tool that may stimulate self-disclosure and deep exploration of self. However, the counselor should keep in mind that such a technique is a means to an end—not an end in itself. Reflection helps the client to examine and explore deep motives, but it does not necessarily change them.

Confrontation.   Confrontation, the direct expression of unpleasant events to the client by the counselor, is employed by the counselor when it is apparent that the client does not want to deal with significant matters. An individual may consistently avoid matters that are emotionally laden, such as sex, intimacy, homosexuality, and guilt, by reverting to various "defense mechanisms." Defense mechanisms prevent the direct confrontation of feelings of inadequacy and low self-esteem and, more specifically, the ideas that underlie such feelings. Typical defensive reactions consist of rationalization, projection, reaction formation, and denial. The following excerpt is an example of the counselor confronting the client's tendency to project blame for something on someone else.

Client: This new guy that I started dating wants me to get high with him on speed.

Counselor: Did he try to persuade you to do that?

Client: No, not directly. But, I can tell that's what he wants.

Counselor: What makes you think that?

Client: Well, I don't know—I just have a feeling. He told me he gets high sometimes.

Counselor: Do you get high?

Client: Sometimes. But only when I am with someone who has the stuff. Never alone.

Counselor: It's almost like you want to be persuaded to do something like that.

Client: I don't know if that's so.

Counselor: It sounds like you don't want to admit that maybe you want to get high, and to take that responsibility off yourself. You seem to be suggesting that you get high only when someone else persuades you—not because you want to. Come on, let's come clean a bit. Aren't there times when that's exactly what you want to do? You, alone? Don't you find it convenient to lay the blame on someone else?

Such a potentially powerful technique as confrontation must be used with great care. It should be used (1) only when a good solid relationship exists between client and counselor; (2) for a special purpose, such as moving a client past a stumbling block; (3) never very frequently; and (4) with great sensitivity to its effect on the client. The counselor must be ready to retreat if it seems too powerful in its effect on the client.

Interpretation. Interpretation refers to a process in which the counselor suggests to the client the possible meanings underlying behavior. Brammer and Shostrom (1978) define interpretation as presenting to the client for consideration a set of hypotheses explaining the meanings of the client's behavior.

Interpretation of client behavior requires a thorough knowledge of psychological processes. As with reflection, confrontation, and clarification, interpretation attempts to bring into the client's awareness many of the client's unacceptable thoughts and feelings. The technique involves going beyond the client's insight. Thus, the aim of interpretation is to make sense out of the client's experiences—experiences of which the client is aware as well as those that may have escaped client awareness. The relationships between the client's present and past behavior are examined and described to increase personal awareness (Greenson, 1967).

Interpretation furthers the development of self-awareness. Effective interpretations by counselors set the stage for further client growth. The counselor should not try to force untimely interpretations on the client if there is evidence that certain material is laden with severe anxiety. If interpretations are not timely, accurate, and made with extreme care and empathy, the client's resistance to counseling may be reinforced. The buildup of anxiety may be so intense that the client may feel that the only alternative is to avoid counseling.

Early interpretations may need to be tentative, and used to stimulate the discussion of new topics. In the later stages of counseling, interpretation may take the form of explanations of the origins, development, maintenance, and functions of defensive mechanisms. Brammer and Shostrom (1978) suggest that counselors make more specific interpretations during the middle stages of counseling. In the latter stages, following a successful restructuring of behavior, the counselor's interpretations should be more general than earlier.

In interpreting the client's behavior, counselors need to (1) state to the client those ideas or thoughts most clearly associated with the client's emotional and behavioral disturbances, and (2) identify the underlying motivations, intentions, and functions of the maladaptive behavior (e.g., resistances, coping mechanisms). Every psychological incident, past, present, or future, becomes potential subject matter for interpretation and restructuring. Interpretation seeks to bring into the client's full awareness the events that have become associated with maladaptive behavioral tendencies.

Reflection, confrontation, and interpretation are powerful counseling and therapeutic techniques. Since these procedures are designed specifically to penetrate the client's resistances and defenses, they are likely to be met with some apprehension on the client's part. It should be noted that interpretation can bring into focus the client's *strengths* as well as *weaknesses*.

An example of *interpretation:*

Counselor: On the surface you seem soft-spoken, and very concerned about others, and as a result many people like you very much. But, having to be so perfectly approved by others sometimes causes you to suffer anxiety. Also, when you think some people don't like you, you seem to get quite upset.

It is particularly important that the counselor does not impose interpretations on the client when the client is not ready to accept them. When this problem occurs frequently in counseling, the client is more likely to see the counselor as the main source of personal growth rather than the client. The goal of interpretation is to help the client learn to rely on personal resources. Interpretations need to be made cautiously, tactfully, and tentatively.

Thorne (1950) suggests some of the following phrases to introduce interpretation: "What do you think of this idea?" "You seem to be implying . . ." "Is this a fair statement to make?"

Unacceptable statements are more likely to be of the following variety: "You should know that . . ." "If you don't see this idea you will be sorry . . ." "I am going to tell you the way it is." "If I were you I would . . ." The principle underlying successful interpretation is to give the client room to back away from a premature, incorrect or threatening interpretation.

When interpretations are offered, they should be corroborated with behavioral data or evidence that would be difficult for the client to deny. For instance, suppose a counselor observed a client to be compulsive about cleanliness, orderliness, and neatness. The following might be said to the client: "You are usually careful, neat, and clean. To what do you attribute this?" If data warrant, the counselor might suggest later: "There seems to be something of your mother's need to be overly critical about matters of cleanliness and order that may have something to do with your own attitudes." Further, if the client has given the counselor evidence of strong feelings of anxiety over sexuality and finds sex dirty and unclean, the counselor might respond: "Can you see how some of your mother's attitudes about matters of sexuality has influenced some of your own? She seemed to have found sex to be a threatening area in her life. Do you think that it is possible that some of her thinking may have rubbed off on you?"

Ideally, interpretation has the effect of helping the client open previously threatening areas for discussion. Once clients become aware of certain behavioral tendencies and their significance, they may be more capable to attempt to restructure or modify them.

Clarification. Clarification, an extension of reflection, is designed to bring into sharper focus or awareness a particular attitude, thought, emotion, or behavior. The counselor uses clarification as a means of helping a client make more accurate discriminations between effective and ineffective behavior.

Counselees often express their thoughts, feelings, and behaviors in vague language that obscures the underlying purpose or intentions behind their actions. Before making a clarifying response, the counselor should consider such questions as "Why is the client trying to ward off feelings of anxiety, guilt, or depression?" "What is being avoided?" The counselor may need to pay particular attention to nonverbal cues that serve as indicators of emotion. The counselor may use some of the following responses to help clarify the client's thoughts, emotions, and actions: "You seem irritable." "You seem afraid." "You appear to be embarrassed." "You seem sad." "You seem to want to hide something." "You appear to be angry."

The counselor's language needs to be simple, concrete, and capable of bringing out emotionally laden material. It is a good idea to stay away from such phrases as "you are" and "it is." These phrases tend to be perceived as judgmental and definite, whereas such phrases as "you seem to" or "you appear" are less so (Brammer & Shostrom, 1978; Ellis & Harper, 1975).

Clarification means to "concretize," to make explicit, to specify. More than to accurately describe a behavior, clarification suggests making explicit the reason, intention, or the function of the behavior (Greenson, 1967). It is therefore a technique that may facilitate further depth of self-awareness and self-exploration.

Restructuring of behavior (working through).   As the client gains in self understanding through self exploration, this knowledge needs to be translated into action. A person who enters a counseling relationship because of personal difficulties has no doubt acquired faulty ways of thinking, feeling, and behaving. If self contradictions and conflicts are to be reconciled so the client can behave more productively, some restructuring of psychological processes is necessary.

Through the use of repeated and accurate reflection, confrontation, clarification, and interpretation, the client can increase self-awareness and self-exploration. These procedures, however, need to be extended into the environment through the use of "in-vivo" (real-life) behavioral tasks. Assignments outside of counseling (e.g., bibliotherapy, assertive responses) permit the client to experience, firsthand, many of the conditions that activated the emotional disturbances to begin with, and at the same time to experimentally apply new strategies for behavior change. The consequences of the new behavior can be assessed and serve as the content for other counseling sessions.

The counselor's major role in restructuring or working through stages of counseling is to help educate the client to restructure attitudes and behavior. The counselor repeatedly confronts and challenges the client's self-defeating thoughts, feelings, and behavior, and tries to show the client how to eliminate undesirable thoughts and the like. The counselor, actively and sometimes forcefully, demonstrates to the client that behavioral change does not necessarily come easy, and that positive reinforcement for new modes of behaving may not be so immediate.

Perhaps for the client a most important result of counseling is to learn to cope temporarily with unpleasant events, such as rejection and the lack of social approval.

In the restructuring stage, the client begins to show signs of gaining self-reliance and independence of thought and action. Gradually, the client relies less on the social approval of others for feeling worthwhile, finding that although the approval of others is desirable, it is not a dire necessity. The client also sees that living more in the present is more productive than worrying about what the future will hold or about the past. Moreover, the client comes to have greater mastery over the environment, realizing, however, that one cannot have everything one's own way.

Working through one's emotional difficulties is by no means an easy task. While there is often a feeling of accomplishment, it still remains difficult for one to give up inappropriate and often irrational tendencies that have developed and been maintained over long periods. Rarely do human beings enjoy facing the truth about themselves. Moreover, ineffective old habits can be comfortable and reassuring despite their ineffectiveness. While involved in the restructuring of behavior, the client shows the incipient signs of hope that the new behavior currently under exploration will have more desirable consequences in the future. The expectation of hope certainly plays an important role in this difficult and demanding period of the counseling relationship.

The counselor also plays a reinforcing role by encouraging the client to do the work required for behavioral change. The counselor balances confrontations and challenges with support and reassurance. Moreover, the counselor reminds the client that new self-knowledge and awareness need to be constantly posed against reality and translated into meaningful action.

New resistances to counseling may be noticed after old resistances have been worked through. Resistance to the working-through process may take the form of being late for appointments, cancelling appointments, making excuses for not completing assigned behavioral tasks, and avoiding emotionally charged topics. It is not uncommon for some clients to terminate counseling while they are in the working-through phase. For some, the experience may be too uncomfortable to tolerate.

The following is an example of the restructuring of behavior. The counselor uses a *rational emotive-imagery* technique:

> **Client:** I tried asserting myself with my husband about being more considerate of me. It didn't work—he continued putting me down. I felt

awful. He told me I was wasting my time in counseling. He thinks it's all nonsense.

Counselor: I heard several things in your remarks. First, the difficulty in trying out new behavior; second, your feeling upset over getting put down; third, some reservation about counseling. Is that right?

Client: Yes, I guess so.

Counselor: Let's see if we can reconstruct your situation somewhat. It is true that at times you may feel you are not progressing. That's understandable. You have also noticed that some things are different now.

Client: Well, yes! That is true.

Counselor: Now. Asserting yourself with your husband has been difficult for you for a long time. Isn't that so? Why should it be easy for you now? Let's go over your situation once again—using the imagery techniques that you have learned about.

Client: Okay.

Counselor: Okay. Sit comfortably, close your eyes, and begin to take slow deep breaths. (When the client visibly relaxes, the counselor reconstructs the actual situation.) Imagine the following scene: you are fixing dinner and your husband comes into the kitchen and begins to tell you how stupid you are for being in counseling. And imagine him saying: "Only nuts see counselors—can't you solve your own problems?" In response to your husband you begin to feel very upset, angry. You want to say something but you can't. You become tense. You feel just like you did when you were a child when your father used to scold you for making mistakes. You imagine that you're about to cry, as you have done most of the time. You're just about ready to cry, but you tell yourself "Stop! I don't have to cry just because my husband is putting me down." Imagine, you begin to tell yourself that "I have every right to work out my own problems in the way I want. I believe I have chosen a reasonable way. Why should my husband approve of me for this? It's his business if he doesn't. I would like to have him approve of me, but if he can't or doesn't, I don't have to drive myself crazy." Now, notice that you begin to feel less anxious and angry. A feeling of calm enters your body and you calmly assert your position to your husband. "George, I know you have a difficult time understanding what I am doing. I would very much like to explain it to you . . ."

Following the working through of the client's negative feelings about her lack of assertiveness, the counselor indicates to the client that she will need to practice her new thoughts and behavior outside of counseling.

Counselor: How did you like the imagery trip?

Client: It was good, but it's tough to get that together out there.

Counselor: Yes, I know. But it is very essential that you continue to practice new assertive behaviors, as well as new thoughts associated with them.

Reinforcement in the counseling relationship. It is well understood and documented that human behavior is influenced by its consequences. If desirable consequences occur following a given behavior, individuals are more likely to repeat that behavior in the future (Skinner, 1971). Behavioral consequences can be considered reinforcers of human behavior; the notion of reinforcement, thus, plays a central role in counseling.

Bandura (1969) suggests that reinforcement and behavioral consequences serve several functions: (1) They impart information that serves as a guide for action; (2) through their possible incentive value they can motivate behavior; and (3) they help to make discriminations between appropriate and inappropriate behavior.

Counselors play a very important role as a reinforcer of healthy behavior. When the client shows signs of positive activity, the counselor needs to acknowledge such signs. In this sense, counselors give feedback to clients about their personal growth (Krasner, 1962). Reinforcement in a counseling relationship may be viewed as encouragement or affirmation of the client's gradual progress toward effective personal development.

Counselors generally give positive feedback when their clients approximate desirable behavioral goals. Positive consequences increase the likelihood that the behavior will occur. Conversely, aversive or negative consequences decrease the likelihood of it occurring. Behavior can be increased, maintained, or strengthened when positive reinforcements are added and negative or aversive reinforcers removed. If positive reinforcers are removed, and negative reinforcers are added, or there is no reinforcement, behavior can be extinguished or minimized.

The achievement of desirable and effective ways of behaving may itself become a source of positive reinforcement for the client. Counselors may reinforce and encourage the client more frequently in the early stages of counseling. During the later stages of counseling, client self-reinforcement is likely to increase (Krasner, 1971; Mahoney & Thoresen, 1974).

Truax (1967) conducted a significant study, showing how counselors reinforce their clients by the way they acknowledge certain behavior. When the client appears to be talking about self-relevant topics, the counselor's attention to these topics will tend to increase the frequency of talking about such subjects. Truax convincingly showed that reflection of feeling is a powerful reinforcer that tends to increase client self-exploration. Also, Tosi, Upshaw, Lande, and Waldron (1971) found that using social reinforcers, such as "good," "that's great," and "tell me more," increased the verbal output of reticent children in a group-counseling situation. Krasner (1962) reviews many additional studies that show how a counselor can influence the behavior of a client through selective reinforcement procedures.

An example of a counselor's use of *positive social reinforcement* to increase client depth of self-exploration and effective coping behavior is:

Client: I have the strangest feelings about myself sometimes.

Counselor: I would be very interested in hearing more about that feeling of yours. (Probable reinforcement.)

Client: At times I feel like I'm going crazy. Like losing control of my emotions. (Increase in self-exploration.)

Counselor: That must be frightening during those times. (Reflection of feeling used as reinforcement.)

Client: Yes, it is very frightening. But I seem to be able to get control of myself. Especially when I realize that the feeling comes when I don't get my way about certain things.

Counselor: That's quite a significant insight on your part (reinforcing insightful thinking), and being able to work through those feelings (reinforcing healthy coping processes) must be very satisfying to you. I think that's a real plus.

Stages of the counseling process

Persons who experience the process of personal counseling seem to progress through several stages. First, there is an increased awareness of self and others. Second, there is an expanded exploration of self and environment (positive and negative behavioral tendencies). Third, there is increased commitment to self-enhancing behavior and its implementation. Fourth, there is an internalization of new and more productive thoughts and actions. Fifth, there is a stabilization of new behavior (Tosi & Marzella, 1975).

More specifically, Rogers (1942, 1959) has outlined a sequence describing the counseling process. This sequence is: (1) the person feels a need for help; (2) the counseling situation becomes defined; (3) the client verbalizes troublesome situations and thoughts and feelings about them; (4) the counselor accepts, reflects, and clarifies positive and negative thoughts, feelings, and emotions; (5) the client becomes more aware of inconsistencies in thinking, feeling, and acting; (6) the client considers possible courses of action; (7) the client initiates constructive behavior; (8) positive actions lead to more accurate discriminations and self-awareness; (9) positive thoughts, feelings, and behavior become more frequent; (10) the client feels a decreasing need for help; (11) the client's thoughts are less likely to produce anxiety; (12) the client responds to others in a more appropriate and flexible manner; (13) the client becomes more spontaneous and self-confident, and behavior is more self-directed.

The goals of counseling

What can a person reasonably expect to achieve as a result of participation in counseling? This question is continually raised by students and educators, as well as by the public. Can counseling help one make a better psychological adjustment to the environment? Does it help the client become a more self-directed person? Does counseling help to reduce uncomfortable symptoms? Do people who experience counseling choose realistic careers? Does counseling help to foster better interpersonal and intrapersonal functioning? Such questions lead to a consideration of the goals and aims of the counseling process. Such goals are developed and defined by the counselor and the client. In chapter 2 we considered several theoretical approaches to counseling. Here we will briefly consider some theories' impact on goal setting in counseling.

Psychoanalytic formulations on goals

Psychoanalytic counselors emphasize the development of emotional insight and understanding into the relationship between intrapsychic processes and overt behavior. Psychoanalytic theory (Greenson, 1967; Munroe, 1955) sees neurotic disorders as based on intrapsychic conflict. Such conflict leads to an obstruction of instinctual drives, resulting in an extreme state of tension. Ego processes, the rational arm of the personality, are unable to cope with the tension and become overwhelmed. A neurotic conflict is an unconscious phenomenon involving unacceptable impulses emanating from the *id*, censored by the *superego*, seeking discharge, and an ego-defense mechanism trying to minimize these impulses. The *ego* serves to keep unacceptable impulses of a sexual or aggressive nature from consciousness. When the ego is overwhelmed and flooded by the demands of the id and superego, it must allow some instinctual discharge. These discharges of tension occur in disguised form and result in symptom formation (phobias, anxiety attacks, psychosomatic symptoms). Neurotic behavior then is a function of intrapsychic forces of a historical nature above and beyond the control of the person (Greenson, 1967).

Thus, a major goal of psychoanalytic counseling is for the client to achieve insight into intrapsychic or unconscious conflicts. For instance, the client comes to realize that the instinctual impulses of childhood which overwhelmed the ego were distorted by the child's superego (tendencies to be perfect, morally good) and that these have been manifested in adult behavior. "One reason I hate my brother so much and feel so guilty is that he reminds me so much of my father who left us all alone." Insight alone, however, is insufficient. A "working through" the translation of insight into actual behavior must occur. Psychoanalysis aims at strengthening the ego to minimize its tendencies to distort reality. The process attempts to make unconscious material (not previously verbalized) conscious.

Counselors with a psychoanalytic perspective view emotional insight as an essential condition for therapeutic change, and utilize those techniques necessary to facilitate insight formation. The idea is to help the client verbalize previously denied and unspoken thoughts. The counselor determines the methods used. These are dictated by psychoanalytic theory. In general, analytic counselors employ insight-furthering techniques, such as confrontation, clarification, interpretation, and working through. These procedures are applied to material derived from free association, transference reactions, and the resistances (Alexander & French, 1946).

Humanistic perspectives on the goals of counseling

Carl Rogers, Robert Carkhuff, Abraham Maslow, Albert Ellis, Everett Shostrom, Fritz Perls—to name only a few—provide a humanistic perspective on the goals of counseling. Carl Rogers's *On Becoming a Person* (1961) describes a conception of counseling and psychotherapy wherein growth trends emerge from within the client. Rogers assumes that given a psychological climate of safety, warmth, and empathic understanding, people move toward self-actualization. Rogers suggests that the actualizing person will exhibit certain qualities—qualities that translate into therapeutic goals: movement away from facades, movement away from oughts and shoulds, movement away from meeting others' expectations, movement away from pleasing others, movement toward self-direction, complexity, openness to experience, acceptance of others, and trust of self.

Rogers did not intend for these general directions to be discrete or independent of one another. In general, these nine growth tendencies may be summarized in terms of self-awareness, self-acceptance, and self-direction, with a full recognition of the importance of others.

More recently, Truax and Carkhuff (1967) have extended Rogers's basic premises on the process goals of counseling. They suggest that, as the process of counseling and psychotherapy develops, a client will show evidence of gaining in accurate empathy (understanding of self and others), genuineness (openness), self-disclosure, confrontation (self-assertiveness), self-respect, and respect for others.

In the humanistic tradition, Fritz Perls (1973), the founder of Gestalt therapy, stresses self-actualization as the major goal of therapy. For Perls and Gestalt therapists (Perls et al., 1951), self-actualization refers to the attainment of high levels of self-awareness, personality integration, maturation, responsibility, authenticity, and organismic self-regulation. Integration in Gestalt therapy—perhaps its most important goal—is the unification of the physiological, affective, cognitive, and behavioral-motoric processes. Integration is achieved through self-awareness or a high level of consciousness. From awareness also flows authenticity and maturity. A "here and now" philosophy is strictly adhered to by the Gestalt therapists. The focus is on the now—not the past or the future. The key ingredient of the process, as previously mentioned, is increased client self-awareness.

Everett Shostrom (1972) has synthesized the works of several contemporary humanistic thinkers, and derived a set of counseling goals based on self-actualization theory. Borrowing from the writings of Carl Rogers, Abraham Maslow, David Reisman, Rollo May, and Fritz Perls, Shostrom devised the Personal Orientation Inventory (1968), the first instrument of its type to specify and measure humanistic goals based on self-actualization.

Shostrom (1972) identified 12 areas that reflect client growth in counseling. Briefly defined, these areas are: (1) *time competence*—the degree to which one is present-oriented, lives in the here and now, is unburdened by past guilt, regrets, failures, and resentments, and is not overly preoccupied with the future; (2) *inner support*—(inner direction) suggests self-directed activity, thinking for oneself, minimized dependence and reliance on others; (3) *self-actualizing value*—accepts values of self-actualized people; (4) *existentiality*—an ability to react situationally and flexibly without rigid adherence to unproven, unscientific principles; (5) *feeling reactively*—sensitivity to one's own needs, feelings, and thoughts; (6) *spontaneity*—freedom to react as oneself; (7) *self-regard*—a liking of oneself because of worth or strength; (8) *self-acceptance*—the affirmation of self in spite of one's weaknesses; (9) *human nature*—seen as essentially good; (10) *synergy*—the ability to transcend dichotomies, to see the opposites of life as being related (e.g., love-lust, work-play, selfishness-selflessness), and to see events on a continuum; (11) *acceptance of aggression*—an acceptance of one's natural aggressive and sometimes destructive tendencies without defensiveness, denial, and repression of them; (12) *capacity for intimate contact*—the ability to establish close, meaningful relationships with others, uncluttered by unreasonable expectation, obligations, and demands.

Behavioristic conceptions of counseling goals

Psychoanalytic and humanistic conceptions of counseling goals take into consideration subjective processes and intra-psychophenomenon, such as self-concept, self-perception, and defensive mechanisms. Many inferences about the existence of such states need to be made by the counselor or therapist. Behavioristic theories are mostly concerned about psychological variables that lend themselves easily to observation, recording, and measuring. Therefore, empirical notions and scientific methods are emphasized. The simplist explanations for behavior are accepted. Covert processes, such as thoughts and emotions, are subject for behavioral analysis and treatment in so far as they can be reliably recorded (Bandura, 1969; Krasner, 1971; Wolpe, 1969).

Behavioral counselors, in full cooperation with their clients, try to make a determination of what behaviors need to be added, strengthened, maintained, and eliminated. Behavioral counselors believe that most symptoms a client presents are brought out and maintained by events in the self or environment, or both. The goals of counseling then have to do with changing the reinforcing conditions that support maladaptive behavior or the situations which elicit it. The counselor focuses on specific response-reinforcement processes rather than on abstract and general psychological ones (Krasner, 1971; Mahoney, 1974).

Terminating counseling

The counseling relationship is terminated when the counselor and client agree that many of the goals, expectations, and objectives set earlier have been achieved or met. The counselor's goal orientations will generally serve as a guideline for what constitutes the development of healthy behavioral patterns. As indicated in other sections, counselors may vary greatly on their concepts of psychological growth and development. Some counselors will terminate their sessions when specific behavioral objectives have been met, while others will end when their clients show a higher level of emotional insight or self-awareness.

In time-limited counseling, the relationship is terminated when specific goals have been met by the client, e.g., increased assertiveness, decreased social anxiety, increased grade-point average. In long-term reconstructive counseling, the sessions are usually terminated when the client shows significant and stable changes in restructuring belief/

value systems and personality as in-depth psychoanalysis or client-centered counseling. Even though a counseling relationship may be terminated, it is a good idea for the counselor to leave the door open in the future for other developmental difficulties that may arise for the client.

There are many other reasons why a client may terminate a counseling relationship. Some may be required or forced to move their places of residence because of a new job, graduation from school, a marriage, or divorce. Or they may decide that counseling requires too much effort and they are not ready to commit themselves to a demanding process. Some client-counselor pairs fit together poorly. Some clients may not be able to relate well to their counselor. Some counselors may be incompetent, and the client perceiving this will drop out of the sessions.

A sensitive and aware counselor may be able to anticipate some of the changes in the client's emotional, social, work, marital, or educational status that could bring about an early termination of the counseling relationship. When such factors appear to be a cause for terminating counseling, the counselor can initiate action to prepare the client for a phasing out of the relationship. When many significant problem areas have not been worked through, the counselor can reinforce the client's positive achievements during counseling, discuss areas that need further work, and suggest further counseling elsewhere, assuming the client is so motivated.

SUMMARY

Research supports the idea that the quality of the counseling relationship is related to positive outcomes in counseling. Regardless of one's counseling theory, counselors need to show a level of understanding, respect, and acceptance of the client as a person. The counseling relationship serves as a vehicle through which a person can gain in self-awareness and self-understanding, while at the same time explore and develop new behavioral patterns.

As we have seen, there is a structure to the counseling process. That is, limitations are placed on counselor-client behavior, time and duration of counseling, and goals. And, if the relationship is structured too rigidly or too loosely, negative consequences may result. The initial interview seems to set the stage for a sound counseling relationship.

The major techniques used by counselors to enhance the relationship are reflection, clarification, confrontation, interpretation, cognitive restructuring, and reinforcement.

Diagnosis and assessment in counseling

A diagnostic or assessment system in counseling is useful when it produces information that relates specifically to some desired set of counseling outcomes, the object of treatment or intervention. A system for assessing human behavior needs to be broad and objective to minimize any tendency a counselor may have to distort or misunderstand the client. A good diagnostic and assessment system, therefore, is designed simply to facilitate the understanding of the client's behavior from both internal and external perspectives and lead to distinctive interventions.

Methods for gathering data for the assessment of human behavior are varied. To a large extent these methods reflect the theoretical persuasions of the assessor. Psychoanalytic and psychiatric systems, based on a medical model, make the assumption that disease entities underlie the symptom of psychological disturbance. Psychiatric taxonomies of psychological disorders dominate systems for diagnosing and assessing human behavior. Counseling psychologists working in community mental health agencies and state hospitals are often required to classify mental disorders according to *The Diagnostic and Statistical Manual* (DSM II and DSM III) endorsed by the American Psychiatric Association (1978).

The modern classification of mental disorders began in the late 18th century with the work of Pinel. Pinel observed patients in asylums and described them as falling into categories of melancholia, mania with delirium, dementia, and idiotism. Later, Kraepelin developed a widely accepted nosology describing various types of schizophrenic reactions. Classification of neuroses came later, in the 20th century, with the work of Janet and Freud.

In 1968, the eighth revision of the International Classification of Diseases (ICD–8) was prepared under the guidance and direction of the World Health Organization (WHO). Psychiatric disorders were included along with physical disorders. The American Psychiatric Association now uses *The Diagnostic and Statistical Manual of Mental Disorders* (DSM III). The DSM III (1978) is a revised version of the DSM I (1952) and the DSM II (1968), which were compiled as a part of the (ICD–8) (1968).

Less medically oriented than psychiatrists, clinical psychologists traditionally have often approached diagnosis using objective tests, such as the Minnesota Multiphasic Inventory (MMPI), and projective tests, such as the Rorschach Ink Blot Test and Thematic Apperception Test. Psychologists have developed increasingly sophisticated statistical and empirical methods for classifying behavioral disorders. Statistical procedures involving factor analysis have been useful in generating meaningful typologies of psychiatric syndromes (Lorr, Klett, & McNair, 1963).

More recently, some psychologists (Skinner, 1938; Franks, 1969; Kanfer & Phillips, 1970; Lazarus, 1971; Ferster & Perrott, 1969) have contributed new assessment techniques based on the functional analysis of behavior. Functional analysis describes behavior in terms of its context—situation, person, outcome. Assessment procedures derived from behavioristic systems focus especially on behavior that is directly observable.

The assessment, analysis, and diagnosis of human behavior is an essential part of counseling. Whether based on psychiatric-medical models, statistical-empirical methods, intuition, or functional-behavioral analysis, some systematic and organized understanding of the many factors contributing to the client's functioning needs to occur prior to intervention. Otherwise, the application of counseling techniques may be blind, based only on trial and error, and indiscriminate. Effective differential treatment is dependent upon differential diagnosis and assessment (Osipow & Walsh, 1970).

With the emergence of behavior theory and existential phenomenological theory, static, analytic, and abstract diagnostic systems have been seriously questioned. Behavior theory, for instance, suggests that information that cannot be accurately observed and reliably recorded should be viewed with caution. For the behaviorist, those events that control behavior are subject to analysis only when they are directly apparent and measurable. Counselors who adopt behavioral theories are likely to be "scientifically" inclined and relatively less concerned with subjective psychological processes that are not directly observable. On the other hand, counselors who lean toward humanistic and psychoanalytic approaches are usually concerned with covert or intraorganismic variables, such as attitudes, values, and beliefs, even though these need to be inferred.

The humanistic movement in psychology embraces a phenomenological method of inquiry. The phenomenological method of inquiry places a priority on describing human behavior, rather than dissecting and analyzing it. The method stresses description first and analysis and evaluation later. Subjective data are considered valid sources of information (e.g., perception, awareness, beliefs, values).

The labeling and classification of events are a logical part of scientific inquiry and knowledge. However, when the labeling and classification of human behavior become too rigid, too technical, and too abstract, they may lead to distorted views of human behavior.

Counseling has de-emphasized the use of medical or pathological models of behavioral classification. Generally, problems have been viewed as either falling into a content area (e.g., educational, vocational, etc.), or a process area such as lack of skill, self-conflict, or choice anxiety. Considerable similarity among the systems of classification is evident. Generally, counseling concerns may be classified as personal, social, physical, and career (vocational-educational).

Hypotheses construction, inferences, and prediction in counseling

Most counselors, regardless of their personal theory, formulate hypotheses, draw inferences, and make predictions about their client's personal-interpersonal functioning. The more sophisticated diagnostic or assessment models are flexible, and allow for change as the counselor increases awareness and understanding of the client's unique system of thinking, feeling, and behaving. Because behavior assessment is experimental in nature, the hypotheses, inferences, and judgments that the counselor makes about the client are tentative, based on probability, and made in light of observable evidence. In effect, the counselor, as any scientist-practitioner, needs to be able to describe relevant client processes, as well as to analyze, to monitor, to intervene, and to predict them. Science begins with what is given (phenomena), then describes, analyzes, and finally seeks to predict and control events. However, there is also an intuitive side to science.

Paul Meehl (1960), in his famous book *Clinical Versus Statistical Prediction,* presents a strong argument for the use of empirical and statistical methods in diagnosis and prediction. At the same time, Meehl recognizes the intuitive side of science and behavioral assessment as indicated in the following five basic steps:

The counselor has some theoretical notions about human behavior and the laws governing behavior. A theoretical system or way of looking at behavior serves as a guide for counselors. If a theory is comprehensive it addresses matters of client thinking (cognition), feeling (emotional or affective states), physical responding (bodily concomitants of emotional states), acting or behaving (behavioral-motoric-overt action tendencies), and interactions with relevant environmental events. An adequate theoretical model will speak to the way a person has been influenced by previous social conditioning (past), the present environment, and a projection of what the future may hold.

A theoretical system itself is a set of hypotheses about the laws governing human behavior. It is therefore not an absolute but an abstraction made by a person to give some order to events. Theory is subject to change when new evidence emerges. Theory needs to be constantly checked against reality if it is to be a reasonable framework for making systematic observations. Thus, while theory may be the counselor's best friend, the counselor needs to be cautious about overtheorizing. When a theory becomes overcontrolling, the risk of distorting and misunderstanding the counseling process increases. The counselor then may see the client as an abstraction instead of a thinking, emoting, and acting human being.

A good theory of counseling will also suggest desirable counseling outcomes or directions. Most theoretical systems of counseling either explicitly or implicitly are goal directed and make statements about the appropriateness of human behavior.

To illustrate differences in theoretical approaches to counseling, consider the following. Psychoanalytic counselors stress emotional insight and personality integration as the goal of counseling. This goal is achieved when an awareness of the personal meanings underlying the maladaptive systems and behaviors is achieved by the client. Cognitive-behavioral counselors place a priority on having their clients replace irrational ideas producing maladaptive behavior with more rational ideas that will produce adaptive behavior. Existential counselors are interested in helping their clients to minimize self-deception and to become more personally responsible for their actions. Counselors practicing behavior modification direct their clients to acquire behavior that is more likely to be positively reinforced than negatively reinforced or punished. Whatever one's theory of human behavior, directions, goals, and means exist either implicitly or explicitly.

The counselor gathers meaningful information. Given a theory or systematic set of assumptions about human behavior, the next step in hypotheses building is collecting information related to client behavior. Information about client behavior is compared with theory.

Information about the client may come from several sources. Psychodiagnostic tests—including personality inventories, interest inventories, behavioral checklists, aptitude and achievement tests, and intelligence tests—provide standardization methods for obtaining data. Psychological tests and inventories generally compare client behavior to various norm groups. Standardized tests aid the counselor and client in the interpretation, the evaluation, and the prediction of behavior. Issues related to the use of testing will be considered later.

Another source of information is the client's history. Data describing the client's cognitive, emotional, physical, and behavioral functioning at various stages of development are important to help understand how clients develop (Tosi, 1974; Kanfer & Saslow, 1965; Erikson, 1964). The counselor asks what significant incidents or situations in the client's life reflect growth-enhancing or growth-inhibiting experiences? What has the client found positively reinforcing and negatively reinforcing? Under what conditions has the client felt frustrated, hostile, sad, or happy? What is the character of the client's relationship to parents, teachers, peers, and institutions? Has the client had major health problems? Is any physical or learning disability present? Historical data are generally collected during the first few counseling sessions or during an intake interview, although facts of historical significance can and do emerge at any time during the counseling relationship.

A third and most important source of information is personal and subjective in nature. The client's self and environmental perceptions expressed verbally or nonverbally provide a most valuable source of material. Verbalizations about oneself are good indicators of how people appraise or evaluate their emotional, behavioral, and situational status. Counselors need to pay close attention to the client's self-verbalizations, listen actively and sensitively to them, and encourage their production. Counselors need also to recognize that a client may not be aware of the significance of many personal thoughts, feelings, and behaviors.

Part of the task of assessment involves counselor efforts to clarify the relationships among the facts collected. For example, the counselor's thinking may include the following questions: Given the client's negative self-view as suggested by repeated self-accusations (cognitive level), is depression likely (emotional level), followed by withdrawal from social situations (behavioral level)? Is the client likely to become frustrated and angry with others? How frequent and intense are the client's thoughts and feelings, and how long are they likely to last? How strong is the relationship among the client's thoughts, feelings, and behavior? How can the client minimize self-accusatory thoughts? What are the relevant environmental factors—home, work, family, peers, or school (Kanfer & Saslow, 1965; Osipow & Walsh, 1970)?

The counselor constructs tentative but specific hypotheses about counselee behavior. In describing relationships among behavioral data (facts) and assessing the strength of association among facts, the counselor generates specific hypotheses. An hypothesis is always tentative and will change in accordance with new data. Hypotheses are predictive statements involving the likelihood that some event will occur.

Recall how important theory was in providing guidelines for observing facts and formulating hypotheses. Keep in mind that hypotheses are operational, predictive statements about behavior. A counselor, for example, might hypothesize that "if John continues to act unassertively in social situations because he keeps telling himself he is socially inept, he is more likely to avoid assertive behavior in the future, experience more anxiety, and reinforce his negative self-verbalizations." The accuracy of hypotheses formation depends on the careful monitoring and observation of the client under various situationally relevant conditions.

Whenever possible, hypotheses need to be stated in measurable, concrete, operational terms. An hypothesis is generated to be tested. Systematic procedures for measuring and testing the efficacy of the counselor's hypotheses have been developed by behaviorally oriented theoreticians and practitioners.

The counselor collects further information, compares facts, and reduces the number of hypotheses to a meaningful few. Throughout the counseling process, the counselor continues to observe client behavior, to gather information, and to formulate a meaningful but flexible model of the client's behavioral patterns. Precautions should be taken to avoid *over*-theorizing and hypothesizing. Parsimonious and factual descriptions of behavior are often more helpful to the counselor and the client than are gross generalizations.

The counselor selects the most tenable hypotheses, makes predictions, and implements the most appropriate counseling strategies. The most meaningful hypotheses will contain certain realistic and empirically verifiable statements about the client's cognitive, affective, physical, and behavioral functioning as these relate to the environment. A counselor may find the formula ($B = f[PE]$) very helpful in developing hypotheses and making predictions. In the formula, *behavior* (B) is a function (f) of the *person* (P) and the *environment* (E). When selecting counseling strategies, the counselor may ask questions like: "If test anxiety is to be minimized in the future, would systematic desensitization be more efficacious than an insight oriented analytical approach? Would a combination of cognitive restructuring and covert sensitization be associated with the most desirable outcomes?"

Behavioral analysis (the functional model)

A functional model of behavioral analysis rejects both strict psychoanalytic and behavioristic conceptions of symptom formation. Functional behavioral analysis looks at the reasons why certain behaviors occur. The counselor explores the following questions: What is the relationship between thoughts, feelings, behavior, and environment? When did a particular maladaptive behavior begin? Under what environmental conditions did it emerge? Was it gradual or sudden? What is the frequency, intensity, and duration of the behavior (Lazarus, 1973)?

Lazarus identifies seven modalities involved in counselor-client interaction that need to be investigated: B—Behavior; A—Affect (feeling); S—Sensation; I—Imagery; C—Cognition; I—Interpersonal relationships; and D—Drugs. (The acronym BASIC-ID applies). He operationally defines these modalities and proposes specific treatments. Osipow and Walsh (1970), Tosi (1974), and Kanfer and Saslow (1965) propose similar conceptual models for the functional analysis of behavior.

The functional analysis of behavior begins with the gathering of data on antecedent and consequent conditions, the relationship of behavior to environmental variables, and the significance or meaning of the behavior (Osipow & Walsh, 1970). Functional analysis describes the stimulus conditions that evoke, reinforce, and maintain behavior within the environment. Reinforcing conditions may be positive—those that increase the probability of a behavior occurring, or negative—those occurring to postpone, to escape from, or to terminate an aversive situation. Behavioral analysis also seeks to determine whether a response needs to be added, weakened, or strengthened. The reciprocal relationship between the individual's behavior and the environment is emphasized. Reinforcing events that are external to the individual, as well as reinforcing events that are internal, are subject to inquiry and experimental analysis.

Kanfer and Saslow (1965) analyze problem behavior in terms of deficits and excesses in client-coping behavior. Coping behavior refers to the thoughts and actions that an individual uses to deal effectively or ineffectively in his environment. A counselor assessing behavior continually asks many questions about the client's coping strategies. Typical questions raised by the counselor are: Under what conditions does the counselee function effectively or ineffectively? What motivates and reinforces the client's behavior? Is he or she independent and assertive?

Beck's types of cognitive distortion

Ultimately, the counselor is concerned with making "clinical" and tentative judgments or appraisals of the client's coping strategies. Coping processes involve cognitive and emotional as well as behavioral factors. Beck (1976) suggests cognitive distortions can be observed in persons exhibiting maladaptive behavior. Beck noted that such persons tend to engage in selective abstraction, arbitrary inference, overgeneralization, magnification and minimization, and inexact labeling. These cognitive distortions tend to prevent an individual from dealing realistically with personal strengths and weaknesses as well as with the environment. Moreover, these distortions may lead to further misconceptions about self and environment. The counselor's role is to help the client correct those misconceptions or distortions that are of a self-defeating nature. Most thinking that is associated with negative emotional and behavioral states can be classified using Beck's scheme.

Selective abstraction refers to a person responding to one feature of a situation while ignoring other important and related aspects. Examples of *selective abstraction* follow:

> I just can't see anything good in my husband. I can't get beyond his drinking. His drinking drives me crazy and that's all I can think about.

or

> I can only focus on my bad habits. I don't see anything I do well.

Overgeneralization is a tendency to draw a generalized conclusion about a specific situation or event. Examples of *overgeneralization* are:

I failed a chemistry examination. Stupid people like me are bound to flunk out.

or

I slept with my boyfriend. I am a worthless slut.

Arbitrary inference has to do with deriving a conclusion from a situation when such a conclusion is not warranted and is without evidence to support it. Examples of *arbitrary inference* are:

My professor challenged one of my ideas in class. I don't think he likes me.

or

I just know that most people see through me when I do something wrong.

Magnification and minimization are cognitive tendencies that, according to Beck (1976), are gross errors in evaluation. These distortions have to do with the underestimating and overestimating of situations and events of a social-psychological nature. Examples of *magnification and minimization* are:

It is awful when things don't go my way. (Magnification.)

Even though I have had a consistent A average in college I feel like a C student. (Minimization.)

Inexact labeling is defined as ascribing inappropriate words to thoughts, feelings, behaviors, and situations. Examples of *inexact labelling* are:

I met John last night and I know that what I felt was love.

or

- When my boss criticizes me I am devastated.

Albert Ellis (1973) approaches behavior disorders by analyzing the rational or irrational basis of the client's value and belief system, and by teaching the client a mechanism for challenging and eliminating irrational philosophic ideas. His approach further includes desensitizing exercises and homework assignments designed to help the client more effectively identify and change irrational premises. The theory is based on the principle that human beings are not passively trained by their childhood experiences, but that they actively accept or reject environmental teaching. Client acceptance of an irrational, self-defeating belief system leads to experiencing self-defeating feelings, which in turn often leads to problem behavior. In these cases the client needs to be reeducated to think and behave more rationally. This behavior therapy approach, known as "rational-emotive," was presented earlier.

Ellis (1975) discusses ten common irrational beliefs that our society teaches which underlie much problem behavior. Ellis holds that the counselor can help the client identify these irrational ideas and modify them. Paraphrased, ten irrational ideas are:

1. One must have love or approval from all significant others. If rejected, one is worthless.
2. One must be completely competent, adequate, and achieving to be worthwhile.
3. People who behave objectionably are bad, wicked, rotten individuals.
4. When one gets seriously frustrated, treated unfairly, or rejected, it is a terrible catastrophe.
5. Emotional misery comes from external pressures. People's reactions to these pressures can't be controlled.
6. One must preoccupy oneself with dangerous or fearsome activities to make oneself anxious about it.
7. It is easier to avoid facing many of life's difficulties and one's self-responsibilities than to face them.
8. Something that once strongly influenced one's life will continue to determine one's feelings and behavior.
9. Things should turn out better than they do. It is awful if one cannot find the solutions to life's realities.
10. Maximum human happiness can be attained passively or by inaction.

Ellis teaches the client to vigorously dispute the irrational belief system that creates self-defeating emotions and behaviors and to correct misconceptions and erroneous ideas that lead to ineffective coping styles. Since counseling is a learning process, it seeks to assist the client in the acquisition of new and more effective ways of behaving, and reinforces the maintenance of those behaviors.

Figure 4–1 provides examples of significant environmental, cognitive, affective, physiological, and behavioral events that may be of use to the counselor in understanding and assessing human behavior (Tosi, 1974). The table points out the type of negative-evaluative thoughts that often occur in various situations, and the resulting emotional, physiological, and behavioral consequences of these negative-evaluative thoughts.

Behavioral Objectives

Behavior may be considered a function of the person and environment interaction ($B = f[PE]$). When an overt behavior or act is observed

FIGURE 4-1
Exemplary person-environment interaction processes suggesting maladaptive functioning

Event	Cognitive response: Negative self-evaluating thoughts	Affective response: Negative emotional state	Physiological response	Behavioral response
John fails an exam in a college class.	He tells himself that he is stupid, and that he will never be able to pass other tests no matter how much he studies.	Worry, anxiety, depression.	Fatigue, always tired.	Poor study habits, underachievement, oversleeping.
Sally wants to stop smoking. She has tried several times before but each time returned to smoking.	Sally tells herself she simply cannot stop smoking because she does not have the willpower.	Frustration, anxiety.	Stomachaches.	Continues to smoke. Blames herself for not being able to quit.
Jim was rejected by his wife when he wanted affection from her.	Jim tells himself that she does not love him any more, and that it is terrible not to be loved by his own wife. He further believes that he must be impotent since he is being rejected by his wife.	Depression, hostility, guilt, self-hate, worry.	Ulcers, headaches, tension.	Withdraws from situation and does not attempt interaction with his wife or he acts out his hostility.
Bill, a young executive, makes a significant mistake in his new job and is reprimanded. Bill has had a goal to advance in the company.	Bill tells himself that he is really dumb for making the mistake. He thinks he will never have a chance for advancement.	Frustration, guilt, self-hate.	Hypertension.	Appears to continue to try to make a good impression in his job; but due to many irrational beliefs, he does not achieve to his full capabilities.

in the environment, concomitant are thoughts, emotions, and physical reactions. Because human behavior is complex, statements about general or specific goals of counseling need to give full consideration to the person, the environment, and the interaction.

Because the scientific method pervades counseling, language is often used which suggests that only those events which can be directly observed are of value to the counselor. If a counselor relies too heavily on rigid objectivity, attention can very easily be directed away from important subjective processes, such as thinking, emotions, values, and attitudes. Therefore, a counselor attempting to specify the goals or objectives of counseling would be wise to employ a model that speaks to the person, the environment, and the interaction.

Behavioral objectives require that counseling goals be stated specifically in clear and concise language, and that they be understood by the client. Behavioral objectives are statements of goals that include cognitive (thinking), emotional, physical, and action tendencies relative to a social environment. Thoresen and Anton (1974) propose three identifying criteria for a behavioral objective in counseling: (1) a behavioral objective specifies the response to be enacted in such terms that it may be observed by the counselor and client and reliably recorded; (2) a behavioral objective specifies a performance criterion (frequency, intensity, and duration levels); and (3) a behavioral objective specifies the conditions or circumstances in which the behavior is to occur. A fourth criterion can also be added to include the counseling strategy to be used.

Behavioral objectives are jointly defined by the counselor and client. Counseling strategies, however, are selected by the counselor. Once some maladaptive behavior is observed, a baseline of that behavior is determined; that is, an assessment is made of the frequency, the intensity, and the duration of the behavior and recorded graphically (see Figures 4–1 through 4–5). The baseline period may vary from one to several weeks, depending on the length of counseling and type of problem. The effectiveness of a counseling strategy will be assessed if desirable changes are observed in the frequency, intensity, and duration of the target behavior, as compared to baseline measures. If the changes are not observed, other strategies may need to be implemented. Efforts should be made by the counselor and client to assure that behavior is *reliably* recorded.

Example. A male client indicates one of his major difficulties is socializing with women. He reports that he is afraid to ask a woman for a date. The counselor and client agree jointly that one goal they will pursue is to increase the likelihood of the client approaching women and asking certain ones for dates (a target behavior). The counselor would need to determine whether the client lacked a social skill and experienced anxiety over the thought of approaching a woman and ultimately avoided the situation or both. Suppose anxiety and a lack of social skill are both responsible for the client avoiding women. The counselor, in cooperation with the client, may proceed to state the following general behavioral objective:

General Behavioral Objective
Given the client's strong tendency to avoid (action) asking women for dates (situation) and his tendency to feel anxious (affect) over the thought (cognition) of asking a woman for a date, it would be desirable for the client to increase the likelihood of asking a woman for a date, and minimize his anxiety through a modification of the thoughts that produce the anxiety.

A general behavioral objective is an inclusive statement about a specific person and environmental interaction. A general behavioral objective can be reduced to *specific behavioral objectives* that speak to the various components of person and environment interaction—cognitions (thoughts, ideas, images), emotions (feelings), and physiological responses (bodily reactions—optional), actions, and situational events. In writing specific behavioral objectives for each component, criterion levels of performance need to be stated as well as the particular counseling intervention to be used to accomplish the objective. The stating of behavioral objectives in general and specific terms serves essentially as an intervention package.

Suppose a baseline of one date per month was established and that the client agreed to try to attain a criterion level of four dates a month. Assume that the client using a 0 to 100 point scale subjectively estimates the intensity of his anxiety level (subjective units of disturbance—S U D) associated with dating behavior to be about 80 (0 = no anxiety, 100 = extreme anxiety). Let's also say that the client sets a criterion level of 20 SUDs as a goal to be attained.

Furthermore, suppose the client reports that he experiences anxiety reactions about five times a day for a total of two hours. Finally, the client expresses that he engages in frequent irrational self-talk about dating (e.g., "Wouldn't it be awful if I were rejected? Wouldn't it be terrible if the woman found me unacceptable? I don't have anything to offer any woman. I know I am a loser. Only good looking guys can get women. I know I am inadequate and all women know that.") The following charts show how behavior is recorded and measured and how counseling may influence positively the client's thoughts, feelings, and overt behavior. Keep in mind that while each process is analyzed separately, they vary together.

Specific behavioral objectives

Cognitive component. To reduce the frequency of irrational self-verbalizations concomitant with anxiety and avoidance of dating from an average of five each day to zero, and to replace the five irrational self-verbalizations with five rational alternatives, using cognitive restructuring. (See Figure 4–2.)

FIGURE 4–2
Cognitive component

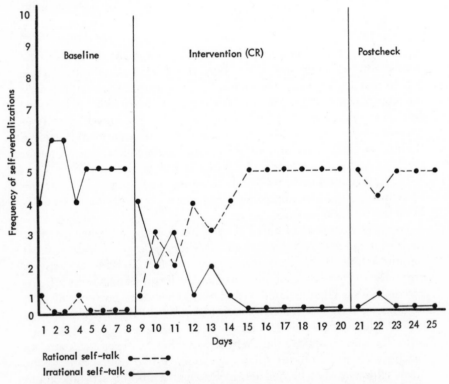

Affective or emotional component (frequency, intensity, duration). (*a*) To reduce the frequency of self-reported feelings of anxiety from five times a day to one time a day; (*b*) to reduce the intensity of anxiety from 80 subjective units of disturbance to 20 units; and (*c*) to reduce the duration of self-reported anxiety from 120 minutes to 5 minutes using a combination of cognitive restructuring and systematic desensitization. (See Figures 4–3, 4–4, and 4–5.)

FIGURE 4-3
Affective or emotional component (frequency)

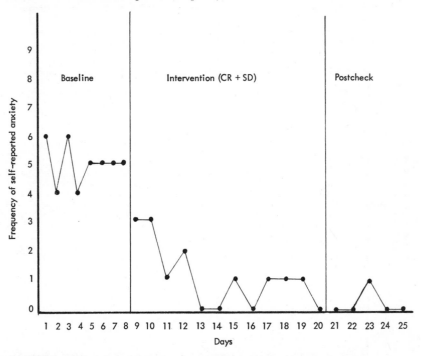

FIGURE 4-4
Affective or emotional component (intensity)

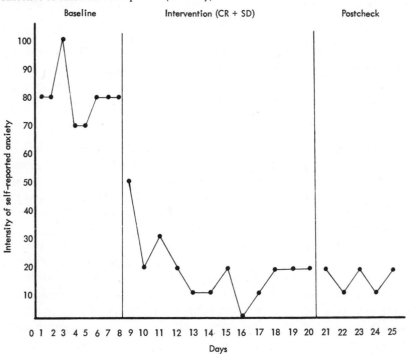

FIGURE 4–5
Affective or emotional component (duration)

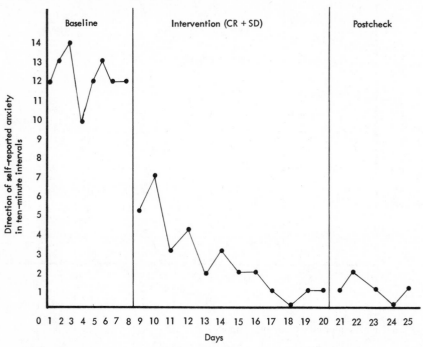

Action component. To increase the frequency of dating behavior from one time per month (four week periods) to four times per month —using cognitive restructuring, and assertive training. (See Figure 4–6.)

Behavioral self-analysis and monitoring

The ultimate objective of counseling is for the client to assume personal behavioral control and responsibility. Self-observation of change during counseling can prove to be a rewarding experience for the client, thus serving as a motivation for continued growth and personal satisfaction. When a client attributes a change in behavior to personal efforts, rather than to some external source, that change is likely to be maintained (Valins et al., 1975). Therefore, a counselor may be very wise to encourage the use of behavioral self-analysis and observation.

Kanfer (1970) reports that the mere counting and charting of the increase or decrease of a particular behavior becomes self-reinforcing and provides impetus for subsequent behavior change. Behavioral self-analysis and the specifying of behavioral objectives are inseparable op-

FIGURE 4–6
Action component

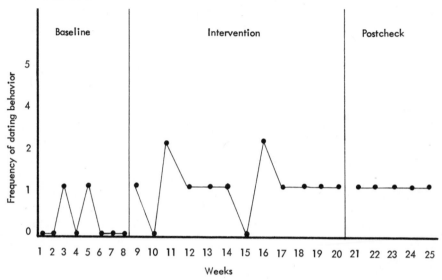

erations. The awareness and discrimination of adaptive and maladaptive behavior is directed toward the implementation of activity that increases one's chances for more productive behavior. Behavioral self-analysis and monitoring provides a client with a valuable feedback that serves to guide behavior efficiently. Moreover, the procedure permits a high level of client involvement.

Nonverbal communication

An important aspect of assessing human functioning has to do with the recognition and understanding of nonverbal behavior. Quite naturally, people communicate with words to express their intentions and thoughts. However, words alone do not always convey the true meanings, feelings, or ideas a person wishes to express. Sometimes people just do not know how to put into words their innermost thoughts and feelings. As a result, people use gestures or other bodily reactions to send messages about themselves to others. As indicated in an earlier section of this book, a counselor listens very carefully to the client's messages—whether these are expressed in words or in other ways.

A counselor needs to be aware of the ways different kinds of people communicate. Members of subcultures differ from one another in their verbal and nonverbal mannerisms and expressions. Counselors, if they are to maximize their effectiveness with diverse groups of people, must be very sensitive to communication patterns. For instance, Anglo-Saxons portray themselves as extremely analytical and aloof, giving little evidence of their emotions. To conclude that such people are unfeeling may be a gross error. On the other hand, black Americans and southern Europeans tend to be openly expressive physically as well as verbally. It would be as much of an error to conclude they are lacking in intellectual capacity. Until counselors have a good understanding of their client's cultural background, they should be very cautious about making conclusions and final judgements about their client's motives, intentions, and behavior. Sue (1978) has proposed a model to use in counseling minority populations that is sensitive to cultural differences. Other investigators (Webster & Fretz, 1978; Westbrook, Miyares, & Roberts, 1978) have found differences between black, white, and Asian-American students in counseling needs and help-giving preferences.

Sociologists continually warn psychologists, social workers, and medical people that an effective counseling relationship may not develop if the counselor lacks a thorough knowledge of the client's customs, traditions, and values. Inferences or interpretations regarding nonverbal behavior elicited by the client need to be made in light of sociocultural factors. Just because one does not express emotions with excessive hand gestures, or the like, does not indicate a lack of deep feelings about some issue.

Counselors may also need to recognize that some nonverbal behavior is meaningless. Tears can represent sorrow, rage, or allergic reaction. The context of behavior is important in understanding its meaning. One way of checking whether nonverbal behavior is meaningful is to reflect the hypothesized feeling the nonverbal behavior may be conveying.

> I notice that when we talk about your father's problem with drinking you seem to move around a good deal in the chair. Does that mean you are uncomfortable with mentioning your father?

> I wonder whether your laughter suggests that you are a bit nervous about certain topics.

Often the client will affirm immediately the counselor's interpretation or reflection, but not always. The client may not affirm or acknowledge the accuracy or inaccuracy of the counselor's reflections and interpretations until later sessions when the client becomes less defensive and anxious. Some potentially meaningful nonverbal behaviors observed frequently in counseling relationships include posture, hand movements, heavy breathing, head movements, ritualistic acts, blushing, eye movements, voice variations, lip movements, and silence.

Psychological inventories and tests in counseling and behavioral assessment

Psychological tests and inventories are used to make decisions about selection and classification of people, to evaluate educational and psychological treatment procedures, and to verify scientific hypotheses (Cronbach, 1970). Psychological tests and inventories are used by counselors working in educational, vocational, and personal social counseling settings for the same kinds of reasons. In counseling relationships, psychological tests and inventories can further serve to facilitate a client's self-understanding as well as comparisons with others. The use of tests and inventories is a standard and objective method available to the counselor interested in assessing the behavioral and psychological status of clients.

Through the use of tests and inventories, the counselor attempts to appraise the personality characteristics, typical behaviors, and potential problems of the client. The interpretation of personality inventories, along with behavioral and problem check lists, can sometimes accelerate an individual's self-awareness and exploration (Brammer & Shostrom, 1968).

Selection of instruments

Cronbach (1970) warns that instruments should be selected and used for the particular purpose for which designed. Counselors, in particular, need to be able to judge instruments in terms of their potential usefulness for client needs. Therefore, the counselor who uses tests and inventories has a special responsibility to stay current with the latest developments in assessment, especially in matters relating to test reliability and validity. The counselor can do this through reading such periodicals as the *Journal of Personality Assessment, Educational and Psychological Measurement,* the *Journal of Counseling Psychology,* the *Journal of Consulting and Clinical Psychology, Measurement and Evaluation in Guidance,* the *Journal of Applied Psychology,* and the *Journal of Applied Measurement,* as well as many others. Test reviews reported in Buros's *Mental Measurements Yearbooks* (1950–1976) are also of considerable importance to the counselor in learning about tests and their characteristics.

Before selecting a test to be used with a client, the counselor should engage in a thorough exploration with the client of the needs that might be fulfilled through testing. This must be done to increase the likelihood that the tests to be selected will be useful to the client and, as a consequence, the test results properly and usefully interpreted. Counselors must beware of "testing for testing's sake." It is tempting to the counselor to appear to be an expert by relying on the extensive use of testing procedures in professional psychological settings.

Some agencies routinely administer standard or semistandard batteries of tests to all incoming clientele. While there are some advantages to be derived from such routine testing, in general the disadvantages outweigh the advantages. Clients frequently fail to respond openly and with proper motivation to routine standardized batteries because proper groundwork for the tests hasn't been laid. Counselors frequently squander client time and professional time in reviewing the results of tests that are administered following such a "buckshot" approach. Client expectations about counselor omniscience and infallibility are often inappropriately increased by the use of extensive and standardized testing batteries. Finally, many instruments contain items that are somewhat frightening to clients, and can increase anxiety in clients already experiencing considerable distress. In sum, tests should be selected with particular purposes in mind, and with as clear an understanding with the client of how the results will be useful to both client and counselor.

Client: Don't you have some kind of test that'll tell me what career I should choose?

Counselor: There are lots of tests that can help you decide, give you more information about yourself; but no test will "tell you" what to do.

Client: Well, what can a test do for me?

Counselor: There is an interest inventory we can start with that might help. It will compare your interests with those of people in a variety of occupations. If we find some similarity between your interests and those of people in certain kinds of fields, those would be good areas to begin exploring first.

Client: Okay, let's start.

Counselor: Before we begin testing, I want to get a better idea of what you expect to discover, and what you'll do with the results if they don't turn out in a way you like. What if some fields are suggested that you think you wouldn't like? Or if no field comes out clearly as one to explore? What then? How will you react?

Another caution for the test user is the importance of using tests for the purposes for which they were designed. While exceptions can sometimes be justified, generally speaking it is best to use intelligence tests to measure intelligence and personality inventories to measure personality and not the reverse. Some counselors have, at times, tried to make inferences about personality based on intelligence measures, and some personality measures have derived scales that allow inferences to be made about intelligence. Such procedures, however, seem to be using "second-best data" and are to be avoided.

Another potential pitfall involved in the selection of instruments has to do with the clear identification of purpose of the test with respect to what one is predicting. Sometimes one is interested in predicting individual behaviors, while at other times group predictions are desired. A counselor trying to help a client identify individual objectives needs to keep in mind the results of studies having to do with the predictive validity of the instrument being used. If the counselor is simply trying to identify the probability of a client belonging to a particular group, then other psychometric questions may be involved. In other words, if one is trying to select the best applicant from a pool of applicants, the kind and type of error that can be tolerated is greater and different than if the counselor is trying to help a client select the best alternative from a field of alternatives.

During World War II, when human resources were strained to capacity, decisions were made to admit applicants of questionable potential to highly specialized training programs. It was reasoned that skilled people were in such short supply no person possible of success should be rejected, even if it meant many potential failures would be admitted. After the war, human-resource needs returned to normal, fewer specialists were needed, and standards were raised so only those virtually sure of success were admitted to specialized training. Even if some potential "succeeders" were missed, we had more than enough people to do what was necessary. It is a question of supply and demand, and economy.

However, when an individual makes a personal decision, it is *all* or *none*. Either they succeed or they fail. Thus, one approaches using tests in counseling for prediction with a different perspective than in a group setting.

Some instruments are used for evaluation, while others may be used more to help describe people; still others may be more useful in their process elements. For example, such instruments as the Strong-Campbell Interest Inventory and the California Test of Mental Maturity are much more likely to be useful in assessing the characteristics and predicting the future performance of individuals than would an instrument such as the California Psychological Inventory, which would be likely to help a counselor describe a client's characteristics.

Process gains can be derived through the use of such instruments as the Self Directed Search (Holland) and the Incomplete Sentences Blank (Rotter); various other projective devices can sometimes be useful in helping clients explore their own needs and desires and values. When instruments are used for their process features, it may well be that the results generated by scores are of secondary utility to the counselors and client, compared to that of the experiences gone through in originally deriving the scores. Some instruments serve more than one of these purposes. For example, the Career Maturity Inventory (Crites) can be useful for assessment and evaluation as well as for process.

There are many kinds of instruments available. One type, of relatively recent origin, are the behavioral inventories. Such instruments are used variously to generate reinforcement hierarchies for desensitization processes (see chapter 5), to assess client strengths and weaknesses, and in general, to canvass client-response repertoires. Counselors often devise their own forms of behavioral inventories, tailored to their clients. The principal virtue of these instruments is that they allow the client to be described in very personal terms.

Since many behaviors of importance do not lend themselves to direct observation by the counselor, for practical reasons (it is not feasible to follow the client for 24 hours at a time) secondary methods to assess behaviors have been developed.

These secondary methods include inventories of specific behaviors (e.g., the Fear Survey Schedule), which require the client to report the presence, frequency, and intensity of concrete responses engaged in. Such methods differ from personality inventories, such as the California Psychological Inventory (CPI) or the Minnesota Multiphasic Personality Inventory (MMPI), in several ways. First, the behavioral schedules do not rely on normative data for their interpretation. Behavior schedules assume it may be significant to know that a client engages in a certain behavior without consideration for the frequency with which people in general engage in the same behavior. Second, the behavioral schedules do not attempt to explain the client's responses in terms of scale-based "traits," such as dependency, sociability, and adjustment (in the case of the CPI), or in terms of diagnostic categories, such as psychasthenia (on the MMPI), or trait scales, such as anxiety (as on the MMPI). In this respect, the behavioral measures are more parsimonious than the personality inventories.

There are several additional shortcomings in the use of the trait-oriented measures. They assume a relatively static adjustment and response style on the part of individuals, and do not pay sufficient attention to situational aspects of behavior. Furthermore, personality inventories fail to recognize that intra-individual variations in behaviors may be wide. Trait-oriented measures tend to cause the counselor to assume that traits may be interpreted in a relatively constant manner across situations. However, it may be misleading to interpret a trait, such as sociability, in a constant manner, because it may not have some meaning even for a single individual in different situations. The individual may discriminate situationally regarding engaging in "sociable" behaviors because of the different value of sociability across situations. Thus, a student may be very sociable (engage in frequent, intense, and effective interpersonal activities) while attending a party on a Saturday night, but appear very unsociable (engage in isolative behaviors) during weekend nights while trying to study. Furthermore, the student may behave in these different ways deliberately, reflecting a stimulus discrimination regarding the desirability of sociable responses in the two situations.

Interactionism

Behaviorally oriented instruments tend to represent an interactionist view of personality espoused by such writers as Mischel (1968). This view sees personality not as a static trait but rather as behavior that varies within a specified range. The amplitude of a particular behavior reflecting personality at a particular time is largely affected by the person's momentary situation.

Such a view of personality minimizes the importance of whether personality is best described as a trait or a state; that is, whether we are striving to find how a person behaves in general or how a person behaves at a particular time. For example, some people are usually anxious. For such people, anxiety might be considered to be a trait that is made worse at times (depending upon the situation). However, we might also properly consider anxiety to be a state that an individual experiences in intense degree under certain conditions (taking an exam), but not ordinarily.

Reliability

Reliability refers to the stability or consistency of a test. That is, if the same test, different form, or if equivalent halves of the same test are administered at two different times under similar conditions to the same group, the scores should be very similar. The reliability and validity of tests are usually expressed as a coefficient (Coefficient of Correlation). A correlation coefficient indicates the extent to which two variables are related. The most commonly used measure of correlation is the Pearson Product Moment (r). Values of the Product Moment Coefficient of Correlation range from 0.00 (no relationship) to ±1.00 (perfect relationship).

When selecting tests, it is good practice to look for high reliability coefficients, generally in the range of .80 to 1.00. If reliability coefficients are too low, there may be problems related to the internal structure of the test. Low reliability coefficients suggest also that the scores the person made on the test tended to be inconsistent. A full discussion of test reliability may be found in Cronbach (1970).

Validity

The validity of a test refers to whether the test measures what it is supposed to. Several types of validity are important for test developers and users: face validity, content validity, concurrent and predictive validity, and construct validity.

Face validity is concerned with whether a test *appears* to be measuring a particular psychological concept, trait, or behavior. Face validity, being the most simple and least sophisticated, is not expressed statistically.

Content validity refers to whether the items on the test are indicators of the particular thing being measured. Content validity is most important to the construction of achievement and aptitude tests.

Concurrent validity, expressed by a correlation coefficient, has to do with the extent the test correlates with some other known and valid indicator of the concept. For example, scores on the Otis Quick Scoring Intelligence Test may correlate .70 with the total score on the Wechsler Adult Intelligence Scales (criterion).

Predictive validity refers to the ability of the test to make predictions about someone's performance on some criterion variable. For example, will high scores on the Otis Quick Scoring Test obtained by a high school senior predict that student's grade point average in the freshman year of college? Predictive validity is also expressed by the coefficient of correlation.

Construct validity indicates whether a particular psychological dimension logically makes sense according to some underlying theory or construct. For instance, if a test is supposed to measure anxiety, are the items consistent with the particular theory of anxiety, e.g., Freudian, behavioral, humanistic.

Factor analysis is a statistical method sometimes used to identify items on a test that theoretically belong together. Sometimes factor analysis can be identified under dimensions of a psychological concept. Factorial validity can be determined through the use of this sophisticated procedure. Factor analysis is a statistical method sometimes used to determine construct validity.

What affects reliability and validity? Among the important items affecting these characteristics are the degree to which good standards of test administration and test scoring are followed. Obviously, if a test has been developed for use in a particular set of administration and scoring conditions, and these conditions have not been faithfully followed by the test administrator, then serious and undesirable effects on the reliability and validity of the resulting scores occur.

A second factor affecting reliability and validity has to do with item selection. The validity and reliability of item selections is particularly affected based on the degree to which the items are related to the criterion that is being predicted and to the performance of various criterion groups. In other words, one cannot reliably or validly predict a behavior if the sample items used to predict it have no reference to the criterion being predicted. If you want to predict how high a person can jump, you might measure leg length (among other things) but not eye-blink rate.

How do you know if a test is adequate with respect to validity and reliability? Validity levels are difficult to assess. This is partly because the criteria for most tests are not clearly stated. Furthermore, even when the criteria are clearly stated, they often are not measured in an ideal fashion. A good test manual, however, will indicate a summary of criterion studies that have been conducted in connection with a test. Depending upon the kind of validity measures one is concerned with, better or worse validity data may be available. Predictive validity—that is, the degree to which the instrument actually predicts the behaviors one is concerned with—tends to be commonly reported, although not always as frequently as one would like. Concurrent validity, or the degree to which the instrument is correlated with other previously validated instruments, tends to be the most commonly reported; but this is probably the least useful to most counselors. Construct validity is the most difficult kind of validity data to obtain and is hardly ever reported. One must make judgments about validity studies largely on the basis of test reviews that are published in various publications and in books like Buros's *Mental Measurements Yearbook.*

Reliability data are somewhat easier to provide and to interpret. For most instruments, reliability below .7 or .8 will probably render the instrument relatively useless. Some instruments report reliability in terms of test-retest, others in terms of internal split half type scores.

The reader is referred to extended discussions on reliability and validity coefficients in more extended treatments of test construction, such as represented in books by Anastasi (1976) and Cronbach (1970).

One final point about reliability and validity that should be remembered: An instrument without satisfactory reliability cannot, by definition, have adequate validity.

Norms

The term *norm* refers to average or normal performance. Norms in psychological testing indicate the average performance of different groups in a particular test, e.g., college graduates, high school graduates, males, females. An individual score(s) on a psychological test is compared to scores obtained by other groups of people.

Cronbach (1970) suggests that the counselor can judge the adequacy of norm groups if the following questions can be answered:

1. Are any of the norm groups representative of persons with whom my counselee should be compared?
2. Is the sample size sufficiently large?
3. Is the sample size appropriately subdivided into smaller groups, e.g., males or females; freshmen, sophomores, juniors, seniors?

When interpreting the results of tests the counselor needs to (a) make clear statements about the nature of the test; (b) encourage the client to give personal impressions and feelings about the test, i.e., what the client thinks the test says about him or her; (c) relate to the client what the test says about him or her; and (d) discuss areas of agreement and disagreement.

Before any test interpretation is undertaken, it is wise to understand the results and to have some notion of what to say to the client. During the interview, the counselor should give a cogent and clear explanation of the test itself and of the norm groups. It is wise to interpret the entire test, including all subscales, so the client can be apprised of strengths as well as weaknesses. Any misconceptions the client may have about the meaning of tests and his or her performance should be corrected immediately. Client participation in the interpretation of tests is almost essential.

Sometimes the client may resist the counselor's interpretation. If such a situation arises, the counselor should not force the interpretation on the client. Forcing the client to face certain "facts" may increase anxiety that may cause the client to block, close up, or withdraw from counseling. It is generally a good idea to set aside several counseling sessions for test interpretation to allow the client enough time to effectively process the information derived from testing. The effective interpretation of tests can open many areas for counseling. Tests in counseling are very often used to facilitate counseling.

The counselor should refrain from authoritarian interpretive statements, such as: "The test says that you are anxious." "Tests don't lie." "If you go to college, you will flunk out." "The test indicates that you are having sexual problems." Statements need to be made on a probabilistic basis where the individual is compared to others. Furthermore, clients should be given an "out" to reject results, if they wish, and the counselor should "tune in" to client reactions to test results. Thus: "Your scores place you above the average relative to this group. What does that mean to you?" "People who score as you did tend to feel more anxious than persons who score lower. Do you feel that describes you?" "Persons with aptitude scores like yours tend to have about a 50–50 chance to succeed in college A, a 60–40 chance to succeed in college B, and an 80–20 chance to succeed in college C." "You seem to have interests very similar to persons who are in medical professions, as opposed to business professions."

What about not using norms in testing? There are some instruments whose use is appropriate without a normative base. The various behavioral inventories that were discussed earlier, for example, lend themselves to valid and reliable use without reference to norm groups. When counselors are interested in client's descriptions of themselves, normative references are relatively unimportant. Therefore, a client's interests, for example, are particularly important to the client in their own right at times and not as they are relative to someone else. For purposes of self-exploration, normative data may be of secondary importance. For purposes of predicting performance and satisfaction levels in comparison to some criterion group, normative bases are important. Counselors should probably avoid the temptation to rely exclusively on normed or unnormed data and instead select those occasions when reliance on norms is useful and select others when it is not.

Some widely used instruments

Figures 4–1 through 4–11 present examples of psychological inventories and check lists frequently used in counseling. They include standardized and objective measures of personality factors, traits, and attitudes, interest inventories, and behavioral check lists. The examples are not meant to be exhaustive but merely representative of the many varieties of instruments. Literally thousands of instruments are available for counselor use—too many to show here.

A brief summary follows of the validity and reliability of the measure, the population for which it is intended, its strengths and weaknesses, and distinctive aspects it possesses. For detailed descriptions of the instruments, the reader is referred to test manuals of the measures. In addition, several excellent books exist that describe interest inventories, such as Super and Crites's (1962) *Appraising Vocational Fitness* (Rev. ed.), Zytowski's (1973) *Contemporary Approaches to Interest Measurement,* Buros's series of *Mental Measurements Yearbooks,* and

FIGURE 4-7

Career interest measures	MMY or date	Description	Uses in counseling	Reliability	Validity	Norms
Kuder Occupational Interest Survey (KOIS)	7–1025	Empirically keyed, self-report assessment of interests in specific occupations and college majors. Individual interests are compared with successful and satisfied groups in specific occupations and college majors.	Grades 11–16 and adult. Educational and vocational guidance.	Good.	Good.	Good. Male and female. Successful adults.
Minnesota Vocational Interest Inventory (MVII)	7–1026	Empirically keyed inventory designed to measure the interests of men and boys in occupations for which a college education is not required.	Age 15 and over. Educational and vocational guidance.	Fair to good.	Fair.	Fair. Men in general in nonprofessional occupations.
Strong Campbell Interest Inventory (SCII) D. P. Campbell, Stanford Univ. Press	1977 SVIB 6–1070	Empirically keyed instrument designed to measure interests, a wide variety of activities, people, and objects. Combination and revision of male and female forms of Strong Vocational Interest Blank. (SVIB). Scales are structured around Holland's occupational model.	Grades 9–16 and adult. Educational and vocational guidance.	Good.	Good.	Good. Males and females. Successful adults.
Career Maturity Inventory (CMI) Crites (includes instrument formerly known as the VDI)	1973	Measures attitudes and competencies associated with effective career development.	Grades 6–13.	Good.	Fair to good.	Good. Grades 6–13.

Instrument	Year	Description	Range			Norms
Ohio Vocational Interest Survey (OVIS) A. D'Costa, D. Winefordner, J. Odgers, P. Koons, Jr.	1969	Help students assess interests and background along 24 world of work interest scales. Organizes interests into data, people, things model. Planning rather than production oriented.	Grades 8–12.	Fair to good.	Little data now available.	Good. Local norms available (sex, grade, geographic region).
Vocational Preference Inventory (VPI) J. L. Holland	1965 1975	A personality measure which assesses vocational interests in the context of Holland's (1973) theory of careers. Allows match between individual and potentially appropriate work environments to be made.	Grade 6–adult.	Fair to good.	Fair to good.	Some norms on college students available.
Self-Directed Search (SDS) J. L. Holland	1972	Designed to provide vocational self-counseling and/or to augment counselor services. Organized like the VPI along lines of Holland's theory of careers.	Ages 8–80.	Good.	Fair to good.	Relates to occupational codes via *The Job Finder*.
Hall Occupational Orientation Inventory L. G. Hall, R. B. Tarrier, D. L. Shappell	1968 (2d ed.)	Helps individual explore career interests in terms of psychological needs in a counseling setting. Scores are reported for 22 needs. Not designed to predict an occupation.	Grades 9–13.	Fair to good.	Fair to good.	None reported.

FIGURE 4-8

Intelligence Tests	MMY or date	Description	Uses for counseling	Reliability	Validity	Norms
Stanford Binet Intelligence Scale L. M. Terman M. A. Merrill Houghton-Mifflin	7–425	Individually administered measure of general intelligence, providing age related deviation I.Q. score.	Ages 2 and over. Educational and vocational guidance.	Very good.	Fair to good.	Good. Male and female. Ages 2–18.
Wechsler Intelligence Scale for Children (WISC–R) D. Wechsler Psychological Corp.	7–431 1974	Individually administered measure of general intelligence. Downward extension of original Wechsler Bellevue containing 12 subtests giving verbal, perf., and full scale score.	Ages 6½–16½. Educational and vocational guidance. Detection of learning disabilities.	Good.	Fair.	Good. Male and female. Ages 6½–16½.
Wechsler Intelligence Scale for Adults (WAIS) D. Wechsler Psychological Corp.	7–429	An individually administered measure of general intelligence containing 11 subtests which yield a verbal, performance, and full scale I.Q. score.	Ages 16–75. Assessment of general intelligence. Aids in psychiatric diagnosis. Educational and vocational guidance.	Good.	Good.	Good. Male and female. Adults.
California Test of Mental Maturity E. T. Sullivan W. W. Clark E. W. Tiggs	1963 (rev.)	Assesses academic potential on five ability scales plus a language total, nonlanguage total, and overall total.	Ages 5–adult. Assesses school learning ability.	Good.	Fair.	K–adult.

FIGURE 4-9

Multiple aptitude batteries	MMY or date	Description	Uses in counseling	Reliability	Validity	Norms
General Aptitude Test Battery (GATB) U.S. Training & Employment Service	7–676	A battery of aptitude tests designed to measure several abilities found to be important to success in many occupations. Composed of pencil and paper and performance tasks.	Ages 16 and over. Employment counseling.	Good.	Fair to good.	Good. Male and female. Adults.
Differential Aptitude Tests (DAT) G. K. Bennett H. G. Seashore A. G. Wesman Psychological Corp.	7–673 1974	An integrated battery of aptitude tests based on the idea the intelligence is not a single ability but rather a number of abilities possessed in varying amount by each individual.	Grades 8–16 and adult. Educational and vocational guidance.	Good.	Fair to good.	Good. Male and female. High school.

FIGURE 4–10

Self-report personality inventories	MMY or date	Description	Uses in counseling	Reliability	Validity	Norms
Personal Orientation Inventory (POI) E. L. Shostrom Educational and Industrial Testing Service	7–121	Self-report instrument designed to assess values, attitudes, and behaviors relevant to Maslow's concept of the self-actualizing person.	Grades 9–16 and adult. Research, personal counseling and therapy.	Fair to good.	Good.	Fair. Male and female. High school, college, businessmen, psychiatric patients.
Adjective Check List (ACL) H. G. Gough A. B. Heilbrun, Jr. Consulting Psychologists Press, Inc.	7–38	An economic assessment of general adjustment and self-concept. Subjects mark all adjectives thought to be self-descriptive.	Grades 9–16 and adult. Personality research. Initial exploration into guidance setting. Very adaptable.	Fair.	Fair.	No normative data in manual.
California Psychological Inventory (CPI) H. G. Gough Consulting Psychologists Press, Inc.	7–49	Derivative of MMPI; designed to measure variables used for the description and analysis of personality in everyday life and social interaction.	Normal population. Ages 13 and over. Personality assessment in educational and vocational guidance.	Fair to good.	Fair to good.	Very good. Male and female.
Edwards Personal Preference Schedule (EPPS) A. L. Edwards Psychological Corporation	7–72	Theoretically derived instrument designed to assess the relative importance within the individual of Murray's manifest need system.	Ages 18 and over. Personality research. Personal counseling with normal populations.	Good.	Fair.	Good. Male and female. College, adult, rural–urban.

Test		Description	Uses			Population
Guilford–Zimmerman Temperament Survey J. P. Guilford W. S. Zimmerman Sheridan Psychological Services	6–110	A personality survey designed to systematically measure normal personality characteristics and general activity level. Constructed through factor analytic techniques.	Grades 12–16 and adult. Personality research. Personal counseling. Educational and vocational guidance.	Good.	Good.	Good. Male and female. High school, college, adult.
Minnesota Counseling Inventory (MCI) R. F. Berdie W. L. Layton Psychological Corporation	6–142	Derivative of MMPI and Minnesota Counseling Scale which measures present adjustment and methods of coping. Edited to be more readable and acceptable to parents and teachers.	Grades 9–12. High school guidance of personal, educational, and vocational concerns.	Fair to good.	Fair to good.	Male and female. High school.
Minnesota Multiphasic Personality Inventory (MMPI) S. R. Hathaway J. C. McKinley Psychological Corporation	7–104	Most popular and sophisticated diagnostic and research instrument designed to assess nature and degree of emotional disturbance.	Ages 16 and over. Research. Differential diagnosis in counseling and therapy. Used in hospital and clinical settings.	Good.	Good.	Male and female. Ages 16–55.

FIGURE 4–10 (continued)

Self-report personality inventories	MMY or date	Description	Uses in counseling	Reliability	Validity	Norms
Mooney Problem Check List R. L. Mooney L. V. Gordon Psychological Corporation	6–145	Straightforward list of commonly occurring problems. Individuals check concerns and expound upon them in their own words.	Grades 7–9, 9–12, 13–16, and adults. Identification of problems.	No data in manual.	Fair.	No norms in manual.
Myers-Briggs Type Indicator (MBTI) K. C. Briggs I. B. Myers Consulting Psychologists Press, Inc.	6–147	Theoretically derived instrument based on a modification of the Jungian theory of type. Scores are taken to indicate individual's preferred mode of operating in the world.	Grades 9–16 and adult. Personality research. Educational and vocational guidance. Normal populations. Marriage counseling.	Good.	Fair to good.	Male and female. College, industrial, professional.
Sixteen Personality Factor Questionnaire (16PF) Cattell	7–139	A factor analytically derived measure of the normal, adult personality. Purports to identify primary source traits, stressing universality and stability.	Ages 16 and over. Research, educational and vocational guidance. Personnel management.	Fair to good.	Fair to good.	Fair. Male and female. High school, general adult.

FIGURE 4-11

Projective techniques	MMY or date	Description	Uses in counseling	Reliability	Validity	Norms
Rorschach H. Rorschach Grune & Stratton, Inc.	7–175	A series of 10 bilaterally symmetrical inkblots which are presented to the individual for his or her spontaneous interpretations. Much skill and experience is required on the part of the examiner in the interpretation of the responses.	Ages 3 and over. Diagnostic investigation of the personality structure as a whole. Used primarily in hospital and clinical setting.	Fair.	Fair.	Fair. Male and female. Adult.
Thematic Apperception Test (TAT) H. A. Murray Harvard University Press	7–181	Test contains 19 structured stimulus cards for which the individual is asked to create a story. The story is to fit the picture, telling about the present situation, what led up to it, and what will happen.	Ages 4 and over. Personality research. Diagnosis and assessment of personality in clinical and hospital setting.	Fair.	Fair.	Fair.

publications by Cronbach (1970) and Anastasi (1976), are examples of very useful sources for the potential test and inventory user. For the applied test user, Goldman's (1971) *Using Tests in Counseling* (2d ed.), Lyman's (1971) *Test Scores and What They Mean*, and Tyler and Walsh's (1979) *Tests and Measurements* are likely to be useful reading for the counselor.

SUMMARY

This chapter has discussed a wide range of diagnostic and assessment approaches that are vital to the counseling process. Without a knowledge of the process of making inferences and hypotheses concerning the client's problem behavior, the counselor would not be able to efficiently help the client. It is therefore important for the counselor to develop skills in these areas as well as in data collection to objectively assess progress in the counseling process. Behavioral analysis techniques as used by Lazarus, Kanfer and Saslow, Beck, Ellis, Tosi, and others are also helpful to the counselor in providing formulas and guidelines necessary in accurate assessment of the client's needs and the counseling goals. A knowledge of behavioral objectives aids the counselor in the development of counseling goals that can be easily measured during the counseling process. Through the use of these diagnostic and assessment procedures, the counselor can be constantly aware of the progress of the counseling process and thus tailor the counselor techniques and goals in a manner that will most efficiently benefit the client.

Planned
behavioral
change

In previous chapters several topics, including theories of counseling, the counseling relationship, behavioral analysis and assessment, and techniques for enhancing the counseling relationship, were presented. We will now try to apply this knowledge to plan behavioral change.

Several of the most current and popular counseling techniques and their application to a variety of problem areas are described in this chapter. Among the techniques reviewed are: systematic desensitization, covert sensitization, covert reinforcement, the Premack principle of reinforcement, assertive training, and cognitive restructuring. Other procedures, such as micro-counseling and social modeling that usually accompany these, are also briefly described. Research supporting the use of some of the techniques described in this section has been reported in previous sections. In some instances, however, research support for techniques not stated in earlier chapters will be included here.

Counselors should find the techniques in this section very useful in bringing about planned and systematic behavioral change. The procedures described here have been shown to be empirically sound. Moreover, the techniques often lend themselves to "time limited" or "minimum change" counseling where the counseling goals are specific and limited. However, these techniques are very useful in long-term reconstructive counseling as well.

Counselors need to keep in mind that the various planned and systematic procedures are implemented in the context of a human relationship. These methods augment the counseling relationship strategies presented earlier. As counselors develop a relationship with their clients characterized by empathic understanding, acceptance and caring, it is much easier to implement structured approaches in the process. This section deals with "how to do it" and shows the beginning counselor some of the basic technology of the counseling process. The prospective counselor may find some of the language in this part of the book a little more technical than in other sections. Technical language, while kept to a minimum, is necessary to describe counseling because it has become a sophisticated procedure.

SYSTEMATIC DESENSITIZATION

Systematic desensitization (SD), discussed in an earlier part of this book, consists of three components: (1) training in deep muscle relaxation; (2) the determination of anxiety-producing stimuli and the construction of hierarchies; and (3) pairing relaxation with the anxiety hierarchy.

Before systematic desensitization is used, a behavorial analysis should be conducted. To have the entire procedure make sense to the client, and to enlist the client's informed collaboration, the systematic desensitization process and associated behavioral analysis must be explained to the client.

The behavioral analysis provides the data to be used in formulating the specific anxiety reaction to be desensitized, and the anxiety hierarchy to be used, as well as to identify the desensitizing elements necessary to counter-condition the client's anxiety reaction. Thus, the first steps involve learning from the client about the situations that produce anxiety. Then, the client is required to estimate subjectively the intensity of the anxiety experienced in each situation on a scale of zero to 100 to permit the counselor to devise a series of step-by-step increases anxiety-producing stimuli. Wolpe (1969) has referred to this scale as indicating subjective units of disturbance, sometimes abbreviated as SUD.

Construction of hierarchies

Using the SUD scale, a hierarchy of anxiety-related stimuli, ranging in intensity from those producing no anxiety to those producing high anxiety, is constructed for each distinctive anxiety-producing situation. These hierarchies should be as real as possible and as concrete as possible in terms of dealing with relevant situations, people, times, and places. This will help increase the effectiveness of the procedure.

The following is an example of a hierarchy that might be associated with test-taking anxiety. This hierarchy is arranged from low-anxiety-producing situations to high-anxiety-producing situations.

1. Getting out of bed the morning of an examination.
2. Thinking about an examination.
3. Looking over class notes in preparing for an examination.
4. Talking to a classmate about an examination.
5. Walking to class to take an examination.
6. Sitting in class as the professor hands out the examination.
7. Actually looking at the questions and trying to respond.

Another example might include dealing with a man's anxiety over asking a woman for a date. The following is an example of some of those situations. Again they are listed from low-anxiety-producing situations to high-anxiety-producing situations.

1. Meeting a woman in class.
2. Thinking about calling her for a date.
3. Deciding to call her for a date for a specific occasion.
4. Dialing her telephone number in order to ask her out.
5. Asking her to go on a date.

An important principle to remember in constructing any anxiety hierarchy is that hierarchies are idiosyncratic in nature, and that it cannot be assumed that a hierarchy appropriate for one individual will be appropriate for another. Therefore, the counselor must always focus on the concerns of the individual client, while still getting hints about possible hierarchy items from experiences the counselor has had with former clients with similar concerns.

Wolpe (1969) suggests that hierarchies are constructed from four main sources, which include: (1) client history, (2) client responses to Willoughby Questionnaire, (3) client responses to the Fear Schedule, and (4) material derived from the counseling interview.

Once the hierarchies have been established, the counselor needs to be sure the client can vividly imagine the scenes depicting the events that are associated with anxiety. If the client has difficulty in imagining the scenes, the counselor may need to spend some time helping the client to rehearse the emotional and behavioral content of the scene. This process is called *cognitive* rehearsal. With some clients, intense cognitive rehearsal may be required.

The concept of *graded structure* is another important part of systematic desensitization. Graded structure implies that hierarchies of performance can be constructed so that the client can successfully approximate desired behavioral goals. With this concept, it is easy to provide the client with immediate reinforcement and feedback about behavior. This allows the client to evaluate his or her own progress (Lazarus, 1971). The concept of graded structure also has implications for conducting systematic desensitization in real-life situations.

Relaxation training

One of the basic building blocks of systematic desensitization is that the counselor introduce to the client a response that is incompatible with the undesired response which the client is displaying. In this connection, Jacobson (1934) found that a relaxation response was incompatible with an anxiety response. Jacobson's approach involves first seeing that the client is seated comfortably, lying almost horizontally, head back and legs extended. The client is instructed to begin a slow deep breathing process with eyes closed. With arms extended, the client is instructed to tense his or her fists, increasing the tension while the counselor counts. The client is instructed to focus on the tension produced by this action. Then the client is asked to loosen the muscles and focus on the relaxation that results. These steps are repeated with each major body muscle group until all muscle groups have been tensed and relaxed and the operator is able to observe visible signs of client relaxation.

Several sessions may be needed before relaxation training can be efficiently accomplished. The number of training sessions will depend upon: (*a*) the willingness of the client to participate in the systematic desensitization, (*b*) the nature and severity of the client's problem, and (*c*) the counselor's skill. One excellent feature of relaxation training is that it can be practiced outside of the counseling sessions and between sessions.

Counterposing relaxation and hierarchies

Systematic desensitization begins when relaxation is paired with graded anxiety-producing stimuli from each hierarchy. Wolpe (1969) suggests that each anxiety-producing scene be presented approximately 5 to 7 seconds with 10 to 30 seconds between items with little or no anxiety and 1 to 3 minutes with items evoking large amounts of anxiety. The counselor asks the client to raise an index finger to indicate whether the scene is imagined vividly. The client may also give verbal feedback.

Systematic desensitization proposes that when a strong relaxation response is paired with a weaker anxiety response, the weaker anxiety response will tend to be inhibited. Therefore, systematic desensitization starts with the least anxiety-producing stimulus on the hierarchy. When the client feels comfortably relaxed in relation to each scene (usually after two or three trials), the next scene in the hierarchy can be presented. Each scene is presented three or four times. If the client continues to experience anxiety in response to a particular scene, the counselor instructs the client to stop imagining the scene, to focus on relaxation, and to move back to a previous scene where the client felt more comfortable. Prolonged exposure to a highly anxiety-producing stimulus may be too painful for the client and thus interfere with the treatment.

The duration of the systematic desensitization sessions may range from 10 to 45 minutes. Systematic desensitization sessions should always begin and end with the client feeling relaxed.

It is generally good practice for the client or counselor to keep a record of the client's progress. A charting or recording of behavior (self-monitoring) as described in an earlier chapter, allows the client to personally monitor progress and goal attainment.

A cognitive approach to relaxation

An alternative to the modified Jacobsen approach to relaxation uses the imagination. The client can become very relaxed while imagining himself or herself in some very relaxing situation. This enables the client to experience the sensations of relaxation and heaviness suggested by the counselor. Using imagery and suggestion the counselor can direct the client's attention to specific parts of the body—arms, legs, thighs, chest, mouth, and fingers—while the client passively concentrates. With most clients, a cognitive-imagery method of relaxation is a very efficient way of achieving a relaxed state in a very brief time. However, when a client has difficulty focusing attention and does not respond well to the cognitive approach, the modified Jacobsonian techniques may be more appropriate. Both the cognitive and modified Jacobsonian techniques can be combined if necessary.

Most behavior therapists use a cognitive approach to relaxation. Starting with the first three steps of the modified Jacobson technique, the counselor asks the client to sit comfortably in a chair, close his or her eyes, and begin to take slow deep breaths. The counselor might then say the following to the client:

> Begin to take slow deep breaths—place the formula—inhale relaxation, exhale tension—in the back of your mind. As you breathe deeply you allow your chest and stomach to expand, filling your lungs with fresh relaxing air. Hold each breath approximately two or three seconds. Then you exhale very slowly. With each deep breath you take you find that your body becomes more beautifully relaxed. Allow yourself to feel the relaxation. Perhaps you feel a sensation of heaviness in your hands—relaxing heaviness that begins to spread through your entire body. As you breathe deeply you feel the relaxing heaviness entering each part of your body. (Name the parts.) With each deep breath you take you find that you go deeper and deeper into a beautiful state of relaxation. (Ask the client to indicate relaxation by raising an index finger. If not relaxed, have the breathing process continue.)
>
> Now that you are beginning to feel relaxed it would be desirable to increase that feeling by beginning to focus on a very comfortable, beautiful, tranquil scene. (The scene that is chosen is usually determined in the interim. The counselor can ask the client about situations or scenes he or she finds to be very relaxing.) Imagine for a moment or so that you are sunbathing on a beautiful white, sandy beach—somewhere in Florida or southern California. The temperature is about 85 degrees. The sun is warm and the colors of the sky and the ocean before you are richly blue. You can hear the relaxing sound of the waves rolling gently on the seashore. You are struck by this most relaxing sensation you are experiencing and this most relaxing scene you are witnessing. As you continue to breathe deeply, you become even more relaxed . . .

Through this approach the client may become very sensitive to the use of imagery, which can be used effectively in the counseling process.

Research support

Studies on the effectiveness of systematic desensitization have been reviewed in the earlier chapter on counseling theory and elsewhere in this book. The effectiveness of this procedure has been well documented in experimental as well as case study research.

Advantages and cautions in the use of systematic desensitization

When systematic desensitization is the treatment of choice, there are many advantages, but cautions should be noted. Lazarus (1971) notes that systematic desensitization will often be effective with persons who suffer from phobias. It is a procedure that does not make insight a prime treatment goal and, therefore, is geared to symptom reduction and behavioral change. Systematic desensitization is a very economical procedure in terms of time and effort. It has been shown to be effective with many behavioral problems. Lazarus (1971) warns that systematic desensitization should not be indiscriminately used, however great the temptation to do so. Considerations should be given to whether the client is (a) able to relax, (b) able to respond with anxiety to hierarchical images, (c) not averse to the procedure, and (d) not getting any secondary gains from his or her phobia or anxiety. Problems in systematic desensitization can be attributed to three factors, according to Wolpe (1969): (1) difficulties in relaxation, (2) irrelevant or misleading hierarchies, and (3) inadequacy of imagery.

COVERT CONDITIONING

The topic of covert conditioning emphasizes Joseph Cautela's covert sensitization, and covert positive and negative reinforcement. These procedures are based on the principles of learning and reinforcement theory. The term *covert* refers to psychological processes occurring within the individual, such as thinking, imagining, feeling, and perceiving. Covert conditioning stresses the role of imagination (similar to systematic desensitization) in the control of behavior.

Several important assumptions underlie the use of covert behavioral self-control. First, the covert processes (thinking, feeling, imagining) are subject to the laws of reinforcement. Second, an individual must be able to tell the difference between the occurrence or nonoccurrence of a covert event. Third, an individual can control the presentation of reinforcers or simply reinforce himself or herself. Cautela (1970a), similar to Wolpe (1969), assumes that aversive and reinforcing events (stimuli) can modify behavior whether they are presented in the imagination or externally applied.

Basic steps in covert conditioning

1. Perform a behavioral analysis

This step is essential. The procedure is almost identical to the one described in the section on systematic desensitization. A determination of significant situations (real or imagined stimuli) that evoke, reinforce, and maintain maladaptive behavior is made. Instruments frequently used in covert conditioning to assess a person's functioning are the Life History Questionnaire (Wolpe & Lazarus, 1966), the Fear Schedule and the Reinforcement Survey Schedule (Cautela & Kastenbaum, 1967). The Reinforcement Survey Schedule yields information about the client's history, personal relationships, and reinforcing events.

2. Identify aversive stimuli and positive and negative reinforcers that are most significant to the client

Events or stimuli that increase or decrease the frequency of a response are called "reinforcers." A positive reinforcer is an event that follows a behavior that increases the probability that the same behavior will occur again under similar circumstances in the future. A negative reinforcer is a stimulus or event that follows a behavior that weakens the response or decreases the probability that the same event will occur under similar circumstances in the future. Positive reinforcers are generally events that are most preferred by the client (e.g., money, candy). Negative reinforcers are most often events that reduce tension (e.g., relief in escaping from an anxiety situation). It should be noted that punishment is often incorrectly confused with negative reinforcement. Punishment involves introducing a negative event (like a shock, a slap, or a harsh word) with the goal of eliminating the undesired behavior. Punishment is rarely, however, used in counseling. A counselor may need to have many reinforcers available so the possibility of a client becoming overly satiated with one is minimized.

3. The purposes, procedures, and principles of covert conditioning should be clearly explained

Because the rationale is not complicated, the counselor can easily explain to the client the basic theory underlying reinforcement techniques. Essentially, the counselor should relate that (1) inappropriate behavior is often a learned habit that has been reinforced over a long time, and (2) the object of covert procedures is to change behavior—to decrease the frequency, intensity, and duration of some maladaptive behavior by focusing attention on old behaviors and what reinforces them.

The counselor may also summarize for the client some of the basic principles of learning and reinforcement in covert self-control. Some examples are:

a. The strength of a behavior or response is a function of the number of times covert sensitization and reinforcement (positive and negative) are used.

b. Learning is more efficient when there is some spacing between practice trials.

c. Learning is more efficient when practice trials are distributed throughout the session.

d. Reinforcement is more effective when it immediately follows a desired response.

e. Reinforcements are more effective when they are realistic and based on client preferences.

f. Reinforcements initially should be applied after every desirable response and then gradually reduced to about an average of one reinforcer applied per five desirable responses (continuous reinforcement to variable reinforcement) (Cautela, 1970b).

4. Train the client in deep relaxation
5. Determine the client's ability to use imagery effectively
6. Initiate covert procedures
7. Emphasize self-observation and analysis
8. Repeat the procedure as often as necessary

Steps 4, 5, 7, and 8 are similar to those presented in the section on systematic desensitization.

COVERT SENSITIZATION

Covert sensitization (Cautela, 1967) is a method for treating maladaptive behavior. "Sensitization" refers to avoiding an undesirable response. Theoretically, covert sensitization is based on an aversive conditioning model. That is, one is to imagine an aversive stimulus (something unpleasant, such as getting nauseous) at the same moment one is about to engage in an undesirable behavior (e.g., overeating or overdrinking). With repeated exposures to controlled covert scenes, the response to the aversive stimulus should become associated with the undesirable response, thereby leading to a reduction of the maladaptive behavior. Covert sensitization is used widely in the treatment of smoking, sexual disorders, alcoholism, weight control, study habits, and test anxiety (Cautela, 1970; Kendrick & McCullough, 1972).

Basic procedure

Five important dimensions underlie covert sensitization (Cautela, 1967). First, the noxious or unpleasant stimuli must occur at about the same time as the maladaptive response. Second, the undesirable response must be positively reinforcing (e.g., love of eating or drinking). Third, the unpleasant stimulus, initially, should be presented continuously with later presentations occurring on a variable or partial schedule of reinforcement. Fourth, it is important that aversive events be noxious. Fifth, to escape the noxious stimuli, one will not be able to engage in the undesirable behavior (e.g., not overeating or over-drinking).

Following the behavioral analysis, and after the client has achieved a relaxed state, the counselor instructs the client to visualize a scene depicting the enactment of a particular maladaptive behavior (e.g., overeating). The client is then asked to visualize the experiencing of some unpleasant effect (e.g., becoming ill). It must be remembered that the idea is to associate the feeling of becoming ill with overeating. The client is instructed not merely to imagine what is happening but to participate emotionally and concentrate on all aspects of the scenes. Following is an example of covert sensitization based on a variation of Cautela (1970c):

> It is a Sunday night. You are alone. You are watching a baseball game on television and beginning to feel stirrings of anxiety. You feel a strong impulse to have something to eat. You begin thinking about eating a pizza. You try to suppress it, but you can't resist and get up and walk to the kitchen, open the refrigerator, and get out all the ingredients for a submarine sandwich. You make the sandwich, open a beer, and begin to eat the sandwich. All at once you begin to feel sick to your stomach. You feel nauseous and you begin to think that you're going to vomit all over the sandwich and the beer, the kitchen, and your clothes. You become so ill that you can't stand the sight of the food and you have to leave the kitchen. Thinking about eating that sandwich or anything else is sickening. As soon as you leave the kitchen you start to feel better and you start to feel relaxed.

With repeated trials and practice, an association between undesirable behavior and aversive stimuli will occur in many instances. Covert sensitization follows an escape conditioning paradigm (negative reinforcement) and is also a self-reinforcing technique. The reinforcer is the reduction of tension following the escape from the noxious situation.

Research support

Mahoney (1974) summarized the research on covert sensitization and suggested that research support for Cautela's covert sensitization is limited. However, despite some inadequacies in the research methods use to study covert sensitization, it does appear to have some merit and empirical support. For example, Ashen and Donner (1968) found covert sensitization to be an effective treatment for alcoholics. After a six-month follow-up, 15 alcoholics treated with covert sensitization abstained from drinking while none of the 8 controls was abstinent. Only nine sessions of covert sensitization of 45 minutes each were conducted. In another study, Juanda and Rimm (1972) found that obese clients using covert sensitization lost significantly more weight than a relaxation group or a control group. Stuart (1967) reported similar results in treating overeating.

Barlow, Leitenberg, and Agras (1969) found covert sensitization to be successful in decreasing deviant behavior in treating a homosexual client. Krop, Calhoun, and Verrier (1972) report using covert sensitization successfully to improve self concept.

Advantages and cautions

Covert sensitization has many advantages. Among them are: (1) intricate apparatus and drugs are not required; (2) it has a potential as a self-directed method; and (3) it is applicable to a wide range of behavioral problems (e.g., sexual deviance, homosexuality, obsessive compulsive disorders, and obesity) (Mikulas, 1973).

Some cautions, however, should be mentioned. Because of the aversiveness of the procedure, a careful explanation of the procedure should be given to the client. If the client shows marked anxiety reactions to the technique, it should be discontinued. Cautela (1970) warns that high levels of anxiety should be reduced prior to the initiation of covert sensitization via relaxation and systematic desensitization. Moreover, a positive working relationship between the client and counselor is necessary. Since covert sensitization has some unpleasant features, the client may try to avoid some sessions. The counselor must, therefore, balance the use of planned behavioral techniques with relationship techniques that positively reinforce or encourage the client for participating in the counseling process. It is generally a good idea for the client to be relaxed at the end of each session.

COVERT POSITIVE AND NEGATIVE REINFORCEMENT

Covert reinforcement is another of the covert conditioning techniques that includes self-reinforcement and imagery. Cautela developed two reinforcement procedures (Cautela, 1970b): covert positive and negative reinforcement.

In covert positive reinforcement, the individual imagines enacting a desirable behavior. After having successfully completed the act, the individual shifts to an image that is positively reinforcing.

Covert negative reinforcement requires the individual to imagine an undesirable situation that terminates when a desirable response occurs. Covert negative reinforcement is based on an escape conditioning paradigm.

Covert positive reinforcement: An example

Positive covert reinforcement as described by Cautela (1970b) involves taking a situation in which there is some anxiety and teaching the individual self reinforcement techniques to overcome the anxiety. This would involve teaching a client to visualize in a positive way dealing with an anxiety producing stimulus. To use positive covert reinforcement in connection with a test anxiety situation, one would first have the client imagine waking up the morning of the test and feeling good about the test, being prepared to take the test, walking to the building where the exam is being given, feeling comfortable and relaxed, going to the classroom, sitting at the desk, and beginning to take the exam feeling confident and feeling comfortable. This procedure allows the client to visualize him or herself in the examination situation and to counter it with the positive feelings of ease, comfort, confidence, and relaxation which presumably with practice should enable the client to gradually overcome the anticipatory anxiety. It is even possible to introduce items in the sequence which indicate difficulty with the exam and positive confident reactions by teaching the client to discriminate between not knowing one or two items on the test and still not failing it.

Research support

Covert positive reinforcement has been shown to be effective in modifying college students' attitudes toward mental retardates (Cautela, 1970b); decreasing test anxiety (Wisocki, 1973); reducing weight (Manno & Marston, 1972) and rat phobia (Flannery, 1972). Cautela (1970b) reports several successful case studies that show results consistent with the above experiments.

Covert negative reinforcement: An example

Covert negative reinforcement uses the same basic principles but in a somewhat different situation. For example, an individual who is uncomfortable in the presence of large groups but who is also even more uncomfortable in some other social situation might be shown that the only way to avoid the more serious negative social situation is to engage in behavior leading to the less seriously aversive condition. The example Cautela uses involves teaching a client who has fear of both open spaces and snakes that the only way to escape from a snake in a cave is to rush out into a large open field. While that example is extreme and not one that is likely to occur in daily life, it does illustrate the principle of moving from a more to a less aversive situation and using that movement as a technique to reduce anxiety.

Here, the client is trained to find the originally fearsome situation to be the only one offering relief from a new, even more fearsome situation. The idea is that gradually the stimulus that originally caused fear will actually acquire positive value because it has offered relief from another set of bad events.

The use of aversive imagery has been successfully used to reduce tantrum behavior, alcoholism, homosexuality, and various fears and phobias (Cautela, 1970d). Reynolds (1968) reports that the effectiveness of aversive imagery or covert negative reinforcement depends on the intensity of the noxious stimuli. Dinsmoor (1971), however, warns that extremely aversive stimuli can disrupt or immobilize the person, preventing escape from the situation. He suggests that a more desirable effect is achieved when escape response occurs immediately after the termination of the aversive stimulus.

Research support

Covert negative reinforcement research has been successful as a conditioning technique in changing attitudes of college students toward the elderly (Cautela & Wisocki, 1969). Evidence of success from numerous other cases have been reported by Cautela (1970) and Flannery (1972).

Advantages and cautions

Covert negative and positive reinforcement offer the same advantages of covert sensitization in terms of self-control and applicability to a wide range of behavioral problems. As in the case of covert sensitization and systematic desensitization, covert positive and negative reinforcement should not be used if a client shows excessive anxiety in reaction to the procedures. It is very important that the counselor starts with relaxation and ends the procedure with the client being comfortably relaxed. The importance of a threat-free counseling climate should not be overlooked.

ASSERTIVE TRAINING

Assertive training is a technique permitting a person to learn to express effective and appropriate behavior previously inhibited by anxiety or faulty learning. Wolpe (1969) theorized that the expression of reasonable assertive responses may inhibit or reduce anxiety because assertive responses are often incompatible with anxiety responses (the principle of reciprocal inhibition).

Assertive behavior consists usually of some degree of aggression but also includes the expression of friendly, affectionate, and other nonanxiety-provoking feelings and behaviors. Assertive behavior differs from aggressive behavior in that assertion is focused, controlled, and minimizes emotion while aggression is usually emotion laden, often used when the person is out of control, and excessive. An example of assertion would be if an individual was waiting in line to talk to a store clerk and notices that a person who came in later gets waited on first. The assertive individual would calmly say, "Excuse me, but I am next." In that same situation, the aggressive individual would be very angry and say, "Can't I get some service here? I was waiting long before him!"

Wolpe (1969) regards assertive training as a special case of reciprocal inhibition. As you may recall, the reciprocal inhibition principle suggests certain stimuli can evoke an anxiety response, but that an anxiety response is not inevitable. Those very same cues may elicit behavior that is incompatible with anxiety (e.g., relaxation, sexual and assertive responses). If incompatible responses to anxiety are made to occur in situations that have previously elicited the anxiety responses, the anxiety response can become weakened and ultimately be replaced with the incompatible response.

Assertive training employs a wide range of techniques. Among these are reeducation, behavioral rehearsal, social modeling, and positive reinforcement. Cognitive restructuring of irrational ideas may also be used (Lazarus, 1971; Tosi, 1974; Jakubowski-Spector, 1973).

Assertive training is often used to deal with a wide range of behavioral problems, such as social and sexual inhibitions, impotence, and depression. Lazarus (1971) suggests that people who may benefit from assertive training are those who find it difficult to say "no," to express positive and negative feelings, to ask favors, to initiate, and to engage and terminate discussions.

Basic procedures

The basic procedures in assertive training resemble other behavioral approaches to counseling. These procedures emphasize specific goals and careful observation of behavior and situational conditions under which the behavior occurs. Assertive training consists of these steps: (*a*) ascertain the specific conditions under which a lack of assertiveness occurs; (*b*) identify specific target behaviors and determine goals; (*c*) determine the appropriateness and inappropriateness of the existing behavior; (d) assist the client in discriminating between appropriate and inappropriate behavior; (e) explore irrational ideas, attitudes, and misconceptions; (f) demonstrate appropriate and inappropriate assertive responses (using live models, symbolic models); (g) engage in behavioral rehearsal; (h) continue practice of assertive behavior; (i) give graded homework assignments that successively approximate the desired behavior; and (j) reinforce appropriate behavior (Tosi, 1974; Wolpe, 1969; Lazarus, 1971; Eisler, Miller, & Herson, 1973).

Assertive training can help a client develop skills involving appropriate verbal behavior, eye contact, gestures, facial expressions, voice tones, and timing of expressive behavior (Smith, 1975). The counselor can also help the client to challenge and confront self-defeating ideas often associated with a lack of assertiveness. Unassertive people often believe that if they are assertive they will hurt others, be rejected by them, look silly, and suffer needless emotional upset as a result (Tosi, 1974). Assertiveness training aims to correct faulty behavior by changing inappropriate emotional responses and by eliminating irrational thinking (Lazarus, 1971).

Before the actual training begins, the counselor, with the cooperation of the client, should establish hierarchies of difficult situations within which the client has been unassertive. Starting with the least difficult situation, the counselor can encourage the client to enact assertive behavior having a high probability for success. This procedure itself is likely to have self-reinforcing consequences. Wolpe (1969) warns that an assertive act should not be initiated if it is likely to be too emotionally upsetting to the client.

Research support

Research reports and case studies demonstrating the effectiveness of assertive training and behavioral rehearsal procedures are numerous. Using behavioral rehearsal and social modeling, Rathus (1972) found that nonassertive college women were less concerned with social anxiety and increased assertiveness when compared to a control group. In a study entitled "Behavioral rehearsal with modeling and coaching in assertion training," McFall and Lillesand (1971) found that subjects participating in all three training methods (behavior rehearsal, social modeling, and coaching in assertion training) were able to refuse unreasonable demands more than control subjects.

Many studies have been reported regarding the efficacy of counseling with socially anxious and unassertive clients (e.g., Hedquist & Weinhold, 1970; Tosi, Upshaw, Lande, & Waldron, 1971; thus, for example, behavioral rehearsal and discussion groups have been used to modify interpersonal skill deficits related to dating problems. In the behavioral rehearsal treatment, male clients learned and practiced dating behavior skills with a female confederate in a role playing situation. The subjects were given feedback on their performance during each of five treatment sessions. The treatment groups were found to be more effective than the control group. While the discussion group did about as well as the behavioral rehearsal group, the results slightly favored the latter.

The efficacy of assertive training involving social modeling in counseling has been demonstrated with diverse client groups. Some examples of these are assertive training in homosexuality (Edwards, 1972); assertiveness training with psychiatric patients (Gutride, Goldstein, & Hunter, 1973); and sexual assertiveness in women (Jakubowski-Spector, 1971. Galassi, Kaska, and Galassi (1975) report that in a one year follow-up of college students who had participated in group assertive training, the initial positive effects were still present. Criterion measures were subjective estimates of anxiety, actual assertive behavior observed in role playing situations, eye contact, and scores on a self-expression scale.

MICRO-COUNSELING AND ASSERTIVE TRAINING

Assertiveness in interpersonal situations has been found to be an antagonistic response to anxiety associated with social inhibition. The general assertive training format consists of several components which include instruction, modeling, role or behavioral rehearsal, practice, feedback from the trainer, and social or verbal reinforcement. These skills can be taught using methods based on micro-counseling. Micro-counseling simply refers to a carefully structured training method that uses miniature counseling-like situations to teach people how to perform certain behaviors.

Micro-training and counseling procedures developed by Ivey (1971), and Ivey and Authier (1978) make use of videotape recordings wherein the client assumes specific behaviors. Prior to videotaping, the client is given a rationale and some instructions concerning the skill to be developed. In most instances, the behavior is enacted by a model. The client then role plays the behavior (e.g., assertiveness). The role playing session is videotaped and replayed. During the videotape replay of the role playing, the counselor or trainer comments and reinforces the client for approximating the desired behavior. The procedure is repeated until the client gives evidence of acquiring the skill.

Research support

One specific study on assertive training and micro-teaching was conducted by Gormally, Hill, Otis, and Rainey (1975). They found that a micro-teaching approach significantly increased assertive behavior on the part of male and female clients. Changes in assertion as determined by judges' ratings, also included more effective eye contact, congruent body movement, voice intensity, voice modulation, delivery style, effectiveness, and posture.

SOCIAL MODELING

Behavior may be learned through direct experiences, simulated experience, or vicariously—that is imitating and modeling the behavior of others. Through imitating the behavior of parents, teachers, and others, people acquire many behaviors. This learning occurs especially when the learner receives positive and negative feedback when exhibiting modeled behaviors. Sex role development, for instance, occurs when a young child is reinforced by both parents for imitating the behavior of the same sex parent. Peer models, especially, are very potent in affecting behaviors in both adolescents and adults.

When used in counseling, modeling can expose a client to many different problem situations in which the model displays appropriate or inappropriate behaviors, or both. Modeling is a particularly useful technique when a client does not know, through inexperience, how to act properly in a given situation. By imitating a model's behavior, a client can observe effective or ineffective behavior in the situation, as well as observe the consequences of the behaviors. Modeling procedures can augment the insight and understanding a client may have gained as a result of participation in a counseling relationship.

Live models

The counselor may act as a live model or use one of the client's peers as a model. First, the counselor or peer model demonstrates the behavior to be performed. Second, the client practices the desired behavior to be performed. Third, the counselor positively reinforces the client for each successive behavior which more closely approximates the desired behavioral goal. Live models are particularly effective when used with guided participation and when the client receives immediate feedback about his or her behavior.

Behavior rehearsal or practice used with modeling allows the client to explore more desirable behavior in a nonthreatening, accepting relationship. If the client fails in some initial attempts to modify a behavior, the counselor can demonstrate the behavior for the client to observe.

Symbolic models

Symbolic models include books, films, and videotape and audiotape recordings. The use of symbolic models gives the counselor a certain amount of control of the time and content of the modeling presentation. Symbolic models have the advantages of convenience and reusability over live models.

Covert modeling

Covert modeling pertains to the use of one's imagination. Covert modeling is a significant feature or component of covert self-control procedures, such as covert positive and negative reinforcement and covert sensitization. Covert modeling can be applied to a wide variety of behavioral problems. These include behaviors dealing with problems of self-control (e.g., delaying impulsive actions), peer pressures to conform, interpersonal behavior, and managing the consequences of behavior.

Research support

Studies have been done showing the effectiveness of the use of live and symbolic modeling in assertive training (Rathus, 1972); phobias (Bandura, 1969); and classroom behavior (Krumboltz & Thoresen, 1969).

Kazdin (1974), in studies on covert modeling, found that the clients who imagined models similar to themselves in age and sex were the most successful using covert modeling. The success of covert modeling further depends on the development of the client's skills in using imagination. Additionally, Bandura (1969) found that certain characteristics of models help learning. The most effective models are more often prestigious, competent, knowledgeable, attractive, and powerful. The greater degree the client identifies with the model, the more potent the model. Of further importance are the client's needs to see the benefit of performing the desired behavior that is displayed by the model. Meichenbaums's (1971) research makes a very interesting and important distinction between *coping models* and *mastery models*. A coping model experiences realistic difficulties in some problem situations, but ultimately gains control of the situation. A mastery model exhibits control over the modeling situation with no difficulty. Meichenbaum suggests that coping models are more effective because they are more realistic.

COGNITIVE RESTRUCTURING

Cognitive restructuring, briefly described earlier, is based on the idea that emotional reactions result mainly from the evaluative thoughts, attitudes, and beliefs a person ascribes to a situation. In other words, by the way they think about things, people create their own emotional, physical, and behavioral responses. Therefore, in order to change behavior, those attitudes that give rise to, support, or reinforce behavior need to change (Ellis, 1971; Tosi, 1974; Maultsby, 1971; Lazarus, 1971). Ellis has proposed the "ABC" method described earlier to teach people how to minimize negative emotions. It will be recalled that it works something like this: Point A represents a situation or an event in the person's life that has become associated with some emotional or behavioral response at point C. At point B the person holds a belief about the situation. This belief is usually based on experiences or on information learned through a prior interaction with the environment. For example, someone rejected and thinking irrationally at B might feel anxious, depressed, and inadequate at C. That same person, also rejected but thinking rationally at point B would feel disappointment, but probably would not feel devastated or inadequate. Examples of irrational thinking at point B might include such self statements as "I can't stand it when people reject me," "It is a catastrophe if I am rejected," or "If I am rejected, it proves I am worthless." Examples of more rational thinking at point B might be "While rejection is unpleasant, it is not a total catastrophe," "I can stand rejection," or "Rejection does not make me a worthless person."

Cognitive restructuring is a method to help people reconstruct situations so that their thinking under pressure becomes more rational than before. A list of ten irrational beliefs is found in chapter 4.

Determining rationality and irrationality
in cognitive restructuring

In cognitive restructuring the counselor helps the client identify irrational or self-defeating beliefs, shows the client how to dispute these, and teaches the client how to replace them with more rational self enhancing beliefs. A question which appropriately arises here is how one identifies a self-defeating or irrational belief. Maultsby (1971) suggests that one can determine how rational a belief is by using five criteria for rational thinking and behaving. First, thoughts and beliefs need to consider objective reality—the facts. If a person took a video-tape picture of the situation, what would actually be seen? Second, thoughts, beliefs, and behaviors need to be life preserving. Third, thoughts, beliefs, and behaviors are directed toward the achievement of personal goals in the most efficient manner possible. Fourth, thoughts, beliefs, and behaviors need to minimize negative emotional responses. Finally, thoughts, beliefs, and behaviors are aimed at helping a person to minimize conflict with significant others.

According to Maultsby, if a person's thoughts, beliefs, and behaviors follow three of these five criteria, 60 to 80 percent of the time the person would rarely have significant emotional conflict. Counselors who use these criteria can demonstrate to their clients a method of evaluating thoughts and behavior. In instances when client thoughts do not fit the criteria, the counselor uses cognitive restructuring to show the client how to replace irrational thoughts, beliefs, and behaviors with more rational, self-enhancing thoughts, beliefs, and behaviors (Maultsby, 1971).

Once the person has outlined more rational ways of thinking and behaving, mental imagery may be used to practice the new rational modes (Ellis, 1973; Maultsby, 1971). Imagery refers to the rehearsing of new rational beliefs in the imagination (recall the example of rational-emotive imagery in chapter 3 on the counseling relationship). More-over, Maultsby suggests that the ABCs of rational thinking can be writ-ten out on paper. He refers to this as systematic written homework. A client can write out As, Bs, and Cs in between counseling sessions, thus reinforcing cognitive restructuring activity.

After a counselor determines what a client may be telling herself or himself (rational or irrational thinking), he or she may want to see whether such ideas fall into Beck's classification of "cognitive distor-tions." Recall that Beck classified cognitive distortions as selective ab-straction, arbitrary inference, over-generalization, magnification and minimization, and inexact labeling. The counselor will no doubt find that behavioral assessment procedures, Maultsby's criteria for rational thinking, and Beck's classification of cognitive distortions should help facilitate the cognitive restructuring of the client's beliefs about self, the environment, the past, and the future.

Research support

Many studies have investigated the relationship between emotion and thinking (e.g., Bergin, 1970; Deci, 1975; Luce & Pepper, 1971;

Rollins, 1975; Norman, 1975). Many theorists and researchers have found that people do talk to themselves and that this "self talk" significantly affects behavioral and emotional states (Thoresen & Mahoney, 1974; Beier, 1966; Kelly, 1955; Meichenbaum, 1971; Payne, 1971). Research on the effectiveness of cognitive restructuring has already been cited in chapter 2, "Theories of Counseling."

COUNSELING FOR SELF-CONTROL

The idea of teaching people how to manage their own behaviors is appealing to both counselors and clients. All the counseling procedures already described in this chapter have implications for self-directed behavioral change or self-management. Recently, a body of theory and research focusing directly on the topic of self-control has emerged out of the work of Bandura's (1969) social learning theory. Mahoney and Thoresen (1974) in the social learning tradition have systematically described behavioral self-control in their writings. Other authors studying behavioral self-control include Ellis, Meichenbaum, and Lazarus. We have already seen many examples of counseling for self-control throughout this chapter and in others. Because of the profound influence this topic has had on counseling practice, we felt it necessary to present it as a separate section.

Dimensions of self-control

Thoresen and Mahoney (1974) define behavioral self-control as a set of procedures designed to direct and manage internal and external actions. In order to master these procedures, the person first must be aware of the variables that control behavior. Awareness of the controlling variables is achieved through the careful self-monitoring of behavior. As we said earlier, people who record their behavior on frequency charts or in diaries can increase the accuracy of self-observation. Self-recorded behavioral data gives significant information about the *rate* of behavior, the *cues* that precede behavior, and the *consequences* of behavior.

After self-monitoring and observation, the individual may implement self-control strategies, such as *environmental planning*. Environmental planning involves modifying the circumstances that precede or give rise to a behavior. Through environmental planning, a person learns about the environment and how to modify it. Some examples of environmental planning are avoiding cigarette machines, buying low-calorie snacks, and carrying small amounts of money to control smoking, overeating, and spending money.

A third self-control strategy is *behavioral programming*. Thoresen and Mahoney (1974) define behavioral programming as altering the consequences of a behavior rather than the events that precede it. The eliciting cues of a behavior are events that usually give rise to the behavior. Thoresen and Mahoney cite the use of self-praise, self-criticism, and pleasant or unpleasant mental images as examples of behavioral programming. These can serve as self-administered internal consequences for behavior. The person can also use external consequences, which may include private contracts (if I do this, I will get that) and special privileges (going to a movie after the performance of some desirable behavior). These can be very effective in reinforcing behavior. (A person trying to lose weight shouldn't use a snack as a reward, however.)

Research support

Substantial research support is accumulating regarding the effective use of self-control procedures in counseling. Thoresen and Mahoney (1974) provide an excellent review of studies on this topic. Good examples of studies demonstrative of procedures described as self-control à la Thoresen and Mahoney are those described in the section on study habit modification. Richards's (1975) investigation (described below) examining self-monitoring and the stimulus control technique, is most illustrative of the approach. Too, the Jackson and Van Zoost (1972) study (described below) shows that self-administered reward is a significant factor in controlling study behavior. Also, the Tosi, Briggs, and Morely (1971) investigation on the use of the "Premack principle" of self-administered reinforcement exemplifies behavioral self-control on academic performance.

Counseling for study habit modification through self-control

Counselors who function in college and university settings work extensively with groups of students who suffer from serious academic deficiencies. Programs on college campuses that are designed to offer remedial assistance to high risk students have become an integral part of student personnel services.

Colleges and universities have become more accessible to students with marginal educational skills during the past 20 years. Many of these students generally enter college with American College Test scores well below the 25th percentile based on national norms. These students experience anxiety over their abilities to do college work. Often they are poorly motivated to study. High risk students have been and remain prime clientele for the counselor. The counselor will need to be acquainted with many educational and psychological procedures designed to assist such students to acquire academic, interpersonal, and social skills.

Study skills can be modified and improved through the use of self-reinforcement procedures and study skills training. One such method of self-reinforcement is based on the *Premack principle* of reinforcement (Premack, 1965). This principle suggests that behaviors which the client finds enjoyable and which the client is likely to display (e.g., socializing with friends) can be used to reinforce behaviors which the client finds less enjoyable and is less likely to engage in (e.g., studying). The Premack principle is particularly useful in counseling situations with students who are low in scholastic motivation. The Premack principle is illustrated by encouraging a student with problems of getting down to studying to set forth a specific (but not too ambitious at first) and concrete study objective, such as reading and outlining a reading assignment. After its completion the student might listen to a record before returning to the next task.

Counselors can help the academically disadvantaged student improve study skills through combinations of self-management and self-reinforcement techniques. Systematic desensitization can also be effective in helping to reduce anxiety toward studying and examination taking. The research studies cited in the next section are good examples of how self-control procedures can be combined with study skill training and used effectively by counselors.

Research support

In a study combining the use of self-reinforcement procedures based on the Premack principle of reinforcement (Premack, 1965) and the Robinson SQ3R study method (Robinson, 1970), Tosi, Briggs, and Morley (1970) were able to assist high risk college students to achieve higher grade point averages than a comparable control group. Students in this study were found to benefit from the counseling treatment when they were able to select their own reinforcement for study.

The Robinson SQ3R study method includes reading comprehension and study skills advice (Jones, 1969; Robinson, 1970). These procedures alone have proven effective in the modification of study habits (Jackson & Van Zoost, 1972).

College student study skills are modifiable by a combination of study skill training and self-control behavioral modification techniques. In a well-designed study, Richards (1975) compared Behavioral Self Monitoring, Stimulus Control, and Study Skills groups relative to modifying studying behavior. *Self Monitoring* required the person to record personal behavior on frequency charts. The client observed and monitored self-behavior change and used these recorded observations for guiding future behavior. The *Stimulus Control* allowed the client to manipulate the frequency of a response; that is, to increase the frequency of a response in some situations and decrease it in other situations. The *Study Skills* technique used the Robinson SQ3R Reading Method. The findings of Richards's study revealed that college students' study behavior can be significantly modified by a combination of study skill training and self-monitoring. The stimulus control techniques did not show the expected positive results. Richards's findings were consistent with studies reported by Thoresen and Mahoney (1974), Kazdin (1974), and Goldfried and Merbaum (1973).

In changing study behavior, the presence of either social reinforcers (from others) and/or self-reinforcers (from self) seem to be associated with desirable outcomes. Jackson and Van Zoost (1972) examined the use of self-administered reinforcement and external reinforcers following the successful performance of academic exercises prepared by the experimenters and covering a number of study skill areas. Academic skill training consisted of (*a*) organization and planning of study, (*b*) motivation and note taking, (*c*) reading techniques, (*d*) essay writing, and (*e*) exam preparation and writing. Reinforcers consisted of money. Students were to deposit $10 by meeting certain attendance and program requirements. Members of the self-reinforcement group paid themselves, contingent upon feedback from the counselors and their own evaluation of the acceptability of questions they had to answer. The counselors determined the maximum amount of money that could be earned for a given session (six sessions total).

Members of the external reinforcement group were paid 50 cents for attending the workshop and $1 for completing the various assigned learning exercises. The group leader evaluated each participant's answers to the exercises and paid them according to some prearranged amount of money. A no-reinforcement group and a no-treatment control group were also involved in the study. Significant gains in study habits, measured using the *Survey of Study Habits*, were observed for both reinforcement groups; the changes were maintained over a four-month period.

Harris and Trujillo (1975) found that study habits of low achieving junior high school students can be modified to increase their grade point average. Using behavioral self-management and reinforcement techniques and group discussions about academic matters, the students were able to achieve more self-mastery over studying. This was shown by higher academic performance for the experimental group, when compared with a control group. The group of students participating in the behavioral self-management group also reported more efficiency in studying than those participating in the other groups. Osterhouse (1972) compared the effectiveness of systematic desensitization, efficient study skills training, insight-oriented counseling, and a "placebo" treatment in reducing the test anxiety of college students. Systematic desensitization proved to be more effective than the control group and the insight-oriented counseling group in reducing examination anxiety. While systematic desensitization was not significantly more effective than study skills training based on Robinson's SQ3R method (1961), results were in favor of systematic desensitization.

SUMMARY

In this chapter on planned behavioral change, the prospective counselor was given an opportunity to discover and explore some of the technical aspects of counseling relationships. In almost every instance, the counseling procedures described are to be used to help persons plan and direct their own behavior. Most, if not all, of these procedures can be taught to a client and can be used by the client independent of the counselor. The techniques need to be thought of as behavioral self-management tools through which persons can continue to monitor, facilitate, and modify their behavior at some future time after the counseling relationship has terminated.

The systematic behavioral change methods described in this chapter are based on the principles of learning theory—in that they require the use of positive and negative rewards to extinguish undesired behavior and to reinforce new behavior. Reinforcement can be externally applied (social reinforcement) or applied to oneself (self-reinforcement). The counselor, therefore, should remember to assess the types of reward system that works best with the individual client if the effectiveness of these procedures is to be maximized.

If students of counseling have a fundamental grasp of systematic desensitization, covert reinforcement, assertive training, cognitive restructuring, social modeling, and self-control procedures, they will be better able to deal with many of the typical problems their clients pose. Certainly, with more study and training, counselors will develop additional skills in the variations of these procedures.

Counselors in actual practice most always combine many techniques to form an intervention package. The result is most often that the client can learn to minimize undesirable behavior and maximize desirable behavior through a variety of means.

Group Counseling

Up to this point we have been concerned largely with individual counseling, or one-to-one counseling. Before a counselor can hope to imagine to tackle the complexities of group counseling, individual counseling must be mastered. Many of the concepts and techniques found useful in individual-counseling relationships are of value in group-counseling situations. However, the group represents a very different kind of social phenomenon that has some properties uniquely its own. Counselors will invariably find themselves working with groups of clients in addition to working with people on a one-to-one basis. Groups, an economical use of professional time, have significant features that inherently may make group procedures the treatment of choice at times.

Counselors are involved with many types of group experiences. There are problem solving/task-oriented groups; encounter groups; therapy groups; career guidance groups; and assertive training groups—to name a few. And there are many different theoretical orientations to group counseling. Most counseling theories stressing one-to-one counseling have been extended to group counseling. In this section we attempt to present some of the essential characteristics of group counseling. Among the topics to be considered are (1) the social psychology of group counseling, (2) the counselor in the group counseling process, (3) growth factors in group counseling, (4) self-disclosure, (5) types of feedback, (6) group composition, (7) selection of members, (8) group size, (9) group cohesiveness, (10) group attendance, (11) structuring the group, (12) counselor behavior, (13) the counselor level of self-awareness, (14) stages of group development, (15) types of group counseling, (16) confidentiality, and (17) research in group counseling.

The social psychology of group counseling

The "group" can be a powerful modality where persons may pose significant aspects of their behavior. People can validate or invalidate many of their ideas, values, and beliefs through the feedback from others. Because of its powerful social reinforcing properties, a group can strongly influence individual behavior. Reinforcement in groups occurs not only through positive and negative social exchanges but vicariously through imitating or modeling the behavior of others.

One major assumption underlying group counseling is that when the forces of the group process are mobilized in positive ways, people may be influenced in positive ways. Through the group process, individuals can gain in self-awareness through self-exploration and reality testing while at the same time receiving valuable feedback about their behavior. The group can be used as a practice setting sometimes. However, the group process can also hurt clients if the members of the group lack acceptance, understanding, and respect for one another. The facilitative conditions so essential in one-to-one counseling are as essential in group counseling.

The counselor in the group counseling process

The counselor's role in group counseling revolves around four basic functions. The counselor may be a psychological educator, a facilitator of changes and personal growth, a monitor of the change or growth process, and a reinforcer of behavior change (Tosi, 1974). Depending on the nature and goals of the group, the counselor may elect to emphasize these functions to various degrees. For instance, a school counselor may serve as psychological educator and facilitator in a group-guidance class that emphasizes career development and personal adjustment. Over the course of several years, the counselor may want to monitor the effects of group guidance through a number of observational procedures, and whenever appropriate, reinforce or encourage healthy behavior and decision making. In a psychotherapy group, a counselor may spend more time helping the members explore areas of their personality that they may have previously avoided. In so doing, a counselor helps members reconstruct self-defeating attitudes and behaviors.

Growth factors in group counseling

Yalom (1975) believes that the main growth factors in most types of counseling consist of the imparting of information, the acquisition of hope, the development of socialization techniques, imitative behavior, interpersonal learning, group cohesiveness, and self-expression. Yalom's own approach to group counseling is eclectic and draws upon psychoanalytic, learning, and educational concepts. More simply, individuals participating in group counseling have the opportunity to develop psychologically in a social context. The group, theoretically, operates as its own social system that encourages personal development through interaction with others. A group most often develops its own set of norms or standards of behavior (structure) by imposing limits on destructive behavior while permitting the expression of a full range of positive and negative thoughts, feelings, and behavior.

Group cohesiveness

As the group unfolds, the members tend to develop an esprit de corps, or a sense of cohesiveness. Cohesiveness or group trust seems to allow for a lessening of barriers to open communication and interaction. When members of a group trust one another, members are more likely to feel free to disclose undesirable behavior, to take risks, and to give and receive feedback about their behavior. Behavioral feedback, as we shall see later, from group members permits the individuals to observe the consequences of their actions in a social environment.

Self-disclosure

For a group counseling/therapy session to operate effectively as a potential change agent, members need to share with others many of their personal concerns about themselves and others. The disclosing of personal feelings, however, does not come easily for most people. Fear about being rejected by others can inhibit people from expressing themselves honestly and sharing their innermost thoughts and feelings.

Jourard and Lasakow (1958) suggest that self-disclosure can occur on at least six dimensions: attitudes and opinions, tastes and interests, work, money, personality, and body. Jourard and Lasakow (1958) have found that a high disclosure behavior occurs in the areas of attitudes, tastes, and work, while low disclosure occurs in the areas of money, personality, and body. People tend to be less threatened by the subjects in the high disclosure areas. Harrison and Lubin (1965) found that females seem more willing to self-disclose than males. This finding was also supported by the work of Jourard and Lasakow (1958). Not surprisingly, people with low self-esteem seem to be less willing to disclose their feelings than high self-esteem people.

Counselors play an important role in determining the extent to which self-disclosure occurs in a group. Yalom (1975) observed that group members tend to be more willing to self-disclose if the counselor also engages in self-disclosure.

Because feedback about one's motives and behavior is often difficult to accept, self-disclosure can be very difficult for many. Therefore, the counselor and other group members need to be very supportive of any individual who is making an honest attempt at self-expression.

Behavioral feedback

We have already mentioned the importance of behavioral feedback in a group. In this section we will try to be a little more explicit about what is meant by feedback.

Behavioral feedback conveys information about the reaction of another person to one's behavior. Such feedback serves to guide behavior and to add to the motivation for behavior change through self-awareness and self-exploration.

The National Training Laboratory has outlined several categories of feedback in a publication entitled *Feedback and the Helping Relationship* (1967). An adaptation of these dimensions presented as polarities are: (1) descriptive versus evaluative; (2) specific versus nonspecific; (3) constructive versus destructive; (4) encouraging versus discouraging; (5) solicited versus imposed; (6) clear versus ambiguous; (7) well-timed versus poorly timed; and (8) accurate versus inaccurate. These dimensions of effective feedback probably serve as the basis for effective interpersonal communication in any counseling relationship—group or counseling relationship. Examples of some feedback dimension are given below.

Descriptive versus evaluative feedback.   When one person responds to something another person says or does in a group, such statements should not convey the message that the individual is good or bad. The group members' behavior can be *described* and the impact it appears to have on others may be specified. Counselors can serve as models for effective feedback. When persons give feedback they should acknowledge that their reactions are clearly based on their own observations and perceptions. Persons providing feedback need to take responsibility for it.

Descriptive   When George moves toward you, I notice that you have a tendency to move away from him.

Evaluative   When George moves toward you, you get defensive and anxious.

Specific versus nonspecific feedback. When feedback is specific it is concrete and to the point. Nonspecific feedback is vague and does not speak directly to an issue.

Specific   When I said that I became upset over your remark about me, I noticed you blushed.

Nonspecific   I don't know where you are coming from when you play with words.

Constructive versus destructive feedback. Constructive feedback will contain all dimensions of effective feedback. Feedback is constructive when it facilitates meaningful and desirable changes in another person's behavior. It is destructive when it is intended to hurt the other person.

Constructive   I feel deeply about the things you just said about me. It must be important for you to express angry feelings toward me.

Destructive   There is another example of your weakness. You must learn to control your anger. You don't care for anyone.

Solicited versus imposed feedback. To know whether feedback is solicited or imposed requires that the person giving feedback possess a certain amount of empathic understanding. That is, the ability to hear and respond to the emotional meaning of another person's words or gestures. Whether another person is or is not asking for information regarding a specific behavior is very hard to determine. Therefore, the counselor may need to engage in a certain amount of trial and error, with the possibility at times of being inaccurate. Imposed feedback may not be based on an accurate understanding of a person and as a result is often met with resistance. Solicited feedback, on the other hand, will more often than not be experienced and interpreted in a positive way.

Solicited   I get the impression that you want me to react to something you said a while ago.

Imposed   I feel compelled to tell you what I think of you. I don't care what you think.

Clear versus ambiguous feedback. The clear versus ambiguous feedback dimension would naturally overlap with specific/non-specific statements. The difference has to do with the clarity of meaning rather than the specificity of the content of words. Clear feedback is generally expressed in simple language that another person can understand. Ambiguous feedback is vague and may obscure the message that is to be communicated.

Clear   My impression of your shyness in this group is that it prevents you from participating in the group.

Ambiguous   My impression of you is that your reticence serves as a symptom of existential anxiety.

Timing and accuracy of feedback. Feedback needs to be well timed. A person receiving feedback is more likely to hear and accept it if it is given at a time when he or she is ready to deal with it. Second, well-timed feedback is easier for the person to see as having personal relevance. Third, well-timed feedback tends to have a stronger reinforcing effect, thereby facilitating self-exploration. As counselors develop professionally, and with much practice, they become proficient at timing their feedback.

Feedback also needs to be accurate to be effective. Accurate feedback almost always is based on observable behaviors so as to minimize many of the misconceptions the receiver may have about himself or herself and others. Inaccurate feedback may lead to confusion and misunderstanding on the part of the receiver.

Group composition

An important issue in group counseling concerns homogeneous versus heterogeneous group composition. That is, how similar or different should group members be from one another. Yalom (1975) suggests that a homogeneous group structure should facilitate: (1) a more rapid identification of problem areas, (2) a more rapid development of awareness of self and others, (3) a shortened duration of counseling, (4) better attendance of sessions, (5) decreased resistance and threat, and (6) the prevention of subgroups. A heterogeneous group structure tends to facilitate: (1) deeper self-awareness and self-exploration, (2) expanded reality testing, and (3) the easy assembly of groups.

Selection of group members

Selecting group members can be a difficult task. A selection process based on the behavioral functioning of members seems to be more preferable than one based on some diagnostic set of categories. How each person can potentially affect the behavior of another person in the group is an important issue in selecting members for group inclusion (Locke, 1961).

In most instances, counselors will work with relatively "normal" persons in group situations. Persons who show signs of being potentially disruptive to the group may need to be excluded. For example, persons suffering from severe personality disturbances (psychotic behavior) should not be included in groups that operate outside of the appropriate mental health facilities. Yalom (1975) suggests that poor candidates for intensive group counseling/therapy are people with: (a) brain damage, (b) strong suicidal tendencies, (c) psychotic disorders, (d) sociopathic behaviors, (e) paranoid tendencies, and (f) severe drug or alcohol addiction. People with these behavioral disorders are very often destructive in the group. Yalom does not imply that such persons cannot be helped with group counseling or therapy. For these people, Yalom suggests that a specialized group treatment involving a homogenous population, a strong leader, and an institutional setting may be indicated.

Many people who do poorly in group counseling/therapy and who terminate early seem to have problems related to emotional intimacy. These people may be extremely anxious about sharing their personal lives with others. They may also have a difficult time hearing about the personal problems of others. In general, poor candidates for either group or individual counseling are persons who are extremely insensitive to the needs of others, who show little respect for others, and who are self-centered and participate in the group with little display of emotion.

Group size

When the group members are compatible in personality, they are more likely to get along with one another and become a cohesive unit (Yalom et al., 1967). Cohesiveness seems to be a significant factor related to the effectiveness of the group-counseling process. Yalom (1975) asserts that on the basis of current reviews of theory and research, cohesiveness should serve as the main guideline for the composition of counseling and therapy groups. Yalom does not suggest that groups be composed of persons who exhibit the same personality patterns, but that groups be composed of individuals who are somewhat heterogeneous. That is, persons in groups who have had restricted social environments will benefit from interacting with individuals who are different culturally, educationally, and economically.

Group attendance

As in individual counseling, regular attendance by the client is most important. Frequent absenteeism from the group can be very disruptive to the process. Expectations regarding attendance should be made clear to each group member at the outset of the group sessions.

Structuring the initial session

The initial sessions of group counseling serve primarily to structure the process. Limits similar to those discussed in an earlier chapter are thoroughly explicated as well as some of the theoretical aspects of group counseling. The counselor, additionally, needs to emphasize the importance of honest communication, as well as respect for privacy and confidentiality about what is said in the sessions.

Group orientation and purpose

It is wise for the counselor to clearly communicate the purpose of the group and to provide sufficient information about the process to help the members orient themselves to it. Group orientation is a logical aspect of structuring.

The group members should have a clear-cut idea of what the counselor's intentions and theories are about the process. If the group is defined as an assertive training, and clearly not an intensive self-exploratory or therapy experience, the members should know that. We believe that counselors who lead their clients into believing that they are to participate in one kind of experience and then provide another kind of experience may be treading on unethical ground.

If the process of the group is to be heavily experiential, as opposed to didactic and problem solving in nature, each member should be aware of that orientation. When counselors employ techniques that provoke intense effect, they have an ethical responsibility to describe those procedures and what they are intended to accomplish. Perhaps as a physician explains some surgical techniques to a patient, the counselor likewise must explain counseling techniques to a client. These explanations should be given in simple and concrete terms that the client can easily understand.

Counselor behavior

As indicated earlier, the counselor enacts several roles in both individual and group counseling. The counselor educates, facilitates, monitors, and reinforces healthy behavior patterns in the client. In so doing, the counselor participates fully in the process. Bordin (1968) has observed that the counselor's involvement will vary on a continuum from objectivity to subjectivity. The counselor essentially must be able to make some sense out of what is going on in the group. The group members also need some intellectual perspective on the group process, and the counselor can help provide that to the members. Behaviorally, the counselor will reflect feelings, clarify meaning, interpret actions, positively reinforce healthy client behavior, confront and challenge ineffective behavior, and provide some perspective on the group process. These procedures most often will stimulate the same type of therapeutic behavior from the group members.

The counselor's level of self-awareness

Group counseling, like individual counseling, can be very emotionally demanding for the counselor. Since the growth process in group counseling is many times very slow, the counselor may react to the group process with personal frustration. The counselor must be aware of personal emotions and needs as a leader of the group in order to be able to effectively cope with her or his own frustrations.

Another part of the group dynamics that may be disturbing to the counselor involves the tendency of certain group members to project their hostility onto the counselor or to simply become very emotionally dependent upon the group counselor. Some of the group members may accuse the counselor of being insensitive, rejecting, demanding, or stupid. If the counselor is not in touch with the goals of the group, and with the developmental process of the group members, he or she may become very frustrated with these group actions in a manner that is not in the best interests of group progress. Many of the members' negative reactions to the group and the leader may be an attempt to control or manipulate the situation in which the group member is feeling insecure or threatened. Therefore, the counselor must recognize such manipulative behaviors and help the client deal with them effectively within the group setting.

Stages of group development

Group counseling, like individual counseling, seems to progress through various developmental stages. These stages are in evidence as people deal with personal concerns over a period of time. Whitaker and Lieberman (1964) identified several common characteristics of group development which occur at specific times. They feel that certain developmental themes occur in groups and therefore must be constantly dealt with during the life of the group. Whitaker and Lieberman (1964) discuss basic themes that occur at the beginning of counseling and periodically at other times during the counseling process. In the beginning of a group, members are uncertain of what to expect and consequently feel anxious about what may happen to them in the group. Because of these conditions, members need to develop a certain amount of basic trust. The initial uncertainty that members may have about the group fosters uneasiness, especially when they fear confrontation from the counselor and the other group members. Members' initial fears may result in some defensive behavior. Defensive behavior develops when people believe they will be criticized or ridiculed by group members. Guilt feelings, anxiety, and anger may result if one does not trust his or her own possible reactions towards other members.

Whitaker and Lieberman (1964) have observed many different kinds of fear reactions that group members have during the initial stages of the group, and even throughout the life of the group. Members often fear: (1) retaliation or disapproval from the therapist; (2) punishment from the counselor; (3) abandonment and an angry reaction from the therapist; (4) attack and criticism from other members; (5) looking foolish; (6) being thought of as crazy by the therapist and others; (7) their own destructive impulses; and (8) harming the counselor. Moreover, Whitaker and Lieberman (1964) warn that other negative reactions of a client can lead to a disruption of the group process. Some of these defensive reactions may involve: a wish to punish or reject certain group members; a desire to be a favorite of the counselor; competitive and hostile feelings toward other group members; hostility toward the counselor; sexual feelings toward another group member or the counselor; and an intense need for help by revealing personal problems.

The client may attempt to cope with some of the above fears and anxieties by denying these tendencies and projecting these feelings onto the group. Another means of coping with many of these feelings and tendencies may be for the client to comply totally with anything the therapist wants.

Later in the development of the group, Whitaker and Lieberman (1964) note that group members seem to become committed to the desire to achieve successful solutions to group conflicts and problems. When this commitment occurs, the group achieves a higher degree of cohesiveness and trust. The group is better able to move toward the attainment of group goals.

In general, we might conclude that groups move through different stages. First, there seems to be the development of basic trust and cohesiveness. Second, the group becomes more committed to achieving desirable therapeutic outcomes. Third, the group seems to then implement behavioral modifying strategies aimed at achieving therapeutic goals. Progress through these developmental stages is not easy. As we have noted, group members must work through many of their fears and defense mechanisms before the group reaches its therapeutic potential.

Types of group counseling

A counselor may work with many different kinds of groups. Some of the most prominent groups are problem solving or task-oriented groups, encounter or sensitivity groups, therapy groups, career guidance groups, and assertive training groups. We will try to highlight the characteristics of these groups in this section.

Problem solving/task-oriented group counseling. In some instances groups are formed to address solving problems that are common to their members. In so doing it may be necessary to learn problem solving techniques that could be applied to situations which are particularly important for the group members. For instance, problem solving techniques could be used to help the group members learn more effective communication and decision making skills. Group members may increase their awareness of their personal reactions to others and the impact they have on others. Therefore, the teaching-learning model, which is used in group problem solving, can be used in many different group problem situations. In such groups the role of the counselor is to help members identify problems, define them more clearly, determine alternative solutions, evaluate alternative solutions, implement the most tenable solutions, and evaluate outcomes. In effect, the counselor serves as a teacher of the decision making process as applied to personal, social, and career areas. The focus in such groups is on a specified task, such as determining an appropriate course of action, choosing a career or college, or reaching a behavioral goal.

Encounter groups. Shertzer and Stone (1976) describe the encounter group as an experience based group designed to facilitate personal development and awareness. Yalom (1975) sees the encounter group as one that helps facilitate self-discovery, untapped resources, or the uncovering of an individual's full potential. In the encounter group, persons can receive feedback from their peers and from the counselor or trainer that can help them better understand the impact of their behavior on others. Members may also deal with defense reactions that prevent them from communicating effectively in interpersonal relations. Encounter groups are not considered therapeutic because the emphasis is not on personality reconstruction or remediation but rather on effective communication. Encounter groups are for normal individuals rather than for individuals with diagnosed psychopathology.

The encounter group may be held in several successive sessions over a period of time or it can be held in one or two very long sessions called "marathons." Marathon groups are designed to increase understanding of one's defenses in order to be better able to interact in an open and honest manner within the group.

The following is an example of an encounter group in which an individual is having a problem disclosing significant information about himself:

Jim: I simply have too many problems and I do not feel that I want to discuss them at this time. I simply do not think that it is good to tell everything about yourself to the whole world.

Facilitator: It sounds to me that you do not trust the members of the group.

Jim: Yeah, that's it. I don't want to tell things that people will tell other people. Anyway, if I tell my real problems in this group the group will just think that I am strange and laugh at me.

Sue: It sounds like you have a conflict about sharing your encounters.

Jim: I never tell people about my problems. I never told anyone except one close friend. Then I watch what I say. People can use things you say against you. I guess I just do not trust anyone. I never have.

John: It sounds like you hold inside a lot of concerns that you want to discuss. I find that I would like you to discover whether you could trust this group.

Jim: If I talk about any problems here I will probably feel even worse that I told the group.

In this group, the facilitator and the group members are helping Jim look at his basic problem of not trusting others. By displaying understanding and reflecting the concerns of Jim, the group assists him to talk about a problem that could be interfering with his everyday growth and happiness.

Group therapy. Shertzer and Stone (1976) describe group therapy as group counseling in which a psychiatrist or clinical psychologist is involved, and whose goal is helping people deal with significant psychological conflicts in their lives that prevent them from living normally. The goals of the encounter group and the therapy group are somewhat similar, except that the therapy group tends to deal with individuals who have more severe personality problems (Yalom, 1975).

The following transcript depicts group therapy wherein a client whose dependency on his parents is now causing how to feel guilt. The presenting problem is related to a vocational problem solving situation but seems rooted in childlike dependence on the parents, which in turn may be causing the client problems in other areas of life.

Ed: I always wanted to become a mechanic, but my dad and mom want me to go to college. I just have no interest in books at all. I guess I don't know what I should do. I really cannot disappoint my parents.

Therapist: It sounds as if you are frustrated because you want to do one thing and your parents expect you to do another.

Ed: Yeah, that's it. And I feel as if I will be cast out by my parents if I disappoint them and do not go on to school. I will feel very guilty. My father is a teacher and he has always taught me about the importance of an education.

Sally: How does it make you feel when you are thinking that you really should go to school just to please your parents?

Ed: Well, I feel confused. But that's always been the case where my parents are concerned. I would like to just go to a vocational school and learn to be a good mechanic. But then if I don't, I will disappoint my parents. Then I feel very guilty—especially since I am an only child and they are counting on me.

Therapist: You seem to be very concerned about feeling guilty over not doing what your parents want. Have you ever talked with your parents about this?

Ed: No. What's the use? If I talk to them they get upset, and when they do I feel more guilty. They have been telling me for years that I must go to school. My mother in particular wants me to be a doctor because they are much more successful than teachers, which is what my father is.

John: It sort of sounds to me that you have decided that you do not want to go on to school, and that you want to try to be a mechanic for a while. It sounds as if your problem is not so much your career as it is your concern over your parents and your concern over your parents' approval.

Ed: Well, I guess so. I have always wanted to please my parents. I do not even want to talk about this with them since they may be upset.

Therapist: Perhaps the group could help you look at some of your guilt feelings.

In the above group session, the therapist is attempting to help Ed work out guilt feelings over his parents so that he can then make a reasonable career decision. In a therapy group, though, the focus of attention would be on Ed's deep-seated emotional problem causing him significant personal conflict.

Career counseling groups. A career or vocational guidance group is one that is usually conducted with a group of people interested in obtaining information about careers and career decisions. Also, career guidance groups can facilitate healthy attitudes and behaviors toward the world of work. Group counseling may include helping the students explore the world of work and deal with problems connected with preparing for a working career. In the earlier example, John was attempting to decide whether he should become a mechanic. This type of problem may also occur in a guidance-oriented group, although a person with guilt feelings as strong as John's may not be able to make a career choice without the help of a more therapeutically oriented group.

Assertive training groups. The assertiveness training group is designed to help persons become more aware of their behavior in social situations and to develop skills so they may be more socially effective. The emphasis in assertive training, as stated in a previous chapter, is to help people express their ideas verbally in situations where they were previously reticent. In assertive training the counselor may take an educator role with the group.

A typical activity for an assertive training session could be a role play of difficult situations, such as asking the boss for a raise or expressing one's dissatisfaction with a certain part of the operation of the organization in which one works. Assertive training could also deal with such areas as expression of one's feelings within the family or other important social situation, and learning to be comfortable with expressing dissatisfaction or approval in situations that may be uncertain. The group serves to socially reinforce effective behavior and to act as a reality testing arena. Assertiveness training, as described earlier, most often occurs in a group setting.

Confidentiality and ethical issues

There is a general acceptance that confidentiality is a prerequisite for the development of trust and cohesiveness in group counseling. Gazda (1978) lists several guidelines to follow to ensure confidentiality in groups. The list includes the following restrictions:

1. Group leaders should not reveal any unnecessary information they have concerning any group member outside of the group. Any discussion of the group should be done for professional purposes only with other professionals.
2. Data collected from the group members for research purposes should be gathered only after the group members have given their written permission.
3. Data that might identify members in publications or in instruction must be disguised to protect the anonymity of participants.
4. Group leaders should periodically remind the group members about the importance of confidentiality in counseling and therapy groups. That is, the personal material discussed in the group must remain in the group.

Whitaker and Lieberman (1964) suggest that group leaders allow participants to help make the rules governing confidentiality. Group participation in this matter helps members to be aware of the importance of confidentiality as a key factor in the group process.

Ethics are an important issue in groups. The counselor should have a thorough understanding of the American Psychological Association's standards for ethical conduct. Counselors must exercise good judgment and at all times operate in the best interest of their clients.

Research in group counseling

Many research studies have investigated different aspects of group counseling. Some of those will be reviewed in this section.

Diamond and Shapiro (1973) examined the effects of encounter group experiences on the participants' level of self-control. Graduate student volunteers were matched for age, sex, and training experience, and were then randomly assigned to one of three encounter groups. A similar group of nine students served as a no-treatment control group. All subjects were given the Rotter Internal-External Locus of Control Scale (Rotter, 1966) before the first group meeting. The results indicated a significant change toward greater internal control of behavior for the three encounter groups. The no-treatment control group did not show the same level of change.

Jew, Clanon, and Mattocks (1972) reported very favorable evidence of immediate and long-term effects of group counseling/therapy with difficult treatment populations. Further studies, which support positive behavioral change associated with group participation, have been reported by Cooper (1972), Dies and Sadowsky (1974), Diamond and Shapiro (1972), Kaye (1973), Hare (1970), Stanton (1975), and Yalom et al. (1967).

One study investigated the effects of marathon approaches to group treatment. Marathon groups differ from other groups in that they last from six to 48 hours or more at a time. Bare and Mitchell (1972) studied three different time patterns for group treatment. One group ran 30 hours of contact spaced over a ten-week period. A marathon group consisted of 24 hours of continuous contact. A mixed group consisted of mass treatment sessions of ten hours followed by spaced two-hour sessions over a period of five weeks. The participants were 165 adults who actively sought a personal group growth experience. Behavioral rating scales were used to determine psychological growth. The results showed that the three groups which had treatment showed significant positive behavioral change over the no-treatment control group. Changes were maintained over a three-month follow-up period. The specific effects of spaced, massed, and mixed time patterns were minimal. Trends in the data indicated that there was less change associated with massed training than with the other two treatment conditions.

Studies have shown that a higher rate of self-disclosure on the part of the leader produced higher rates of self-disclosure in group members (Dies & Sadowski, 1974; May & Thompson, 1973; Strassberg, Gabel, & Anchor, 1975).

Behavioral feedback as an important process in groups has also been documented. A study of Jacobs et al. (1973) and Schaible and Jacobs (1975) indicated that positive feedback was perceived by participants as more desirable than was negative feedback. Jacobs et al. (1974) discovered that positive feedback was given the highest credibility, while emotional feedback in general was found to have less impact upon the group members. Tosi and Eshbaugh (1978) found that behavioral feedback about group members' performance on facilitative conditions, such as empathy, genuineness, respect, and concreteness, enhanced the effects of cognitive restructuring and communication training in the development of interpersonal facilitative skills (empathy, respect, genuineess) and self-actualization.

A detailed summary of research in groups may be found in *The Theory and Practice of Group Psychotherapy* (Yalom, 1975) and *Group Counseling: A Developmental Approach* (Gazda, 1978).

Leadership style in group counseling

On the matter of leadership styles in group counseling, Goldstein, Heller, and Sechrest (1966) concluded from their review of numerous studies spanning educational, psychological, and industrial contexts, that a group-centered approach (i.e., client-centered) to leadership results in more favorable member feelings and attitudes about the group than a leader-centered group. Further research by Yalom (1975) supports this contention. Goldstein, Heller, and Sechrest, however, warn that more studies in group-counseling situations are needed to reach any firm conclusion.

There is, however, a rather directive trend developing in group counseling that emphasizes an active-directive-educational approach by some counselors. Rational-emotive group counseling, in particular, is one example of a more leader centered group experience (Maultsby, Stiefel, & Brodsky, 1973). Most group counselors today probably vary their leadership styles on a continuum from moderately directive to moderately nondirective.

Sprinthall (1977) and his associates at the University of Minnesota developed a set of group procedures they call "deliberate psychological education." Deliberate psychological education deals with the training of large groups of people in psychological matters related to personal adjustment. Sprinthall uses a teaching-experiencing model or an educational approach to psychological processes in the school environment. The leader of the group is a teacher or counselor who uses educational methods combined with psychological ones.

Some additional ideas about group counseling

Group counseling/therapy can serve as an adjunct to individual counseling. It is particularly useful as a reality testing base. Individuals can test out new ideas and behavior and receive helpful feedback from the group. Also, the group allows for a sharing of many different perspectives on personal problem areas. Group counseling is usually (often) conducted as an adjunct to individual counseling.

Another important fact that should not go unrecognized is that group counseling is economical in terms of the counselor's time. And, if the client is paying a fee for counseling, group counseling can be very economical.

We do not believe that group counseling will replace one-to-one counseling. Group counseling may augment the effects of one-to-one counseling and for some counselors and clients be a preferred mode of treatment.

SUMMARY

In this chapter the various aspects of group counseling were presented. The counselor plays a very significant role in group counseling. Therefore, the counselor should be aware of the parameters of the group process that are likely to promote success. In the group counseling process the degree of self-disclosure on the part of group members is very important to the success of the counseling process. In general, group members are more willing to self-disclose if the counselor self-discloses. The rate of self-disclosure seems to have a direct relationship to the level of self-esteem in the client.

The selection of individuals to participate in group counseling is a very important consideration related to the progress and growth of the group. For example, a very psychologically disturbed person should not be placed in a group of relatively normal people, since he or she often tends to disrupt the group's progress. People who show commitment to participation on a regular basis are good candidates for group experiences.

Groups progress through developmental stages. Initially, group members have concerns about confidentiality, being personally attacked, and not being accepted by the group. Members may exhibit defensive behavior to escape group participation and to protect their self-esteem. As the group evolves, members show more cohesiveness and commitment to the achievement of group and individual goals. Members also display higher levels of trust.

Groups are classified in many ways. Classification includes encounter groups, counseling/therapy groups, career guidance groups, and assertiveness training groups—to name a few. Although the process and goals of each of these types may differ, the basic communication patterns and dynamics are often very similar. Counselors need to clearly define for members the type of group they intend to conduct in terms of both process and goals.

Issues pertaining to confidentiality and ethics need to be addressed in the group to preserve the trust of the members. Counselors are ethically bound to use good judgment and to function within the limits of their training.

Some of the research conducted in the area of group counseling was presented in this chapter. Research can provide the counselor with valuable insights into the group process. In general, the research in group counseling, while often suffering from methodological limitations, seems to support the notion that group counseling is a relatively effective treatment modality.

Educational-vocational development and career counseling

Any person engaged in the labor market, about to enter the labor market, or about to enter the complex world of secondary or higher education is faced with a fantastic array of educational pathways and vocational opportunities. The *Dictionary of Occupational Titles* (1977) lists more than 20,000 types of jobs; the process of deliberating among the many possible choices often leads to confusion, anxiety, and despair among many people, young and old.

Many societal and personal factors significantly affect vocational development. Social factors, for instance, limit and influence the number of choices about careers open to an individual. Specific societal factors most often influencing vocational development and choices are economic conditions, geography, climate, sex, race, age, and social class membership. The degree to which various alternatives are actually available to individuals is largely a consequence of the social factors just identified.

A second major factor affecting vocational development is individual or personal in nature. Personal factors describe the individual's personality attributes, interests, and abilities. These may include skills and physical characteristics, as well as the individual's ideas, attitudes, beliefs, and capacity to successfully perform a variety of thinking and behavioral tasks. The combination of social and individual conditions merge in an idiosyncratic way for each individual and result in a particular vocational development style and outcome (Senesh & Osipow, 1973).

To help people cope with the complexity of making educational and vocational choices, the practice of career counseling has developed over the past 75 years. The counselor is seen generically as one who has the background and knowledge to assist the individual in an analysis of both the world of work and personal attributes. The analysis includes a logical integration of the results in ways that will enable the individual to make rational decisions concerning how to spend his or her vocational life, and how to implement these decisions.

An implicit assumption in the vocational development process is that careers are seen as the way to the "good life" (Osipow, 1969). However, occupational and occupationally related decisions are made in the context of considerable anxiety. Anxiety is created when persons are faced with the responsibility of making wise choices and decisions and accepting the consequences of their choices. The need to choose a career wisely often means to move up socially. For many people the fear of failure to improve social, educational, and vocational level is debilitating. Work choices are undesirable when they lead to unsatisfying vocational activities, or when they expose a person to tasks for which the individual has little potential for success.

Occupation to a large extent determines an individual's lifestyle (Blau & Duncan, 1967; Havighurst, 1964). Not only are occupational decisions socially bound (Gross, 1964; Caplow, 1954; Osipow, 1973), in that they reflect the social status of the chooser, but they also have extremely important implications for the eventual social position of the chooser. Income, style of consumption, tempo, and cycle of living depend upon the occupational role of the individual.

A person's particular career situation reflects the culture at the moment of choice. The vocational decisions that people made in the depression of the 1930s were markedly different from those their younger siblings made in the 1940s during and immediately subsequent to World War II. These decisions in turn were substantially different from those of their nephews and nieces in the 1950s and 1960s, who were choosing in a fairly affluent economic environment, and these in turn are different from the choices made in the economically confused 1970s. Educational preparation and emphasis also varies from one generation to another and exerts its own significant impact on the range and nature of vocational choices and aspirations of people.

Another aspect of vocational decision making that requires attention is the developmental nature of careers. As Super (1963a) points out, the tasks that confront individuals about vocational selection and preparation are a function of the person's particular stage of development. There is very good reason to believe that the degree to which one is able to make sound vocational decisions during college is in part a reflection of the successful negotiation of earlier, and somewhat scaled-down, educational decisions. Super has developed an elaborate description of developmental tasks and stages through which individuals must pass in the course of their vocational life.

The developmental nature of vocational behavior underscores the significance of change within an individual. The expectations, preferences, and capabilities of individuals change over the life span as a function of their experiences and competencies in dealing with the demands placed upon them. It is necessary, however, not only for individuals to cope with personal changes but also with a rapidly changing environment. New jobs are introduced and old ones phased out, sometimes right from under a worker. Young people must make choices about career paths with the uncertainty that these paths will reliably lead to the anticipated occupational ends. Parents must deal with the unfamiliar careers that their offspring are considering.

Changes in occupational structure, the pressures to make early choices, increased attention to mid-career change, and social concern about full and equitable employment opportunities for various subgroups all contribute to the increased importance of the work of the career counselor.

The evolution of ideas about work

In ancient cultures, work was seen to be a necessary but onerous responsibility that the individual was required to fulfill. In fact, a return to biblical references to work reminds us that as part of the original punishment of Adam and Eve was, among other things, labor for their sustenance. Other biblical references to work exist, all of which indicate first that work is hard and can be viewed as man's atonement for being human. Reading early biblical literature, it is possible to note occasional statements about the nature under which work should be undertaken, rules about when it should be done, instructions to fathers about their responsibilities to teach their sons a trade and to help them select the work that they will do, and many other signs of concern about work.

As Williamson (1965) points out, it is possible to find other evidence of efforts during ancient times to deal with the need to become vocationally placed. After the Hebraic period, Greco-Roman culture seemed to take the attitude that one was born into an occupational class. There was an elite educated ruling class with very clearly understood obligations and privileges, along with a slave class with equally clear responsibilities and privileges. Some individuals were considered to be a worker class, but the number of these was relatively small in ancient times.

Attitudes toward work and work selection and expectations of potential rewards from work changed very slowly from the Greco-Roman period through the Middle Ages until technology began to develop, requiring skilled and differentiated human resources. Although Hershenson (1974) and Zytowski (1972) have pointed out that in literature references to work abound as far back as A.D. 1400 and even earlier, that until the time, generally, of technical acceleration, people worked the land and farming did not require much selectivity about work activities. If people did not farm, and sometimes even if they did, occupational roles were inherited from parents either in terms of knowledge of specific skills, in terms of the possession of certain kinds of material properties, or in terms of social roles along sex lines.

With the advent of technology, which began to accelerate noticeably within the last few hundred years, more and different kinds of job activities began to develop. As a result, a means had to be developed to move people from the occupations of their parents into the occupations required by the current marketplace. Despite this need, however, training until relatively recently was still often casual, and people did not have much invested in their preparation for the trades in which they found themselves. Despite the lack of material investment, it was not easy for a person to change work because of the somewhat rigid social custom. Some changes were possible, however, partly because of an economic environment that permitted some hardy individuals to strike out in new directions and follow the physical frontiers of an expanding world. Many such people moved from the "Old World" to the Western Hemisphere and took along the old occupations but shaped them into new forms to meet the peculiar needs of their new surroundings. Other people moved from the east to the west in the "New World," once again starting with old occupations, but forging new opportunities for themselves in response to available options found on the scene.

In response to the need to develop career planning at a more sophisticated level, Parsons (1909), as well as others at the end of the 19th century, began developing ideas and methods to help individuals focus their attention on the matter of career decision making, training, and occupational change. While at the present time the ideas of these pioneers in vocational development seem simple and perhaps inadequate, they fundamentally set the stage for vocational counseling and psychology in much the same way that Freud set the stage for understandings about personality and psychotherapy. Career counselors have built upon Parson's fundamental notions and expectations, and nearly all of the techniques and constructs in use in vocational counseling today can trace their roots to the fundamental work done by Parsons and his colleagues.

The aftermath of World War I accelerated the study of interests and shifted the importance of interests in understanding vocational development from a casual one to one of increasing centrality, this change very largely the result of E. K. Strong's development of the Vocational Interest Blank. World War I made it essential to mobilize large numbers of men and to assign them efficiently to tasks, thus further enhancing the importance of developing a technology of differential psychology. The vocational guidance movement in the 1930s created an almost desperate need to understand and improve vocational placement effectiveness. Much of the government's resources were invested in developing a technology to measure individual attributes that would be useful in classifying people into occupational activities. Thus, in the 1920s the early development of the Strong Vocational Interest Blank took place, and in the 1930s the major developments were the elaboration of the Strong, the Kuder, and a heavy investment in research, much at the University of Minnesota, dealing with the creation of aptitude and ability tests and prediction of success in occupational training and on the job. Entire batteries of instruments were devised during this period to classify people into occupationally relevant categories. Also, it was during the Great Depression that the basic work for the *Dictionary of Occupational Titles* was conducted, and the work fundamentally underlying the later development of the General Aptitude Test Battery took place.

In the 1940s, World War II made it necessary once again to extend the technology available to classify individuals into occupational categories, and to identify those who would be most responsive to highly specialized training or work in sensitive areas. After World War II, the need to counsel returning veterans to take their place in society reinforced the importance of vocational counseling.

Only as the 1950s began was there a shift from the fundamentally empirical technological approach in the study of careers to an approach conceptually richer. During this transition period we see the beginning of concern with the creation of theories of career development (Osipow, 1973) in the early work done by Ginzberg et al. (1951), Super (1953),

Roe (1957), Holland (1959), and others. These theoretical efforts were designed to develop an understanding not only about the assignment of individuals to occupational categories but also to develop a better understanding of the forces that shape the ways people acquire the characteristics that make them suitable for assignment to a particular category. Moreover, for the first time a concern was noted toward understanding the career development process beyond that of initial selection and entry—but to include its eventual implementation, the individual's effectiveness and satisfaction, and its course through the life span. This emphasis continues basically unchanged to the present time.

A conceptual basis for career counseling

Two ingredients can contribute to our knowledge of how careers unfold and what can be done to facilitate this unfolding process. First, an extensive and satisfactory theoretical literature is needed from which hypotheses about human development can be made. A theoretical base helps to understand as well as to predict behavior in general. Second, we need to have a similarly good theoretical basis from which to predict and understand career development. Fortunately, we are in a favorable position, with respect to both of these conceptual requirements. There is a rich conceptual literature for vocational psychology (see, for example, Crites, 1969; Osipow, 1973).

Throughout the various theories of career or vocational development are many common themes (Osipow, 1969). The major conceptual theme in all career theory is developmental in nature. Most people agree that career development is a process that occurs over time in a reasonably organized and systematic manner. Among the major proponents of the developmental view are Super, Starishevsky, Matlin, and Jordaan (1963), Ginzberg (1951), and Tiedeman and O'Hara (1963). In one way or another, these theorists build upon the concept that life proceeds in predictable stages of development and growth (Buehler, 1933), each of which requires special attention.

A second theme is that career development is significantly influenced by the cultural-social-economic environment of the individual. As indicated earlier, the social class background of the individual, the economic status faced when considering entry into the labor market, and the attitudes toward work reinforced by one's subculture, interact to operate significantly upon vocational preferences, choices, eventual implementation, and overall effectiveness and satisfaction. Personal background will influence not only the content of choice and its level but also the quality of implementation and feedback from the choice itself. People who usually deal with life intuitively and impulsively are much more likely to need to make drastic changes in their career plans than people who make data (information) based decisions. Also, high ability people are more likely to find it possible to implement their plans than low ability individuals. Considerable data from sociological studies (e.g., Blau & Duncan, 1967) substantiate this notion. In addition, the viewpoint has support from data based on theorists, such as Holland (1973), who emphasize the person-environment interaction in vocational life.

A third major theme related to career development is that in Western cultures individuals have considerable potential for self-expression in work. This can be done through self-concept implementation (as per Super, 1963a & b), the matching of individual aptitude and personality traits with those demanded for success and satisfaction by particular jobs (e.g, the trait-factor approach), in terms of the exhibition of behaviors associated with cognitive styles (e.g., the tendency of individuals to perceive their environment in somewhat idiosyncratic ways, or to solve problems in some characteristic manner), or in terms of finding congruence between self and occupational environments as described by Holland (1973)—to mention but a few.

Finally—and very important, though frequently not fully understood by individuals—the freedom to choose widely and to satisfy personal goals in work often elicits anxiety about the work choice. One characteristic response to the anxiety associated with choosing work and the training for it is seen in the impulsive style. An individual exhibiting such a style tends to make choices impulsively, without much or adequate data, and without any serious effort to relate significant personal attributes to the relevant aspects of work. The motive for this careless approach to work choice is the desire to avoid anxiety. Once the choice is made, such people seem to reason, no anxiety will be felt because they will move toward a goal. Unfortunately, too often the choices made this way are poor ones—they do not engage the individual's greatest talents or interests and prove over time to be unsatisfactory and in need of revision. Thus, over the long run, the individual is exposed to even greater anxiety and strain than would have been faced initially if the trouble had been taken to think seriously about the choice, despite the anxious discomfort felt.

A second type of response to the anxiety is to become immobilized. Persons who become so overwhelmed by the uncertainties of career choice often ask themselves, "Will I be able to implement my decision through training? Do I have the necessary talents to succeed? Will I find my choice satisfying? Will the economy support me in my occupation throughout my life span?" In consequence, people can be paralyzed by fears. As a result, some individuals never quite seem able to make a choice final enough to implement. Such individuals suffer considerable psychic pain, continue to be indecisive, and make numerous false starts. In some ways, these people suffer consequences similar to those of the impulsive type. "The paralysis" approach to deal with choice anxiety results in anxiety and waste in the long run. Both types of people seem to actually bring about many of the negative consequences that their responses are designed to avoid.

Concepts of human development applied to careers

The basic developmental concept most frequently used by vocational theorists is Havighurst's developmental task. The concept was borrowed, transformed, and elaborated by Super (1963c) into the vocational developmental task.

Developmental stage theories have been described by many writers (e.g., Buehler, 1933; Blocher, 1966). Developmental theories include the concepts of Gesell, who proposed the idea that development occurs in rhythmic, sequential patterns (Gesell, Halverson, & Thompson, 1949; Gesell & Ilg, 1946; Gesell, Ilg, & Ames, 1956). Freudian theory also includes the notion that life progresses in stages. What is distinctive about psychoanalytic theories of development is their basis in libidinal energy (e.g., Freud, S., 1953; Freud, A., 1958, 1965). Neo-Freudian approaches to human development (e.g., Adler, 1917, 1927, 1931) substitute the concepts of inferiority, a striving for adequacy, and overcompensation as motivators to growth rather than libido. Harry Stack Sullivan (1953) discusses human development in terms of stages in growth in perception and adaption.

Havighurst (1953) has proposed the concept of the developmental task defined in terms of its physical, cultural, and individual aspects. During adolescence, a time of critical growth in vocational behavior and attitudes, these developmental tasks emphasize heterosexual development, independence from family, and educational-vocational commitments. All three of these, however, seem interwoven; for example, independence from family is facilitated by certain kinds of vocational decisions and inhibited by others, and rapid heterosexual development enhances the motivation for independence from family and thus requires vocational autonomy.

Erikson (1963) has proposed a theory of development oriented in the context of conflict management and resolution. His theory includes eight stages of development, each with its own distinctive focus.

In one form or another, these developmental theories have been applied to the career area—usually by describing how people deal with life-stage demands as they relate to careers.

Despite the richness of thinking of the writers mentioned earlier, the various life stages postulated may adequately *describe* what goes on in the life of an individual; but they do not provide anything substantial by way of *explaining* the events with an underlying concept (other than that of growth) (Horrocks, 1969).

Thus, a twist given to the concept of developmental stages by Tiedeman is especially interesting. He emphasizes the transition points between stages as areas of significant growth. These periods of discontinuity, as Tiedeman refers to them (1951), are the times of great change when old familiar behaviors may not work effectively in new surroundings. As a result, the points of transition between one life stage and the next, between one environment and the next, between elementary school and junior high school and between high school and the job, between being single and being married, and the like, are highly likely points of stress on people. These life-stage transitions require individuals to make numerous difficult decisions, and as a result, deserve attention. While these periods are those of most potential stress, they are also those of most potential growth, since the individual, once discovering that old behaviors are no longer effective, must find new styles of response.

Several theoretical systems have been proposed suggesting the existence of vocational developmental stages. These include, most notably, the proposals of Super (1963a and b) and Ginzberg et al. (1951). The Ginzberg proposal describes vocational development in terms of three periods called "Fantasy" (first to about 11 years), "Tentative" (11 to about 17), and "Realistic" (18 to 22 or 24).

Super's stages and periods are similar, though more detailed, and the timing is slightly different from Ginzberg's. Super describes vocational development in terms of crystallization from about age 14 to 18, specification from 18 to 21, implementation from 21 to 24, stabilization from 25 to 35, and consolidation from 35 on (Super, 1963c). The implications of these stages are similar, however, in that vocational growth is seen to be systematic, predictable, and accumulative. The concepts have led to the clarification of the concept of vocational maturity to describe the progress of an individual through these stages. A number of tests have been developed to measure vocational maturity, most notably Crites's Career Maturity Inventory (Crites, 1973), Super et al.'s Career Questionnaire (Super, Bohn et al., 1971), and Westbrook's Cognitive Vocational Maturity Test (Westbrook & Parry-Hill, 1973); in addition, interview schedules have been devised to assess vocational maturity—for example, Gribbons's and Lohnes's Readiness for Vocational Planning Scales (1968).

A great amount of research has been conducted to assess the validity of construing vocational development in terms of stages, such as those proposed by Ginzberg and Super. The overwhelming impression from the data (summarized and reviewed in Osipow, 1973) is to establish firmly the notion that vocational development can be viewed in terms of stages, such as those proposed, although the timing may vary from setting to setting and generation to generation. Consequently, measurement of vocational maturity can be potentially useful in evaluating effects of interventions designed to enhance vocational development.

A recently developed application of social learning theory to career development has been proposed by Krumboltz, Mitchell, and Jones (1976). This approach builds on interaction between genetic factors, individual environment, learning, cognitive emotional responses, and performance skills. Assumed is that at each decision point in an individual's life the person has multiple options. The object is to identify the factors that shape the number and nature of these options, as well as to influence the individual's responses to the options.

The major variables presumed to influence the individual's options and responses to them are the special characteristics that result from genetic heritage, such as: intelligence, musical ability, physical appearance, race, and sex; environmental conditions and events, such as job opportunities, training opportunities, neighborhood, community, and the like; the individual's learning history, which includes instrumental learning experiences and associative learning experiences; and finally, task-approach skills, which are those skill standards that the individual brings to bear in problem situations, such as values, work habits, and cognitive processes.

The social learning approach specifies the circumstances that *enhance* an individual's preferences for activities, as well as those circumstances that *depress* an individual's preferences for activities. A second set of propositions concern the development of the individual's performance and emotional responses, and a third set involves the learning histories associated with the development of implementation behaviors.

The propositions focus on the identification of reinforcers in the environment. One of the principle reinforcers are the role models available to the respondent. Therefore, application of the social learning approach depends heavily upon the development and use of models. The models differentially reinforce positive, as opposed to negative, behaviors. The counselor deliberately introduces films, videotapes, and live models that display desirable behaviors.

The approach is principally conceptual and has not been widely applied systematically, although there have been examples of applied research in which this thinking is evident (e.g., Thoresen, 1966; Thoresen, Krumboltz & Varenhorst, 1967; Krumboltz & Schroeder, 1965;

Krumboltz & Thoresen, 1964; Krumboltz, Varenhorst & Thoresen, 1967; Krumboltz, Mitchell, & Jones, 1976).

Career counseling

Traditionally, career counseling has involved the matching of individuals with jobs after the fashion first proposed by Frank Parsons (1909) many years ago. Typically, a variety of aptitude and interest measures are administered and then interpreted to the client with respect to the implications of the results for vocational training and placement. Interpretation usually is done using an interview method.

The overall approach ordinarily involves an intake interview, where some background information about the client is obtained and a testing plan is formulated. This is then followed by a testing session, which may be more or less extensive, depending upon the decision made in that first interview. After a short intervening period, during which the tests are scored, a second interview is held, in which the test results are explained and the implications discussed in terms of the particular decision points that are pertinent for the client (e.g., an educational decision or a job entry decision). Occasionally, a third interview might be necessary to further elaborate the implications, or to follow up earlier recommendations. Normally, the approach rarely goes beyond two or three interviews. A group variation of this approach has been developed in more recent years in which a standardized test battery is administered, explained, and interpreted in a group setting. Some opportunity for individual interaction between the group leader and the individuals comprising the group is usually provided.

For the most part, individuals exposed to these traditional approaches are self-referred—they themselves choose to come for counseling. In recent years some institutions, however, have developed programmatic referral systems in which tests are administered on an institutional basis and the results interpreted (as indicated earlier in the group method) to all the individuals in the institution. When this latter is done, it tends to have as its main focus the confirmation of old choices or the prevention of difficulty arising from an inappropriate original decision.

One of the assumptions of the traditional approach is that most careers move in a straight line. In the straight-line career an individual identifies the career path to follow relatively early in life (late adolescence). The person may need help in reassessing this decision before implementing it educationally and vocationally. Assuming that the entry field is appropriate, the career moves in a relatively straight line in the same content area for the rest of the person's life. Presumably, little attention to career decision or career development problems will be required from that point on.

Unfortunately, the "straight-line career" assumption does not hold up too well for many individuals, especially in our current economy. As noted earlier in this chapter, external events frequently disrupt these straight-line careers (wars, economic catastrophies, and personal physical trauma). Also, in the normal course of events, individuals often find that their decisions must be modified, sometimes to rather drastic degrees, as they grow older and their personal characteristics change as well as their personal objectives. For many individuals entering their career area later than the adolescent period, such as women, the straight-line career is especially inappropriate.

As a consequence of the recognition that the straight-line career model and the testing and interviewing method may not be most appropriate, new counseling approaches have been developed. These approaches focus on various critical choice points or life-stage transitions that most people experience. For example, a period in early adolescence associated with the transition to high school from junior high or eighth to ninth grade is a frequently identified transition point that has implications for careers and their educational correlates. A second critical point is 12th grade, when planning for the post-high school years is accelerated. Entry into the labor force, at whatever point, is another transition that is critical, and with reference to careers, the preretirement years would be another example.

The methods used by practitioners applying the developmental transitional factors vary widely, but most involve some use of the interview testing method, and an emphasis on what might be considered the "process" element. Process refers to the attempt to cause the individual to focus upon the subjective elements associated with decision to be able to identify those outcomes that are most suitable and comfortable for the individual. In other words, "process" describes the underlying thoughts and feelings of people.

Career education

Career education as an approach to vocational counseling in the broadest sense seems to stem from assumptions based on life-stage development. The career education approach is built upon the expectation that improved career decisions would result if individuals gradually accumulated information about careers from early childhood. The ideal career education approach involves teaching youngsters to observe, interpret, and evaluate their environments and themselves as they act in the environments. The objective of this method is to develop a ready fund of knowledge and experience that the individual can draw upon handily at each decision point when it comes. If an individual has a pool of knowledge and experience (not *only* factual) available, when critical decisions about educational programs and careers must be made, hopefully such decisions would be relatively easy to make and be based on valid data. Many career education programs have been developed and are functioning today. These programs appear to have at least face validity, although no comprehensive outcome studies about the long-term implications of career education programs on the quality of career decisions have yet been conducted.

The programs described are all interview based and interpersonally focused. While they may vary in the degree to which they focus on data about the individual and the environment, some of the newer approaches also spend considerable time dealing with the development of skills with which to implement preferences.

Analysis of career counseling

A very useful overall analysis of career counseling forms has been published by Crites (1974). Crites has developed a two-way matrix to demonstrate the various approaches to career counseling. He calls this a "taxonomy" of approaches.

On the horizontal dimension he lists five major counseling approaches: trait and factor, client-centered, psychodynamic, developmental, and behavioral. On the vertical axis he divides the scheme into two major categories, each with three subcategories: *models* (diagnosis, process, and outcomes) and *methods* (interview techniques, test interpretation, and occupational information).

Crites analyzes each of the five approaches to career counseling in terms of the six content elements. The trait and factor method, described earlier, emphasizes diagnosis (testing) and choice (outcomes). It relies heavily on the communication of occupational and personal information by test interpretation and the interview.

The principal difference between the trait-factor method and the client-centered method is the substantially increased focus on the process elements of the client-centered method and its de-emphasis on external items, such as test information.

Similarly, the psychodynamic model focuses on internal needs and motives. It aims to identify these for the individual to permit better control over decisions.

The developmental model is very much like the material described earlier in this chapter associated with Super. Developmental thought focuses on life-stage transition points; its methods resemble career education approaches to vocational development counseling.

Finally, the behavioral approaches strongly resemble the social learning approach described earlier. Here the counselor focuses on problem identification and the development of appropriate client responses to deal with problems. This approach is further characterized by its attempt to be objective and to focus on external events and goal setting.

All these approaches rely heavily on tests, interviews, and interpretation by the counselor to the client. Superficially, the various approaches may look very similar, although in their goals and their rationale they are very different. Because many of the methods overlap, counselors sometimes make the mistake of assuming that there is really no differentiation in counseling methods for career development.

In another publication, Crites (1976) encourages a differential counseling model for what he calls "comprehensive career counseling." In this approach Crites focuses on interviewing techniques, test interpretation, and occupational information. He proposes that in order to determine what interview techniques and tests should be used, and what and how to introduce occupational information properly, the counselor must first do a "differential diagnosis." There is some interaction between testing and differential diagnosis, as well as interviewing. Crites proposes, among other things, that career-counseling problems relate to indecision versus indecisiveness. Therefore, these two concepts must be properly differentiated to approach the counseling task correctly.

Overall, career counseling seems to deal with several subcategories of events: (1) *exploration*—subdivided into motivation to explore, skills to collect self and environmental data, and the processing of these data once they have been collected; (2) *goal setting*—setting and specifying the desired outcomes; (3) *implementation*—identification of skills to be developed, the actual development of the skills, using these skills to implement decisions, and the evaluation of the outcomes of the action.

The above process can be repeated (and probably is) throughout the life span as the individual moves from one decision point to another, constantly exploring, goal setting, and implementing.

Some of the common problems that career counselors encounter in their work deal with information deficits, decisional problems in terms of indecision or indecisiveness, anxiety over the need to make a good decision, and skill deficits in the face of potentially satisfying decisions. Many of the decision problems have been incorporated in the development of the Career Decision Scale (Osipow, Carney, Winer, Yanico, & Koschier, 1976; Osipow, Carney, & Barak, 1976; Osipow, 1979). This instrument gives the client an opportunity to indicate the events blocking their capacity to make a decision or reach closure about a career. Some of the barriers described involve skill deficits, approach conflicts, information deficits, interpersonal conflicts, anxiety, "obessiveness," impulsiveness, implementation deficits, and lack of support. Other barriers may exist, but these are good examples of some of the problem areas clients often disclose.

The counselor must identify the developmental stage related to problem areas and tailor the resulting approach accordingly. Intervention itself probably takes a different form for an adolescent than for someone at midlife.

In many respects the principal means for the delivery of career counseling remains the interview. Increasingly, however, settings other than late adolescent school situations and the early adulthood job situation appear to be developing for career counseling. These new settings involve early school years via the career education model and the midlife period as more emphasis is given to recycling people and careers throughout the life span. New methods appropriate to these new settings are being devised.

Goals for vocational and career counseling seem to be expanding. Originally, counselors sought to specify a point of job entry by developing exploration, self-awareness, and decisional skills, broadly defined, with the job entry point as the major criterion to assess career counseling. Now there is less reliance on psychometric methods than before and more reliance on promoting behaviors that might be useful in skill development and implementation. Overall, it must be recognized that the nature of the career counseling intervention necessary is very much dependent on the job economy. Where jobs are plentiful and people must and can select from among many attractive alternatives, the career counseling task is different from the situation in which jobs are scarce and individuals must adapt their personal resources to a limited range of possibilities.

Future trends

The rate and quality of change of occupational differentiation, which stimulated interest in career counseling and the study of careers to begin with, is now accelerating (Toffler, 1970). As Toffler suggests, it may well be that in some respects the accelerating rate of change in the occupational world may prove to be too difficult for people to deal with successfully. The Industrial Revolution expanded the work opportunities available to people through the creation of factories serving new industries and the associated new products and techniques. Currently, the service industry is expanding with similar consequences; that is, the development of new industries, new products, new services, and new careers.

Toffler suggests that the accelerating rate of change makes it even more imperative now than before to help individuals consider serial careers. This need is in contrast to the practice, until very recently, of assuming a continuous straight-line career. The rate of change in occupational technology was such that a person was not seriously confronted with the need to develop more than one or two career options during a lifetime. At one time, an individual might select a position, trade, or profession for training and enter it with the expectation of remaining in it for an entire lifetime, with possibly one or two modest work changes. Now, however, it is increasingly common to see men and women change their careers drastically, not only once, but several times during their lifetime. Sometimes even highly trained and specialized individuals are observed to do so. Sometimes the means to generate these changed occupations require very elaborate and intensive training in midlife. The day may not be far off when it will be the rule rather than the exception for individuals to seriously consider vocational decision making in very fundamental terms not only during their adolescence but also again during their thirties and forties and beyond. Because of the obsolescence of job-related skills and techniques it may be necessary to develop the means to help individuals make decisions that will lead to multiple careers more effectively than ever before.

It is clear that there is a great social need to develop the means and the understanding that will allow vocational specialists to become as effective as possible in fostering career decisions and processes throughout the life span.

As a result of the rapidly changing vocational world, career counselors have moved from a limited concern with one-time decisions about vocational plans to a more elaborate concern with the development of attitudes toward careers. In addition, professional counselors strive for their clientele's understanding of the use of one's skills and resources in fostering careers, as well as the ability to plan serial and multiple careers and shift job roles with age as individual and social characteristics demand.

SUMMARY

This chapter has presented two conceptual bases for understanding career counseling and adjustment. The first of these derives from studies of human behavior in general; the second from understandings gleaned from vocational psychology. Both frameworks are easily applied to thought about career counseling, because of their developmental aspects. Studies of human behavior have characterized human growth in terms of developmental stages. Vocational psychologists have similarly characterized vocational development in terms of stages of choice and adjustment to work.

In addition, the concepts about career development must be viewed in a social-economic-cultural context, in that individual vocational decisions and events are significantly influenced by the social framework within which people live. Within the limits imposed by social variables, however, personal attributes are expressed in vocational behaviors. People attempt to find work that enables them to use their most relevant abilities, satisfy their interests, and express personality traits and styles. In striving to implement these personal qualities in work, many people are beset and sometimes immobilized by anxiety. The overriding force of anxiety, individuals' reactions to it, and the effect of decision making in an uncertain, somewhat uncontrollable environment, provide the context within which most developmental and remedial vocational counseling occurs.

In the last 75 years, interest in vocational behavior and development has moved from an assignment and classification task to the understanding of a process and its facilitation. Despite this shift in emphasis, basic methods remain unchanged: we test, we talk, and we assign. Our tests may be a little better than they were 50 years ago, that is, more valid and more reliable; our counseling technology includes computers and, thus, may be faster, more complex, and more extensive. Our "talk" may be more cognizant of problems that offer the promise of shifting the emphasis in vocational development from testing and assignment to individual development. It is this last change that is perhaps the most significant and possibly the most interesting.

Essentially, the structure of most career counseling includes some exploratory activity where data are collected primarily using test and interview methods. These data are then collated and some summary statement of vocational possibilities and probabilities associated with them is generated. The counseling part of the process concerns itself primarily with both large and small decisions. Anticipating the need to make large decisions at a somewhat remote point in time, the individual is led to make a series of small decisions, each of which in effect leads logically to that larger decision, but each of which can be tested somewhat independently of the final outcome. This reality testing permits some basic shifts in directions toward the large decision to be made before that large decision becomes inevitable.

Exploration and decision define the process of vocational counseling in its typical form. The process includes self-exploration, information seeking, trial behavior, implementation efforts, which are reflected in career selection and the elaboration of these exploration and implementation efforts (reality testing), and finally, the confirmation of a large decision. The cycle may be repeated any number of times in accord with each of the large decisions that the individual must make during a career life.

Counseling:
Special applications

8

The work of the typical counselor has historically been confined to the normal ranges of personal problems related to educational, vocational, and personal adjustment. While this emphasis on the "normal" continues to be characteristic, many counselors work cooperatively with psychiatrists, physicians, social workers, and clinical psychologists in mental health settings wherein a given clientele may display a full range of behavioral disorders. Sometimes in the course of working with the "normal" the abnormal appears.

Counselors play an increasing role in the community mental health movement. Persons displaying severely disordered behavior now have treatment options in their own community. Many do not need to be confined to state hospitals and institutions. Because more than ever before counselors will encounter a more seriously disturbed population, they need to know about major adjustment problems and the environmental factors that influence their development.

This chapter presents a brief description of some of the most frequently observed behavioral disorders. The intent is to augment material presented in the earlier chapter on behavioral assessment. The chapter also looks at the counselor's role in sex, marital, and family counseling, substance abuse counseling, crisis intervention, and rehabilitation counseling.

Counseling: Major psychological disorders

The American Psychiatric Association describes and delineates the various psychological disorders. Counselors who work in community mental health settings will no doubt have to become familiar with the diagnostic classification system developed by the World Health Organization—*The Diagnostic and Statistical Manual of Mental Disorders* (DSM II, III). The DSM II and III consists of diagnostic categories of psychological disturbances. The counselor should refer to the DSM II and III for specific definitions of each major psychological disorder. A sample of classification is given next:

Psychoses Not Attributed to Physical Conditions (DSM II):
Schizophrenia
295.0   Simple type
295.1   Hebephrenic type
295.2   Catatonic

Major Affective Disorders
296.0   Involutional melancholia
296.1   Manic-depressive manic
296.2   Manic-depressive depressed
296.3   Manic-depressive circular

Paranoid States
297.0   Paranoia

Neuroses
300.0   Anxiety
300.1   Hysterical
300.2   Phobic
300.3   Obsessive-compulsive
300.4   Depressive

Personality Disorders
301.0   Paranoid
301.1   Cyclothymic
301.2   Schizoid
301.3   Explosive
301.4   Obsessive-compulsive
301.5   Hysterical

The DSM II and III go on to classify alcoholism, drug dependence, sexual deviations, psychophysiological disorders, transient situational disorders, behavior disorders of childhood and adolescence, and others.

Psychotic behavior

Psychoses refer to a set of extreme behaviors depicting a withdrawal from reality, with severe personality disorganization in thought processes and emotional states (Freedman, Kaplan, & Sadock, 1976). Psychotic reactions are sometimes divided into functional and organic classifications. The functional psychoses include schizophrenic, manic-depressive, and paranoid reactions. The organic psychoses refer to senile, toxic, arteriosclerotic, infectious, and traumatic. Distinctions between functional and organic psychoses need to be made.

Freedman, Kaplan, and Sadock (1976) suggest that many factors contribute to the psychoses. Sociocultural, biological, life stresses, traumatic experiences, genetics, early physical disease, child-rearing practices, and family interaction patterns generally all influence the development of seriously disturbed behavior. The degree to which each of the cited factors contribute to a particular psychotic reaction is still debatable.

Psychotic behavior: An instance of a counselor interacting with a person exhibiting acute paranoid schizophrenic symptoms

Counselor: Hello, I'm Dr. Smith. What is your name?

Client: I don't have a name.

Counselor: Why don't you have a name?

Client: Well, If I told you, you wouldn't believe me.

Counselor: What are you doing here? Could I be of help to you?

Client: Not really, I have a special mission that no one understands.

Counselor: A special mission?

Client: Yes, I have been told by God that I am the second coming of Christ. God told me that before I could complete my mission on earth—that is, bring world peace through him—I would have to suffer great persecution and affliction. My time is not now.

Counselor: Are you saying you are Christ?

Client: Yes, in the spirit and the body. I am presently attracting many disciples to help me with my mission.

Counselor: How do you attract these disciples?

Client: They hear it in my voice and see the light in my eyes.

Counselor: What did you do before your divine conversion?

Client: I was an auto mechanic.

Statistical approaches to the diagnosis of psychotic behavior

Lorr, Klett, and McNair (1963) have used complex statistical methods of clustering, typing, and labeling various behaviors that describe psychotic reactions. These researchers derived ten basic psychotic syndromes through statistical methods. The syndromes are called excitement, paranoid projection, hostile belligerence, perceptual distortion, anxious intrapunitiveness, retardation and apathy, motor disturbances, conceptual disorganization, disorientation, and grandoise expansiveness.

The syndromes are based on the work of Lorr, Klett, and McNair (1963) as adapted by Rosenbaum and Beebe (1975); they show the likelihood of the syndromes association of occurrence together. Placed around a circle, the syndromes closest to one another occur most frequently together. Syndromes opposite one another occur less infrequently. The circular arrangement would, for example, reveal a person exhibiting behaviors classified as paranoid projection to be more likely to show anxious intrapunitiveness and grandoise expansiveness than to display motor disturbances, disorientation, and conceptual disorganization.

The syndromes proposed by Lorr, Klett, and McNair represent phenomenological descriptions of very maladaptive behavior. Phenomenological description, however, does not specify causes, etiology, and treatment. An advantage of the system is that classification is based on the statistical probability of observing various relationships among maladaptive behavior. Moreover, the system encourages one to view severe personality disturbances as consisting of clusters or syndromes than as belonging to a single category.

The counselor should keep in mind that psychotic syndromes and the specific behavior defining them represent exaggerated forms of self-defeating behavior that are of a high frequency, intensity, and duration. Accurately diagnosing psychotic behavior requires much skill.

Counseling strategies for psychotic reactions

The prognosis for acute psychotic reactions is far better than it is for the more chronic forms (Retterstol, 1971). For persons suffering from acute psychotic reactions, counseling is often helpful. Most important is that the counselor be able to establish a trusting relationship, wherein the client can see some hope for improving his or her condition. Very important are the counselor qualities of experience and training, a healthy personality, and expertness. The counselor's attitude toward very disturbed clients needs to be positive and encouraging (Wolman, 1976).

The use of cognitive restructuring and behavior therapy also show promise with psychotic reactions (Beck, 1976; Reardon, Tosi, & Gwynne, 1977; Ellis, 1971). Cognitive and behavioral interventions, as earlier indicated, are aimed at modifying the thinking and behavior of the client. The use of major tranquilizers (prescribed by physicians or psychiatrists) also play a helpful role in treatment. Before counseling can be initiated with persons exhibiting psychotic behavior, it is often necessary to bring their symptoms under control. Medication can help to reduce anxiety and minimize bizarre symptoms (Wolman, 1975).

Counselors working with psychotically disturbed people need a high level of personal awareness and maturity. Freedman, Kaplan, and Sadock (1976), for instance, warn of the difficulty in treating psychotic behavior. Because of this, a counselor may experience many intense and negative emotions, such as anger, despair, rage, lust, anxiety, and disgust. A counselor can very easily become disenchanted with the counseling process and therefore communicate to the client many negative attitudes. Personal confidence and trust in one's self certainly are necessary ingredients for working with severely disturbed persons. A counselor is looking for the approval from clients, but he will rarely receive it. It is a sound practice for the counselor to have an ongoing consulting relationship with colleagues about some cases that may pose personal difficulties.

One of the special roles the counselor may play is in helping family members better understand and respond to the disturbed person's behavior. Because of a general lack of understanding and acceptance of severe behavioral disorders on the part of the public, a counselor may have difficulty in trying to explain these reactions to the client's family, employers, and friends. A counselor may spend many hours educating significant persons in the client's life about the nature of emotional disorders. Additionally, the counselor may provide members of the family individual counseling. This is one role the counselor will often play in a mental health team.

The prospective counselor who intends to work in settings that provide treatment for severe behavioral disorders would benefit from further reading on the topic. Among some of the most informative writings on severe personality disorders are *Interpretation of Schizophrenic* (Arieti, 1955), *Direct Analysis* (Rosen, 1953), *Collected Papers on Schizophrenia* (Searles, 1965), *Prognosis in Paranoid Psychosis* (Retterstol, 1971), *Depression* (Beck, 1967), *Depression and Human Existence* (Anthony & Benedek, 1975), *Modern Psychopathology* (Millon, 1969), and *Syndromes of Psychosis* (Lorr, Klett, & McNair, 1963).

Psychoneurotic behavior

In the so-called psychoneurotic reactions, anxiety is the most prominent major symptom. Anxiety is best described as being exaggerated, nonobjective, inappropriate fear. Unlike in psychotic reactions, severe personality disorganization and gross distortion of reality are not observed in psychoneurotic behavior. Persons suffering from neurotic symptoms are often aware of their behavior. To avoid becoming overwhelmed by anxiety, they will resort to a variety of defensive mechanisms that offer temporary relief from symptoms. Repression, displacement, and conversion are typical defensive mechanisms associated with psychoneurotic behavior. Neurotic reactions are classified as anxiety, hysterical, phobic, depressive, neuresthenic, and hypochondriacal (DSM II, 1968). Neurotic classification has been reinterpreted in the DSM III.

Neurotic behavior: *An example of a counselor with a person exhibiting obsessive-compulsive symptoms*

Counselor: Mary, tell me what's been bothering you lately.

Client: Well, I don't know if I know really. It's just those crazy thoughts that don't go away.

Counselor: Could you be more specific?

Client: Well, I think I am going to get venereal disease when I come into contact with garbage. When I think about garbage, I can't get that out of my mind ever. I feel like I am going crazy. I can't stop myself. When does this end? I have to wash my hands all the time.

Counseling strategies for the neuroses

Most persons exhibiting neurotic behavior patterns are excessively anxious and adopt many different defensive mechanisms that avoid confronting and resolving their difficulties. Avoidance behavior may consist of obsessive preoccupations, phobias, and self-depreciation. By avoiding the sources of one's difficulty, anxiety and tension may be reduced temporarily. A self-reinforcing mechanism is then set up that perpetuates a vicious, self-defeating behavioral cycle (Beck, 1976; Lazarus, 1966; Goldfried & Sobocinski, 1975). When counseling people with what are often referred to as neurotic disorders, a counselor (*a*) needs a thorough knowledge of the etiology of various neuroses, (*b*) must be able to discriminate between the various types of neuroses and recognize similarities among the types, and (*c*) be able to employ differential counseling strategies for different types of symptoms.

Behavior modification procedures based on systematic desensitization and some of its variants, such as covert sensitization, have been particularly promising in the treatment of neuroses where the symptoms are relatively clear-cut (e.g., phobias, obsessions, and compulsions) (Stern, 1970; Wisocki, 1970; Boulougouris & Bassiakos, 1973; Lazarus, 1974). Depressive neurosis responds particularly well to active-directive approaches based on cognitive restructuring and in-vivo desensitization (Beck, 1976; Mahoney, 1974; Wolpe & Lazarus, 1966). Intrapsychic techniques emphasizing insight and awareness are often useful for dealing with conversion and dissociative disorders (Millon, 1967). A multimodal approach to the treatment of neurotic behavior (Lazarus, 1973) seems to be quite effective. Multimodal systems are eclectic and combine approaches from many different theoretical perspectives.

In most neurotic disorders, repression and denial of unacceptable thoughts, feelings, and behavioral tendencies are the major defensive mechanisms. A counselor needs to approach repressed material with a degree of caution. If the counselor's confrontation of denied and repressed material is premature, the client may be overwhelmed with anxiety and terminate counseling. On the other hand, if the counselor fails to present relevant material, the counseling process may be stifled, the client may feel treatment is not helpful and may terminate. A balance of increased self-awareness and symptom relief should be achieved.

Psychophysiological disorders

Psychophysiological reactions are exemplified by peptic ulcer, colitis, essential hypertension, migraine headache, bronchial asthma, and neurodermatitis. Millon (1969) suggests that when these conditions are prolonged they could lead to irreversible organic or tissue damage. Persons who are subjected to persistent environmental stresses, or who are unable to resolve intrapersonal conflicts, are more likely than others to be afflicted with these disorders. The gastrointestinal, cardiovascular, and respiratory systems are frequently the locale for psychophysiological reactions (Alexander, 1950). Psychophysiological reactions, unlike the neuroses, do not circumvent psychological distress or reduce tension through ritualistic acts, obsessions, or phobias. One is most often unaware that psychological factors are the sources of the tension and therefore tends to somaticize them (Freedman, Kaplan, & Sadock, 1976).

Millon (1969) concludes that psychosomatic disorders (*a*) arise as a consequence of the failure to release tension; (*b*) keep the person unaware of psychological conflicts; (*c*) inhibit expression of unacceptable thoughts and emotions; (*d*) function to obtain secondary gains in the form of sympathy and attention; (e) arise out of conflict between needs for dependence and independence. Specific causes for specific psychosomatic disorders are difficult to identify.

Counseling approaches to psychophysiological disorders

Counseling approaches that employ biofeedback, autogenic training,* imagery, and relaxation training have shown promise in the treatment of psychophysiological disorders. Systematic desensitization (see Chapter 5), for example, has proven to be very effective in the treatment of these disorders (Wolpe & Lazarus, 1966). Case reports (Cooper, 1964; Sergeant & Yorkston, 1969; Stedman, 1972; Creer, 1971; Niesworth & Moore, 1972) and experimental studies (Rachman, Hodgson, & Marks, 1971; Alexander, 1972; Moleski & Tosi, 1976; Paul, 1969) do provide convincing evidence of the merits of behavior therapy that use muscular relaxation training, assertive training, reciprocal inhibition, and cognitive restructuring.

Case studies employing relaxation training, biofeedback, and autogenic training as a treatment for migraine headaches have shown marked success (Budzynski et al., 1973; Sargent, et al., 1973). Experimental studies seem to confirm case study reports. Biofeedback methods have been used as a treatment for essential hypertension (Brenner & Kleinman, 1970; Shapiro et al., 1969). Case studies further reveal the effectiveness of operant conditioning techniques emphasizing self reinforcement with neurodermatitis (Leitenberg, 1976), stuttering (Moleski & Tosi, 1976), and bed-wetting (DeLeon & Sachs, 1972; Lovibond, 1972; and Stedman, 1972).

For a further detailed and comprehensive discussion of behavior therapy approaches to psychophysiological disorders, see Wilson and Franks (1973; 1974; 1975), *Behavior Therapy: Theory and Techniques*, Vols. 1, 2, and 3; Leitenberg (1976), *Handbook of Behavior Modification and Behavior Therapy; Theory and Practice in Behavior Therapy* (Yates, 1975), and *The Therapist's Handbook* (Wolman, 1976).

---

* Note: Biofeedback and autogenic training methods are self-management techniques in which a person can be trained to control various physiological processes, such as heart rate, pulse, constriction of blood vessels. The techniques use relaxation training combined with passive concentration. Biofeedback uses mechanical devices that measure galvanic skin responses, muscular tension, and skin temperature. The subject is able to monitor his or her physiological responses via feedback provided by these instruments. Both approaches are aimed at controlling the autonomic nervous system. For a more detailed exposition of these methods, see Luthes *Autogenic Therapy* (1969–1973) and Barber et al. *Biofeedback and Self Control* (1971).

Transient situational disorders

Transient situational disorders consist of acute reactions to environmental stress. Examples of transitional disturbances may be anxiety associated with military combat and depression associated with a loss of a job. These reactions may occur at any developmental stage. When the environmental stresses have been removed, a person's negative reactions will tend to subside (DSM II, 1968).

Counseling strategies for transient situational disorders

Counseling/therapy of a supportive or reconstructive nature may be indicated, depending on the severity of the condition. Crisis intervention and time-limited counseling may also prove beneficial.

Limitations of diagnostic classifications

Sundberg and Tyler (1962) point out several serious inadequacies with the official psychiatric classification system: (1) The etiology or causal factors as well as differential treatment are not referred to directly. The mental disorders are not directly related to specific theories of behavior. (2) Classification systems, such as the DSM II, are often not for descriptive purposes. A categorical diagnosis may be used for administrative handling of a client, i.e., placement. (3) Any taxonomy often excludes exceptions or variations in people. There is a tendency to force people into categories. (4) Diagnostic categories in general lack statistical reliability. (5) Diagnostic taxonomies do not cover a wide range of human problems. The DSM III, however, compared to the earlier DSM II and DSM I, has remedied this to some extent.

Whatever one's personal theoretical orientation to counseling may be, it is not possible to escape the fact that some persons are seriously disturbed emotionally. Perhaps all human beings suffer from some sort of psychological disturbance—even the so-called normals. Psychology and related disciplines for years have argued for and against various theories of emotional disturbance. Academic arguments, as important as they are in understanding emotional disorders, do not deny the existence of emotional disorders and can provide reasonable perspectives. The practicing counselor will encounter directly persons who indeed are suffering—whatever the cause, etiology, or motivation of their suffering. In this section, we have tried to highlight important behavioral symptoms that reflect disordered thinking, feeling, bodily response, and overt behavior.

Family, marital, and sex counseling

Counselors working in mental health agencies, university counseling centers, rehabilitation settings, pastoral counseling centers, or in private practice work with groups consisting of unrelated individuals. A great deal of counselors' work, however, is with families, married couples, and with couples who are contemplating marriage, living together, are divorced or separated. Currently, premarital, marital, family, and sex counseling are becoming integral parts of centers offering psychological consultation.

Marital counseling

In recent years, marital and family relationships have been studied intensively by contemporary behavioral scientists. An ever-increasing divorce rate suggests that many people are becoming disenchanted with marriage. Traditional marriage and family norms and values have been challenged by the feminist movement. Steinman (1974) observed that as women worldwide become more educated, their demands for equal rights with men increase. Educated women aspire toward values that include self-actualization outside of the roles of wife and mother. Steinman predicts that a certain amount of conflict between the sexes will be the consequence of changes in sex role stereotyping resulting in an alternation of the power structure of male/female relationships. The sexual balance of power will shift toward equalization.

Eastman and Reifler (1972) reported that the presenting concerns of couples seeking marriage counseling at the University of North Carolina Counseling Service involved mainly extramarital affairs, sexual incompatability, separation, and divorce. In the Eastman and Reifler study, premarital clients (30 percent of the total sample) were mostly concerned with deteriorating relationships and decisions over whether to marry.

Because of their training in life-span development and awareness of the impact of social forces on human behavior, counselors play a special role in assisting couples who experience sex role and value conflicts. Counselors can assist couples in the exploration of new and more effective ways of communicating with one another.

The practice of marriage counseling is a specialized area of family counseling and provides professional psychological assistance to individuals and married couples, singly and in groups. The marriage counselor applies psychological principles and techniques for the purpose of modifying interpersonal conflicts resulting from maladaptive attitudes and behaviors associated with family life (Silverman, 1972). In contrast to individual counseling, in marital counseling the counselor attends not only to one individual but to the system, a unit of two or more individuals. The counselor also deals with the many interpersonal conflicts between husband and wife, including "intrapersonal dynamics" (thoughts, feelings, and actions) of each party. Silverman (1972) states "marriage counseling keeps in its sight its objective of enabling marital partners and their children to achieve the optimal adjustment with their welfare as individuals, as well as members of a family, and as citizens in society."

As in all forms of counseling, the counselor's personal beliefs and values affect performance in marital and family counseling. The counselor's ability to know and accept his or her own value system and the divergent value systems of others may be one of the most essential factors in being a successful marriage counselor. The counselor must ultimately answer some very important value questions: where I stand on extramarital sex; on divorce and separation; on open marriage; on cohabitaiton and swinging; on couples living together who are not married; on sex roles for married people; on abortion (Ziskin & Zisken, 1975).

Sex counseling

Sex counseling, while often a part of marriage counseling, is not limited to marriage. In contemporary times, the need for sex counseling for adults has been well documented (Eastman & Reifler, 1972) as well as for adolescents (Elias & Elias, 1975). Sexual problem areas of adults seem to involve impotence, premature or delayed ejaculation in males, and fridigity in females. Sexual problems of adolescents seem to center on guilt and anxiety over masturbation, petting, and sexual intercourse. Elias and Elias (1975) reported some interesting findings on adolescent sexuality:

On sexual self-concept. Of both sexes, 62–81 percent experience significant anxiety over their attractiveness to the opposite sex and worry about eliciting approval from their peers. Roughly 38 percent of the adolescent sample agreed with the statement that they frequently feel ugly or unattractive.

On petting and sexual intercourse. Findings show 11 percent of the interviewed females and 31 percent of the interviewed males stated they had engaged in sexual intercourse (female age range 11–18; male age range 14–17). Of those female adolescents who reported that they engaged in heavy genital petting, 87 percent were involved with the same person. Of the males, 16 percent reported the same.

On masturbation. Respectively, 33 percent and 77 percent of the females and males masturbated with a frequency of once a month to daily.

Adolescents and adults vary in their sexual experiences and practices and react emotionally in very different ways. Anxiety and guilt reactions over masturbation and premarital sex appear to be the most common emotions. Even after years of marriage, many couples suffer from feelings of anixety and inadequacy over their sexuality.

Sex counseling and programming

An illustrative example of sex-counseling programming is found at the University of California, San Francisco. The Sex Advisory and Counseling Unit of the Human Sexuality Program provides counseling services for persons having problems of sexual arousal, erection, orgasm, and ejaculation. Based on a relearning model, counseling is short-term, intensive, and focuses explicitly on sexual needs, behavior and communication skills. Couples and individuals who are heterosexual, homosexual, or bisexual are accepted for treatment. Treatment combines individual and group counseling. Behavioral contracts, outside homework assignments, and educational self-help sessions are routinely used. A noteworthy aspect of the program is its emphasis on reeducation (Vandervoort & Blank, 1975).

Sex research and counseling has been advanced through the work of Masters and Johnson (1970; 1966–1974). A thorough discussion of their major research and treatment techniques may be found in *The Human Sexual Response* (1966) and *Human Sexual Inadequacy* (1970). Masters and Johnson's work is a valuable source of information for counselors. In brief, the Masters and Johnson treatment for sexual incompatibilities, such as impotence and frigidity, consists of a variety of innovative techniques.

The treatment procedure begins by taking a detailed and accurate sexual history. The sexual history consists of specific information about early sexual experience, family attitudes toward sex, personal beliefs on sex and marriage, and the marital relationship.

In the initial phase of sex counseling, a male/female diagnostic team determines the degree of sexual incompatibility in the relationship. The male counselor interviews the male marriage partner at the same time the female marriage partner is interviewed by the female counselor. The counselors exchange, discuss, and evaluate the material derived from the initial interview. In the second session, the male counselor interviews the female client and the female counselor interviews the male client. The counselor team and the couple meet together in the third session for an open discussion of any sexual incompatibilities. Counseling and physiological techniques used for the treatment of sexual incompatibility are thoroughly explained. If the counseling team determines that the couple is sufficiently commited to overcoming their difficulties, sex counseling begins. If the couple does not wish to cooperate fully with treatment, they are directed toward other sources of help (Stahmann & Hiebert, 1977).

More recently, Helen Kaplan (1974; 1975) composed two volumes dealing specifically with sex counseling. The *New Sex Therapy* and the *Illustrated Manual of Sex Therapy* introduce counselors to an eclectic approach to sex counseling. Kaplan has attempted to integrate neopsychoanalytic concepts, behavior therapy, and the methods and research of Masters and Johnson.

Counseling approaches and techniques that are especially suited for treating sexual disfunctions are rational emotive therapy and cognitive behavior therapy, systematic desensitization, covert conditioning, and assertive training. Such procedures make extensive use of recent advances in sensory-imagery, relaxation, and cognitive restructuring. Rational-emotive therapy (Ellis, 1974), for instance, incorporates as one of its main techniques Rational Emotive Imagery (REI), a cognitive restructuring technique. Ellis reports on the success of REI in the treatment of sex and love problems in women and men (Ellis, 1974; Ellis & Harper, 1975). REI consists of vivid imagining and the rational restructuring of thoughts and emotions related to disturbing events. The person is to imagine engaging in irrational self-talk about the situation, to experience negative emotional states (anger, hostility, anxiety), and to observe self-defeating ways of acting. Following the self-defeating sequence the client is to observe the same situation, but this time is to engage in rational self-talk and to imagine the experiences of having more desirable emotions and behavior. Ellis contends that irrational ideas typically associated with anxiety, sexual difficulties, and suppression of sexual feelings are "wouldn't it be awful if I could not satisfy my partner," "in order to be worthwhile sexually, I must be perfect in every respect." REI, a cognitive restructuring type of desensitization, is to be repeated and practiced by the client on a frequent basis (Maultsby, 1971; Ellis & Harper, 1975).

Since such sexual problems as impotence and frigidity generally have multiple causes, treatment procedures need to be diverse and varied for men and women (Kaplan, 1974). Lazarus (1973) views sex counseling as a multimodal process that consists of the *correction of misconceptions, graded sexual assignments, systematic desensitization, assertive training, aversion-relief therapy,* and *rational or cognitive restructuring.* He further asserts that if sex counseling with couples is to be optimally effective, cooperative sexual partners are indispensable. Interpersonal difficulties stemming from hostility, jealousy, and passivity may interfere with effective sex therapy. Therefore, before sex counseling can be initiated, personal counseling may be required. For additional information on sex counseling, the reader is referred to Sadock, Kaplan, and Freedman (1976), *The Sexual Experience*.

Family counseling

Family counseling, unlike individual counseling, aims at modifying the family system. Individual changes in behavior are secondary to change in family systems and dynamics. "Conjoint" family counseling refers to a modality wherein each member of the family is involved collectively with one another. Counseling sessions involve all members of the family at the same time.

Among some of the most noted theorists and practitioners of family counseling are Nathan Ackerman (1970), Virginia Satir (1964), Gerald Zuk (1971), and John Bell (1970). These writers share their emphasis on (*a*) the family as a system; (*b*) active-directive authoritative intervention; (*c*) the breakdown of pathological (self-defeating) communication processes; (*d*) the family assuming responsibility for behavioral change; (*e*) openness of communication; (*f*) insight and awareness; and (*g*) the development of effective communication patterns. A detailed discussion of the theory and practice of family counseling may be obtained by reading the works of the theorists just named.

There are many other approaches to family counseling with which the prospective counselor may want to become familiar. Robert Liberman (1972), for example, uses a behavioral approach to family therapy. Emphasizing behavioral analysis of maladaptive behavior patterns in family transactions, Liberman sees the family counselor as a social reinforcer of adaptive behavior who implements the technology of behavior therapy.

Another approach, described by Robert MacGregor et al. (1964), is Multiple Impact Therapy. Multiple Impact Therapy involves the use of a team of counselors who work with the family as a unit, individuals, and various combinations of family members.

The beginning counselor will probably be exposed to a proliferation of theories and techniques of family therapy. Our own observations have led us to conclude that counselors are likely to develop their own perspectives on family intervention in time and with experience. We have observed that experienced counselors who operate out of behavioristic, Gestalt, psychoanalytic, client-centered, rational-emotive, or transactional analytic frameworks function very effectively as family counselors. Experienced counselors, regardless of theoretical orientation, begin to look more alike than different with respect to their counseling behavior (Fiedler, 1950).

At times it will be difficult for the counselor to separate marital, sex, and family counseling. No doubt the counselor will be engaging in all three at particular times.

Substance abuse counseling

Substance abuse counseling refers to working with persons in the context of the counseling relationship who suffer from the psychological and behavioral effects of the abuse of drugs and alcohol. Counselors play an increasingly significant role in drug and alcohol treatment centers throughout the nation. It has become more apparent to the professional counselor that people who use alcohol are likely to use drugs, and vice versa (Eshbaugh, Tosi, & Hoyt, 1978 a, b).

The major problem that counselors contend with in substance abuse counseling is dependence—psychological or physical, or both. Psychological dependence means the development of a craving for a substance because of the pleasurable effects that are derived. Physical dependence suggests a biophysiological change wherein the body requires the presence of a substance to avoid an unpleasant withdrawal.

Classifying alcohol problems

The Cooperative Commission on the Study of Alcoholism (Plaut, 1967) points to an important distinction between "alcoholism" and "problem drinking." This commission suggested that the term alcoholism means "a condition in which an individual has lost control over alcohol intake in the sense that he/she is consistently unable to refrain from drinking or to stop drinking before getting intoxicated." This definition suggests that there is a "loss of control," an inability of a person to stop drinking once started. The definition also implies an inability to abstain from drinking.

"Problem drinking" refers to a repetitive use of alcohol, resulting in significant negative psychological, physical, and social consequences. Kissin (1973) estimates that there are 9 million alcoholics and problem drinkers in the United States. This is compared to about 250,000 "hard core" drug addicts.

Rosenbaum and Beebe (1975) identified and defined several categories of problem drinkers. The *reactive* drinker resorts to excessive drinking to seek relief from some emotional state, such as anxiety or depression. The *schizophrenic* drinker uses alcohol for self-medication. Alcohol serves to mask many psychotic symptoms, such as delusions and hallucinations. The *cyclothymic* drinker is very vulnerable to psychological rejection, with significant shifts in mood ranging from elation to depression. A fourth type is the *heavy drinker under pressure*. Under high-pressure conditions, such as examination taking and military service, some people resort to excessive drinking to reduce tension. A fifth type is the *heavy drinker without funds*. This type of person shows up at a hospital to be cared for while they wait for their disability check so they can buy alcohol. Rosenbaum and Beebe also add to their classification the *middle-aged alcoholic in crises*, the *woman problem drinker*, and the *young drinker*.

Two recent studies conducted by Eshbaugh, Tosi, and Hoyt (1978a, b) used multivariate statistical procedures to type male and female alcoholics and problem drinkers with respect to MMPI profiles. The results of their research tend to support the observation made by Rosenbaum and Beebe (1975).

Criteria for the diagnosis of alcoholism

The National Council on Alcoholism poses major and minor criteria for diagnosing alcoholism. The diagnostic system is comprehensive and considers physiological dependence, psychological dependence, and major alcoholic associated physical illnesses. Some of the major criteria are presented below.

Physiological dependence. Physiological dependence is evidenced by a withdrawal syndrome when the intake of alcohol is ceased and not substituted by any other drug. When physiological dependence on alcohol exists, withdrawal from the substance most often results in gross tremors, hallucinosis (differentiated from psychotic hallucinations), withdrawal seizures, and delirium tremons. Other evidence of physiological dependence is based on consumption of alcohol and blood alcohol levels. Blackout periods are also common.

Clinical features. There are many physiological effects of excessive drinking of alcohol. One of the most prominent diseases associated with heavy drinking is cirrhosis of the liver. Other physical conditions that may result are hepatitis, gastritis, anemia, and cerebral degeneration. Prolonged use of alcohol may also affect sexual functioning, produce maladies of the small intestine and fatigue.

Drug dependence

Drug dependence applies to persons who are addicted to drugs other than alcohol, tobacco, or caffeine (Freedman, Kaplan, & Sadock, 1976). Withdrawal symptoms may or may not be the only evidence of dependence. Most often drug dependence is psychological rather than physio-logical, and is a means through which a person tries to adjust to stress.

Those drugs, excluding alcohol, that people can become dependent upon are opioids (e.g., heroin, marijuana, amphetamines, barbiturates), proprietary drugs (e.g., cough medicines), hallucinogens (e.g., LSD, mescaline, glue, and gasoline).

Counseling approaches

Counselors who work with drug and alcohol related problems should expect to encounter enormous resistance from their clients. Most often, people who resort to excessive use of drugs and alcohol tend to be passive-aggressive and try to deny many of their psycholog-ical conflicts. Many drug addicts and some problem drinkers exhibit antisocial features, in that they are often very manipulative and impul-sive. Counselors need to know themselves well and their own tendencies to be manipulated by the so-called slick client.

Too often substance abusers who undergo counseling give the im-pression that they progress well. Then, without notice, they fall back into old habits. Counselors sometimes believe they have failed these clients and as a result doubt their own competence. It is not uncommon for beginning counselors to feel considerable anxiety and self-doubt about their ability to function professionally when they do not see positive gains made by their clients.

In time, most counselors learn to become more patient and tolerant of themselves and their clients. Certainly, the counseling relationship stimulates counselors to think about areas of their own personal and professional development. We highly recommend continued profes-sional and personal development experiences for counselors to help them cope more effectively with the emotional demands of the coun-seling relationship.

Reality-oriented and behavioral approaches to counseling seem to be more appropriate with substance abuse problems (Rosenbaum & Beebe, 1975). Combinations of reality-cognitive and behavioral tech-niques focus not only on unrealistic attitudes about substances and their harmful effects but on managing behavior (Cautela, 1970; Sobell & Sobell, 1973; Vogler, Lunde, & Martin, 1971). We have already cited some evidence of the efficacy of covert sensitization in the treatment of alcohol abuse. Often physicians and social workers need to be directly involved in the treatment of substance abuse problems. It is our view that counseling approaches be multifaceted. Counseling strategies should include educational, vocational, medical, and sociological com-ponents. Counselors will have to avail themselves of all community resources possible to maximize therapeutic benefits for the substance abuser.

Community resources

The National Council on Alcoholism (NCA) provides pretreatment evaluations of persons with drinking problems. The NCA is a public service and can be found in most large cities in 50 states. The major function of the NCA is evaluation, not treatment.

Alcoholics Anonymous (AA), another national organization, addresses the problem of treating the "excessive drinker" or person with alcoholic problems. Chapters of AA are located in practically every city in the United States. AA offers long-term help for the drinker and very often is the only treatment modality that is available to a person during or following hospitalization. Most hospitals treating alcohol disorders use AA as a resource.

Additionally, the problem drinker can find help at residential treatment centers, such as rehabilitation centers and halfway houses. Outpatient clinics of hospitals, physicians, psychologists, and counselors are also major resources for these problems.

Drug treatment centers are typically found in most communities. Many of them are funded through mental health programs. The VITA drug treatment center in Columbus, Ohio, for example, has a comprehensive methadone maintenance program that makes use of an interdisciplinary treatment model. Psychologists, physicians, social workers, and nurses make up a team whose goal is to help the drug addict make a more satisfying adjustment to the community.

Rehabilitation counseling

The rehabilitation counselor works with a special group of clientele who not only present vocational and personal problems but have additional complications of disablement or disease. In the many public and private rehabilitation agencies, the persons served are often of low socioeconomic status and background.

Rehabilitation counselors are one of the several sets of professionals who provide rehabilitation services. Rehabilitation counselors work in conjunction with physicians, nurses, physical therapists, occupational therapists, speech and hearing therapists, social workers, clinical psychologists, guidance counselors, prosthetists, vocational counselors, special education teachers, correction therapists, and lay persons.

The concept of rehabilitation generally aims at the restoration of an individual to a level of former capacity, most often in a social, emotional, physical, or a vocational capacity (Lofquist, 1957). Rehabilitation services are found in hospitals, vocational schools, industrial plants, sheltered workshops, and special schools, and are sponsored by both state and private agencies.

Today and in recent years rehabilitation counseling and training programs throughout the nation have received substantial local, state, and federal financial support. This has not always been true historically. A favorable attitude toward rehabilitation probably began with the almshouses. Those facilities provided care for petty criminals, vagrants, the disabled, and the mentally ill. As early as 1791, Dr. Benjamin Rush included work and vocational rehabilitation as an integral part of the therapy of patients at the Pennsylvania Hospital. The momentum for rehabilitation increased with the development of special schools for deaf, crippled, and mentally retarded children from 1775 to 1900.

The 20th century saw enormous growth in social, vocational, and physical rehabilitation. For instance, at the turn of the century, the Ohio legislature enacted several bills that provided funds to local schools for the education of disabled children. Other states were soon to follow Ohio. Additionally, workers' compensation laws for the vocational rehabilitation of veterans have added impetus to rehabilitation counseling.

Today, private agencies augment state and local rehabilitation programs. Among some of the more prominent private rehabilitation groups are the American Red Cross, the National Tuberculosis Society, Goodwill Industries of America, and state Bureaus of Vocational Rehabilitation.

Training requirements for rehabilitation counseling are demanding. The rehabilitation counselor needs to have a good working knowledge of the principles of psychology, sociology, social work, law, education, medicine, and psychiatry. Working with handicapped clientele, the rehabilitation counselor's major roles are in the assessment of the capabilities of his clientele, the development of plans of action, the utilization of community resources, and the coordination of the rehabilitation process.

Teamwork is an essential part of the rehabilitation process. The rehabilitation counselor is often coordinator of the process, and therefore needs to work effectively and cooperatively with other professionals representing different disciplines.

The most frequently observed disabilities seen by the rehabilitation counselors have been summarized by Lofquist (1957). Among these are the diabetic, the amputee, the heart patient, the hypertensive patient, the paraplegic, the cancer patient, and the skin patient. Added to this list are the disabilities related to vision, hearing, tuberculosis, and mental health.

A very important objective of rehabilitation counseling is vocational placement. In most rehabilitation agencies, the placement of the client health.
in a job for a reasonable time is regarded as the single most important criterion for successful rehabilitation. The counseling process is intended to facilitate successful job placement while simultaneously focusing on problems of personal and social adjustment.

Realistically, most rehabilitation counselors' major roles and functions involve occupational and vocational activities. Rehabilitation counselors, therefore, need a high level of expertise in matters pertaining specifically to work and work adjustment. The rehabilitation specialist is required to have a thorough knowledge of available occupational information, reference materials (e.g., *The Dictionary of Occupational Titles*), the use of psychological tests, community resources, and the vocational counseling process (Lofquist, 1957).

Characteristics of rehabilitation counselors

Sussman and Haug (1968), in a study of 324 rehabilitation counseling students, found the typical student to be white, male, under 30, middle class, with some previous experience with disability. The proportion of women entering rehabilitation counseling, approximately 32 percent, is higher than graduate students in general, approximately 18 percent. A high percentage of black students also enroll in rehabilitation programs.

Rehabilitation trainees have diverse educational and work experience backgrounds. Undergraduate fields of study vary widely, with the majority of them having majored in psychology, education, and humanities. More frequently than not, rehabilitation counseling students have worked in people-related fields before entering graduate school. For about one third of the students it was a second career. Financial support for students of rehabilitation from the Vocational Rehabilitation Administration has been quite good. Nearly half of the students surveyed received 90 percent or more of their graduate school expenses, with more than 75 percent receiving at least 50 percent (Sussman & Haug, 1968).

Crises intervention counseling

Crises counseling is a brief intervention used in emergency situations, wherein a person is experiencing some acute emotional problem, such as a depressive or anxiety reaction, generally associated with some specific environmental situation. Some examples of crises situations include a person threatening suicide, an anxiety attack (hyperventilation), a rape victim, a family quarrel, a depressive reaction associated with news of a divorce, and a drug overdose—to name only a few. Crises intervention is designed to reduce symptoms or simply bring a problem situation under control.

Often the strategy of crises counseling is to focus on modifying the environment or a specific event that activates the crisis. Sometimes this amounts to removing a person from the crises environment. Most often, however, counselors will help persons in crisis reinterpret their experience by correcting any misconceptions they may have about themselves and their situation. Tosi and Moleski (1975) developed a cognitive-behavioral model of crises intervention, which places a priority on helping persons correct family perceptions and ideas about the crises situation, to focus on self-control of emotional states, and to consider effective ways of coping and managing the environment.

Counselors doing crises intervention need to be particularly sensitive to the social, psychological, physiological, and behavioral aspects of the client's concern. The crises counselor needs to be able to recognize when other professionals, such as physicians, psychiatrists, and social workers, are needed to assist the client. Most often counselors functioning in agency or hospital settings may be asked to be part of a crises intervention team.

We believe that certain personal attributes of counselors contribute to their effectiveness in crises intervention. First, it is desirable for the counselor to assume a relatively calm posture and to provide an accepting psychological climate. Second, a counselor must be able to accurately assess the client's problems and take decisive therapeutic action in a brief time. Crises counseling is no place for the "wishy washy" counselor. Of great importance is that the counselor is able to develop rapport with the client quickly and, ultimately, help the client identify and use effective problem solving strategies. In some instances, counselors may use relaxation techniques to calm a client if talking about a problem does not bring relief. At other times, some psychotropic drugs administered by a physician or psychiatrist may be indicated.

Crises intervention counseling can make heavy emotional drains on counselors. Crises counselors may be required to work nights as well as days with little time to prepare for their clients.

The immediate goal of crises counseling is to ameliorate symptoms and to focus on "here and now" concerns. The counselor, however, will generally direct the client into long-term counseling if that is warranted. The beginning counselor may find the book *Psychiatric Treatment: Crises, Clinic, Consultation* by Rosenbaum and Beebe (1975) very helpful.

SUMMARY

Counselors function in many diverse settings. These settings are primarily educational, vocational rehabilitation, medical, or community mental health agencies.

Because of different expectations in each context, a counselor's activities may be varied. A counselor's activities may range from doing intensive one-to-one counseling or therapy to job placement, depending on the place of employment.

In this chapter we examined the counselor's role in dealing with major psychological disorders, marital, family, and sexual problems, rehabilitation, substance abuse, and crises intervention counseling. The intent of the chapter was to expose counselors-in-training to many of the methods used by practitioners in various specialties.

Counseling outcomes, issues, trends, and ethics

9

Is counseling effective? Is there evidence indicating that counseling works? What are some of the problems associated with evaluating the outcomes of counseling? Do conflicts of interest exist in evaluating the outcomes of counseling? This chapter is designed to explore those questions. Obviously, the "bottom line" is whether people's lives are improved through counseling.

Is counseling effective?

Studies of counseling and therapy outcome have increased over the past years for a number of reasons. One stimulus has been the controversial work carried out by Eysenck. Eysenck (1952, 1961, 1965, & 1966) identified 24 research studies involving 8,053 neurotic cases in which a wide variety of psychological treatments had been followed. In reviewing these reports, Eysenck found that two thirds of all neurotics who enter psychological treatment improve substantially within a two-year period. On the other hand, he found that an equal proportion (two thirds) of neurotics who never enter active treatment show improvement over about the same period. Eysenck concluded that since persons receiving medical care seem to make as much progress as people receiving psychological treatment, psychological treatment interventions do not seem to make much difference. Eysenck concluded that psychological procedures had not lived up to expectations or claims.

However, there were problems associated with Eysenck's work and many critics quickly arose to comment. Perhaps the most thorough of these reviews was carried out by Bergin (1971). Bergin identified significant flaws in Eysenck's methodology that served to reduce the impact of the work. For example, Bergin pointed out that Eysenck had used a very stringent set of criteria, which yielded the lowest possible improvement rate, that the clients across the various studies were not necessarily comparable, that the various studies lacked equivalent criteria of outcome, that there were large variations in the amount and quality of intervention received, there was considerable variation in the nature of onset and in the duration of the disturbance, definition of disorder and criteria for improvement were imprecise, there were differences in the duration and thoroughness of follow-up, recidivism, and finally, that medical treatment may in itself be a form of treatment.

Since the Eysenck work, Bergin (1971), Emrick (1975), Luborsky, Singer, and Luborsky (1975), Smith and Glass (1977), and others have reviewed the outcome literature and found, in general, that counseling and psychotherapy have a positive effect. The Smith and Glass (1977) review, in particular, presents interesting evidence that counseling works, at least to some extent. These authors inspected 1,000 outcome studies and thoroughly reviewed the findings of 375 controlled studies. Their findings for about 25,000 control and 25,000 treated clients across 375 studies and 833 variables show that on the average a client receiving counseling or therapy was better off than 75 percent of the untreated controls after treatment. In other words, in general, as a function of psychological treatment the average client will move from the 50th to the 75th percentile when compared to the average untreated control subject. The clients' mean age was 22 years, they were involved in treatment for 12 hours, were being treated by professionals possessing about 3½ years of experience, and were followed up about 3¾ months after the treatment.

To take a more specific look at the content of counseling and therapy outcome, Smith and Glass (1977) focused on various types of measured outcome. For example, they found, for a variety of fear and anxiety variables across a number of studies, that the average client was better able to cope with fear or anxiety after treatment than 83 percent of the control subjects. For self-esteem variables, it was found that the average client showed more positive benefit than 82 percent of the untreated controls. For adjustment variables, the results indicated that the average client post-treatment tends to be better off than 71 percent of the control subjects. The adjustment variables were measures of personal functioning, defined by such things as hospitalization, alcoholic or various illegal activities. Finally, for school or work achievement variables, Smith and Glass found that the average client tends to be more productive than 62 percent of the untreated control subjects.

It must be kept in mind that the studies used in reviewing the above four outcome areas were not comparable on a number of other variables (type of counseling/therapy, duration, counselor/therapist experience, and the like). This fact clearly limits the impact of the Smith and Glass study. However, these data do indicate to some extent that counseling and therapy are effective and associated with positive client benefit.

In another interesting analysis, Smith and Glass (1977) looked at outcome studies evaluating the effectiveness of different types of counseling and therapy. Few outcome reviews have attempted such an analysis. The relative rank of some of the approaches evaluated are reported below. Keep in mind that the studies used to review the outcome effectiveness of the counseling approaches were not comparable on a number of variables, and for this reason the relative ranks reported must be viewed with caution. However, without question the outcome findings suggest positive client benefit for a variety of counseling or therapy approaches. In other words, all the treatment approaches "work," at least to some extent.

Wolpe's Systematic Desensitization ranked first. After this form of counseling treatment the average client was found to be "better off" than 82 percent of the control subjects. Ellis's Rational-Emotive (RET) approach ranked second. Under RET the average client was judged to be healthier than 78 percent of the untreated subjects. The Adlerian approach finished third, with the average client found to be better off than 76 percent of the control subjects. Rogers's Client-Centered approach and Stampfl's Implosive approach tied for the fourth rank with 74 percent. Rank five was filled by the Psychodynamic approach, with a 72 percent rating. Eclectic approaches that tend to be psychodynamic in nature notched the sixth rank, with a 68 percent rating. The Gestalt approach ranked seventh, with a 60 percent rating. Again the evidence indicates that with some variability the different approaches to counseling and therapy tend to promote positive client benefit.

One other simple fact from the Smith and Glass (1977) data needs to be mentioned here. Smith and Glass explored the interesting notion, espoused by many psychologists, that behavioral approaches to counseling are more effective in terms of outcome and client benefit than the nonbehavioral approaches. To investigate this issue, Smith and Glass (1977) looked at outcome studies across the behavioral approaches (implosion, systematic desensitization, and behavior modification) and across the nonbehavioral approaches (client-centered, rational-emotive, Adlerian, transactional analysis, psychodynamic, and eclectic). Clients under the behavior approaches were seen on the average about two months after treatment to determine outcome effects. Clients under the nonbehavioral approaches were followed up about five months (on the average) after treatment. The findings indicate that after summing the studies for the behavioral and nonbehavioral approaches, no difference in outcome effectiveness appears. Behavioral approaches may be more effective for certain clients with specific types of problems. Similarly, nonbehavioral approaches may be more effective for certain clients with specific types of problems. However, the general notion that behavioral approaches are more effective or superior to nonbehavioral approaches does not "hold water."

In summary, a number of reviews across numerous outcome studies rather clearly indicate that counseling and therapy has a positive effect on clients. Stated more simply, despite its detractors, the overall evidence indicates it works.

Problems in outcome research

Much of the outcome research until recently has been primarily concerned with the gross effects of counseling and therapy, i.e., does it work. The research in many respects has assumed a uniform effect or impact with little regard for specificity of variables, such as type of treatment, goals of treatment, counselor/therapist training, duration of counseling, client problem, outcome criteria, and the like. Currently, researchers (Kiesler, 1966, 1968, 1971; Paul, 1966, 1967; Bergin, 1971) tend to agree that future outcome work needs to ask if any particular counselor and type of counseling is effective for a client with a particular problem in a specific situation.

Another troublesome issue associated with outcome research has to do with the concept of spontaneous remission. Spontaneous remission is the tendency for individuals to show improvement without formal treatment. This spontaneous improvement rate of about 30 percent varies considerably across different types of illnesses, and suggests that some counseling and therapy processes tend to occur naturally (Bergin, 1971). Bergin (1971) points out that true spontaneous improvement is difficult to assess because people with problems tend to seek help informally from other than psychological helpers, such as doctors, ministers, family, and friends. People may also try some form of self-help, such as thinking about things, trying a different behavior, denying the problem, or some form of prayer. As Bergin (1971) points out, these are forms of coping behavior that attempt to reduce unhappiness. The point being made is that some counseling effect may be gained by people who have not been exposed to formal counseling treatment (Bergin, 1971). This simply means that subjects included in control groups in counseling outcome research tend not to be controls at all, but recipients of informal and self-help forms of treatment that tend to be therapeutic in nature (Bergin, 1971). Thus, spontaneous improvement, self-help, or informal help from a nonpsychological helper greatly confounds the role of control groups in outcome research.

A third problem associated with outcome work has to do with the effects of bad counseling. We previously mentioned that certain counselor personality qualities (empathy, warmth, and genuineness) tend to be associated with positive client benefit. Evidence indicates that these counselor characteristics are linked to positive client benefit across a variety of counselors, regardless of theoretical orientation (Truax & Mitchell, 1971). However, the reverse also seems to hold. Evidence shows that counselors low on empathy, nonpossessive warmth, and genuineness account for a vast majority of the deteriorated cases (Truax & Mitchell, 1971). While the findings are not clear, they suggest that more disturbed clients seem to contribute to the deterioration effect (Bergin, 1971). Thus, some clients after treatment will be worse than they were before treatment. For research purposes, the impact of the deterioration effect on subjects in the experimental treatment groups is similar to the impact of spontaneous improvement on the subjects in the control groups. Subjects showing harmful effects from counseling treatment will tend to counterbalance or offset the positive benefit displayed by other clients as a function of treatment. On the average, for an experimental treatment group, differences between clients showing positive gain and clients showing deterioration are virtually wiped out (Bergin, 1971). On this issue there is clearly a need for research on the interaction of counselor and client characteristics as they are linked to harmful effects of deterioration (Bergin, 1971).

A fourth problem area for outcome research is related to the measurement of change as a function of the treatment. Various personality measures are generally used to assess a number of person variables, but little effort is made to assess environmental conditions or the interaction of person-environment variables. It is usually assumed that personality traits (dependency, anxiety, achievement, dominance) are the prime determinants of behavior. Outcome research needs to recognize that human behavior tends to be influenced by many determinants in the person and in the situation. Thus, a focus on person variables alone is likely to lead to predictions and generalizations of limited value (Mischel, 1977).

Finally, an urgent need exists for reliable (consistent) and valid (accurate) criterion measures for evaluating the effects of various counseling treatments upon different problems and client types. Outcome evaluation needs to be based on overt behaviors and internal states of experience. Both contribute important outcome data. Below are some outcome criteria reported by Bergin (1971) that to some extent have proven to be worthwhile in counseling and therapy outcome research.

1. Assessment interviews use a standard interview evaluation of client status before, during, and after counseling and therapy.
2. Client self-evaluation with checklists and self-ratings have frequently been used. Many of these scales are homemade and have reliability and validity problems; but some have been standardized and tend to be more useful, e.g., the Leary Interpersonal Checklist and the Gough and Heilbrun Adjective Checklist.
3. Counselor rating scales have some reliability and validity problems, but are still of some value.
4. The assessment or observation of covert behavior has proven useful in determining whether or not a specific behavior has been acquired or eliminated as a function of treatment.
5. A number of different tests and inventories have been found to be useful in assessing client change:
    a. Personality inventories used include the Minnesota Multiphasic Personality Inventory (MMPI), the California Psychological Inventory (CPI), the Sixteen Personality Factor Questionnaire (16PF), and the Personal Orientation Inventory (POI).
    b. Self-concept measures of self-esteem and self-acceptance are frequently used, e.g., Kelly's Role Construct Repertory Test.
    c. Projective techniques exploring the client's fantasy life have modest use, e.g., the Thematic Apperception Test and the Rorschach Inkblot Test.
    d. Interest inventories have been found to be of value in measuring client change, e.g., the Strong-Campbell Interest Inventory (SCII), the Kuder Occupational Interest Inventory (KOII), and the Self Directed Search (SDS).
    e. Some attempt is being made to use mood scales to assess counseling outcomes, e.g., Wessman-Ricks Mood Scales. The thought is that people may be characterized by their moods and that different people tend to have different mood patterns.

6. Various measures of self-regulation and self-control have been used effectively in outcome research, e.g., measures of temporal perspective, delaying gratification, long-range planning, and goal orientation.
7. Peer ratings seem to be making a comeback as a measure of client change. A limitation of this technique is that it requires a situation in which peers have regular opportunities to observe each other's behavior.

Some recent promising work has attempted to become more specific in evaluating the outcome of counseling and therapy. A number of investigators (Rogers, Gendlin, Kiesler, & Truax, 1967; Truax & Carkhuff, 1967; Carkhuff, 1972; Carkhuff & Berenson, 1977) have made good progress in linking counselor personality qualities and positive client benefit. Other behavioral researchers (Lazarus, 1976; Lazarus & Wilson, 1976; Wolpe, 1973, 1976; Ullmann & Krasner, 1965) are studying what specific treatments are most effective with specific behavioral problems. Analogue outcome research (Heller, 1971) carried out in a laboratory setting has been able to control and define more specifically than before a variety of relevant variables. For example, one such model has applied social psychological concepts to counseling and therapy on the assumption that in many respects counseling is a social influence process. These and other new approaches to counseling outcome research are attempting to be more specific in the research task by explicitly defining control groups, looking at the effects of good counselors, and using reliable and valid criterion measures. They are attempting to ask hard questions about what treatments are effective under what conditions.

Conflicts of interest

All counseling and psychotherapy is designed to move the client toward some kind of standard or norm. Strupp and Hadley (1977) suggest that there are three major vantage points or norms from which counseling and therapy outcome may be judged, i.e., society, the individual client, and the mental health professional. Usually treatment evaluations are based on one of these perspectives, namely the client's sense of well being. From its vantage point, society is primarily interested in social control, i.e., behavior stability, predictability, and conformity to the folkways and mores. Recently, society has shown increased interest in outcome studies mainly because of the trend for third-party (insurance) payments for mental health care (Strupp & Hadley, 1977). As insurance companies, taxpayers, and the possibility of national health insurance begin to sponsor and support therapeutic treatment, interest in the definition, evaluation, and treatment accountability grows. Social agencies want understandable information that what they are paying for is worthwhile within a standard framework of behavior stability and predictability.

The individual client is mainly interested in being happy, feeling content, or experiencing a sense of well being (Strupp & Hadley, 1977). It is with increased frequency that clients enter counseling for the purpose of improving self-awareness, finding a meaning in life, or to be more self-accepting. Within this framework, concern lies with the client's emotions, affect, or feeling state.

From the mental health professional's vantage point, the goal is to have the client move toward health (Strupp & Hadley, 1977), defined in terms of some theoretical model of personality. Such models have been developed by Rogers, Freud, Ellis, Carkhuff, Glasser, and others. These models were reviewed in the theories section of this text. For many professionals the belief in or commitment to a particular theoretical model is vital to successful treatment.

Thus, according to Strupp and Hadley (1977), the outcome of counseling and therapy may be viewed differently, depending upon the vantage point from which the outcome is evaluated. No conflict arises as long as each view or perspective is considered separately. However, if we evaluate the outcome of counseling and therapy from more than one of the perspectives, conflict easily develops. For example, a person may define himself or herself as mentally healthy independent of the mental health profession's opinion. A variety of other combinations exist, suggesting conflict in mental health judgments and in the evaluation of counseling/therapeutic outcomes. According to Strupp and Hadley (1977) clients may be viewed as mentally healthy or mentally disturbed and the counseling and therapeutic treatment as positive or negative in impact depending upon the perspective used to evaluate the outcome, that is, individual goals, mental health expectations, or societal expectations. Therefore, in order to get the best picture of an individual's mental health, one should evaluate all three dimensions (society's, the individual's, and the professional's view) (Strupp & Hadley, 1977).

Counseling in social institutions

We are in the last two decades of the 20th century, and it is clear that counseling is a major institutional effort in our society. The fact that counseling is "big business" is reflected in the extensive range of human services that is available in a wide variety of agencies. Counselors can be found in large numbers in institutional practice, community agencies, private practice, and, very significantly, active in research efforts and program development.

As noted in Chapter 1, counseling as a social institution has to a large extent replaced other human resource support systems. Counselors seem to be the person of first choice to go to for help for a large number of individuals in our society, in comparison with former times when family members, clergy, and sometimes people in the medical profession tended to fulfill this function. A consequence of this impact on society, the importance of counselors to the well-functioning individual in the social system, is a very large financial investment, in training, paying for services, and creating institutions in which counselors can work. The counseling field is becoming increasingly formalized and the functions within it are becoming increasingly more differentiated. The present chapter discusses the trend toward formalization and its implications.

Kinds of counselors

As noted in an earlier chapter, counselors are frequently "hyphenated" in title. They are school-counselors, rehabilitation-counselors, counseling-psychologists, and only occasionally just counselors. These various counselors differ in very significant ways, yet have substantial overlap and similarity in terms of their training, the settings in which they work, the skills that they possess, the typical clientele, and what they choose to emphasize by way of their professional service goals.

School counselors. Variously called school counselors, guidance counselors, counseling specialists, and sometimes just counselors, these individuals are usually found in the public schools, K through 12. Their work usually focuses on programming, scheduling, some personal adjustment counseling for students, consultation with other professionals, such as teachers and administrators, and the administration of school-wide or systemwide testing programs. Their training typically is beyond the master's degree and sometimes the doctorate. They usually come to their work with a background of public school teaching and undergraduate training in education. They typically have considerable sophistication in the area of assessment, interviewing, guidance practices, and human development. While their emphasis may vary from one setting to another, they tend to have some background in psychology or educational psychology. General goals for clients are to help them function effectively, to make valid decisions, and to minimize developmental disruptions. It is sometimes hard to know whether the clients of school counselors are the individual students in the institutions or the institutions themselves. By self-definition, both the students and the counselors tend to view the students as the principal clientele; the institutions benefit as a consequence.

Rehabilitation counselors. Rehabilitation counselors generally have a master's degree, although occasionally they have a doctorate. These professionals are found normally in settings focusing on retraining individuals who have suffered some psychological or physical handicap, or both. The emphasis is on assessment, retraining, and counseling support. Rehabilitation counselors usually have a background in one of the behavioral sciences as undergraduates, although some come to the field from education. Their master's degree focuses on special topics, such as testing assessment, interviewing, counseling, personality development, special aspects of physical disability or behaviors, and job placement.

The clientele served are similar in type to those of school counselors—institutions and the individuals served by those institutions. Productive reemployment and the reduction of disruption resulting from disability are emphasized as goals.

Counseling psychologists. Counseling psychologists tend to be found in a wide range of institutions generally dealing with older adolescents and adults. Counseling psychologists can be found in university settings, community mental health agencies, and, more frequently these days, in private practice. The undergraduate background is typically in psychology, but this can vary broadly. The graduate training leading to the doctorate is a counseling psychology program, which focuses on providing a basic background in psychology with special skills added in understanding personality development, interviewing, career development, and assessment. Training emphasizes research skills and theoretical conceptions as well. The clientele is very diverse, depending upon the particular setting, and therefore becomes very difficult to specify succinctly.

The principal differences among these three kinds of counselors are in terms of the age of their clientele, the settings in which they work (ranging from the institutional public setting to the private or university setting, or both), population (which ranges from normal to abnormal in terms of physical and psychological development), and a focus on remediation as opposed to facilitation.

Professionalism

A profession is a "vocation requiring knowledge of some department of learning or science." Using the above definition as a starting point, it is clear that counseling has moved into the professional realm. One reflection of this movement is the very sophisticated and complex professional counseling organizations that have been created.

A principal organization that affects more than just counselors is the American Psychological Association. This organization consists of approximately 50,000 members representing all the very diverse fields of psychology. Within the American Psychological Association, Division 17 (Counseling Psychology) represents counseling interests. This interest group consists of approximately 2,500 individuals who have designated themselves as counseling psychologists. They must meet certain minimal qualifications that the division has established before they are admitted into membership. Division 17 is very active in promoting counselor training, conducting convention programs of interest to counseling psychologists, and generally representing counseling psychology in the larger framework of psychology so that professional standards, ethical statements, accreditation of programs, and the like are developed with significant input from knowledgeable people in counseling psychology.

Another organization associated with counselors is the American Personnel and Guidance Association. This group consists mostly of people generically working in counseling related situations. The APGA consists of several subgroups, which vary in the degree to which they are related to counseling. Some of the groups that seem more clearly to have counseling related functions are the American College Student Personnel Association, the National Vocational Guidance Association, and the Association for Counselor Education and Supervision. However, many individuals in APGA have multiple division memberships and are represented in a variety of organizations.

Similar to the American Psychological Association, APGA represents the interests of counselors and tries to be sensitive to the issues involved in counseling services. It represents the interests of the public in counseling as well. To that end, APGA is concerned with ethics, training, and research in a manner similar to the American Psychological Association and Division 17 of APA. In fact, there is a considerable overlap of the membership of Division 17 of APA and the American Personnel and Guidance Association.

Professional organizations become professional partly as a result of their promulgation of ethical standards governing the behavior of people who identify themselves as members of the profession. In the counseling area, both the APGA and the APA have for many years had elaborate codes of ethical behavior governing their members. The APA publishes a case book of ethical standards governing the practices of psychologists in general, all of which would apply to counseling psychologists to some extent, and some of which apply in great detail.

Similarly, the APGA has published sets of ethical standards for its practitioners.

Ethical standards generally deal with the fair treatment of the clientele, proper presentation to the public in terms of one's professional preparation and qualifications, and descriptions of the appropriate use of tests, methods, and various other devices so that these are not misrepresented or misapplied. In general, ethics concern themselves with the treatment of clients in a manner that does not exploit them for private gain by the professional. Because clients in a professional relationship are highly vulnerable to abuse (Osipow, 1970) such protection is necessary.

Besides ethical standards, the societies have means available to apply sanctions to members who violate them. For example, the APA has a Board of Social and Ethical Responsibility, which has a subcommittee on ethics. This subcommittee formally hears any complaints made about the ethical practices of psychologists who belong to the APA.

More recently, ethical standards applied to research settings have been developed, partly as a result of pressures from federal agencies for the humane and appropriate treatment of individuals in research settings, and partly because research activities have come to be recognized as an area in which an individual can be mistreated and exploited. In addition to the federal guidelines for the proper treatment of subjects in experiments, the APA has published a book (1973) dealing with ethical matters associated with using human beings in research.

In addition to the ethics applied to research and practice, the American Psychological Association publishes a book on standards for the use and development of tests, which also has ethical implications in that instruments not meeting the standards prescribed would not be considered to be ethically used in clinical or counseling kinds of situations. Also, the APA has recently published a statement on standards for the practice of professional psychology for agencies and for other specialty practices (APA, 1972).

Licenses and certification

Besides prescribing ethical standards, most of the professional organizations have for many years exerted pressure to formalize by law the qualifications needed to present oneself to the public as a counseling psychologist or as a counselor. By 1979 48 states and the District of Columbia had in effect a statute governing the practice of psychology. In some states this is a license; in some states it is a certificate. (The difference between the two is that a license generally refers to not only using the title of the profession, such as psychologist, but also prescribes certain practices in great detail. Certification restricts the use of a title, but is less specific in regard to the practices associated with that title.) The laws vary considerably from state to state and are implemented by Boards of Examiners of Psychology, which themselves vary in the way they regulate the practice of the profession. Counselors sometimes come under the laws applied to psychologists but sometimes do not. A current controversial issue is the degree to which people trained out of psychology departments but who possess an extensive psychological background are eligible for licensure or certification as psychologists. In reaction to this, legislatures in many states are considering separate counselor licensing laws; at least one state has passed such a law. Obviously, the practice of counselors and psychologists in many cases are very similar, if not identical.

Most states that require licensing first admit the candidate to the psychology examination on the basis of a credentials check (courses taken and degree earned) and then administer a written and oral examination to the candidate. Most states have some postdoctoral supervised period as a requirement as well.

Standards

As mentioned earlier, the American Psychological Association has published standards for professional practice for agencies and individuals (APA, 1977). These standards generally regulate the practices of the agencies with respect to confidentiality of records, appropriate training and supervision of the professionals employed in the agency, proper representation of their services to the public, adequate physical and financial sources to perform the services advertised, and the evaluation and valid use of techniques for public consumption.

Some states have licensing laws that describe specialty standards which go beyond licensing a generic psychologist or counselor. Where specialty standards exist in state laws, the candidate is able to obtain a license type of certification, which indicates further skill and advanced training in the specialty areas as long as the candidate conforms to the proper practice associated with it.

One of the prime reasons behind the extensive efforts of associations and state boards has been to regulate the entrance into psychology and counseling of individuals who profess to practice its skills. This regulation has become necessary in increasing degree because of the willingness of many insurance companies and the federal government to provide third-party reimbursement for the provision of psychological services. However, because of the great variety of psychological service deliverers that exist, the third-party payers have insisted upon ways to regulate and identify appropriate recipients of these monies. Licensing boards, certificates, and, more recently, the National Register for Health Providers in Psychology, have served to screen and document the eligibility of individuals who are appropriate recipients of a third-party reimbursement for the provision of psychological services. While these methods cannot assure competence per se, they do represent at least some external judgment with respect to the appropriateness of the professional training of the individual concerned. However, the whole movement of third-party reimbursement and the identification of appropriate recipients continues to be controversial and changing.

Training and credentialing

As noted before, a number of issues have emerged relating to the certification or licensing of people in the counseling profession. A number of terms associated with these issues need to be addressed in order to fully understand some of the current controversy that exists.

Accreditation versus licensing. There is some confusion in the minds of many about the difference between being a graduate of an accredited program and eligibility for a professional license. The difference is simple. Accreditation reflects the status of a training program. Accreditation reflects the approval by a third body that the concept and implementation of the training program is minimally acceptable professionally, that the qualifications of the faculty associated with the program are adequate, and that the resources of the institution associated with the training program are stable and sufficient. Accreditation does not imply that all graduates of the program possess appropriate competencies. This judgment is determined by licensing individual graduates. The licensing or certification process presumably examines the qualifications of individuals in respect to minimum standards for professional functioning. Ideally, licensing examinations would directly assess the competencies associated with successful professional practice. In fact, it is rare to be able to devise an examination that actually is field validated. Some of the few such examinations that do exist are airline pilot examinations, automobile drivers' tests, and a few others where there are very explicit behaviors associated with competency.

Professional competency in psychology is abstract, and, therefore, very difficult to assess through examination. Nevertheless, on the basis of background credentials and some general conceptual knowledge, licensing exams have been developed which at least provide *minimal* assurance that the licensed professional has some knowledge of the professional field, even though it does not assure the public that the individual can use that knowledge effectively in a professional situation. Part of the controversy that exists currently regarding licensing has to do with the issue that the licensing examinations do not measure competency to perform as a professional but rather emphasize academic knowledge.

A recent trend in psychology is the proposed creation of a National Commission on Credentialing and Training in Psychology. This commission would be charged with the development of standards associated with training programs in professional psychology that would provide guidance to licensing boards regarding the admission of candidates for examination (APA, 1978). Unfortunately, many of the most central issues associated with licensure problems remain unresolved despite the current status of the National Commission. Solutions to the controversy remain some years away.

The principal stresses and strains associated with the current controversies on licensing reside between individuals who have their degree in psychology programs, and who experience less difficulty in being admitted to examination for the license of psychology, than do individuals who have their degrees from departments of education, for example, or from other professional schools than psychology but whose training appears to be directed toward professional psychology. In many states these latter individuals have experienced considerable difficulty in persuading licensing boards that their training is appropriate to the profession of psychology, and that they should, therefore, be admitted to examination for the license as a psychologist. The response of the American Personnel and Guidance Association to this has been to create a counter-licensing movement for counselors, so that counselors can practice independent professional work without being subject to the supervision and approval of psychology licensing boards. Once again, the solution to this problem remains some years in the future.

Private practice

As noted earlier, a recent development of social significance is the great increase in the number of independent private practitioners in clinical and counseling psychology. Also noted, one of the major forces behind the private practice movement is the third-party reimbursement by insurance companies. The availability of insurance payments for the provision of psychological services has made it possible for many middle-income individuals to obtain the services of private psychological counselors for their concerns. Low-income families have traditionally used social agencies for needed psychological counseling services, and wealthy people could always pay for needed care, but middle-income families have frequently found it very difficult to obtain mental health services. Insurance reimbursement has made it possible for the full range of socioeconomic classes to hire the services of professional psychologists when needed. In any major city, one can find increasingly long lists of private professional psychologists in the Yellow Pages, some of whom are general practitioners and others are those who restrict their practice to specialty areas, such as children's services, marriage and family, problems of the adult, and the like.

Discussion of how one begins to engage in private practice is beyond the scope of this book. Many private practitioners have begun their work in part-time practice while in institutional practice or teaching positions. At some point, many of these individuals decide for a variety of reasons that they wish to terminate their institutional affiliation and move into the private practice arena full time. There are many pitfalls associated with independent private practice in professional psychology, and movement into this area should not be done without thorough investigation by the practicing professional. Psychologists are vulnerable to malpractice suits, as are other independent private practitioners, and one must be prepared for variations in case loads and income, the complexities of office leases, and the isolation from other professionals.

Private practice may or may not be the trend of the future, but it is clear that, increasingly, psychological services are being provided in this manner.

Continuing education for professionals

A critical issue facing all professional practitioners in psychological and mental health services has to do with how to keep up to date and avoid falling into stereotyped professional practices. The most reasonable solution to slow down the process of obsolescence has to do with a variety of continuing education activities.

Increasingly, state licensing boards are considering requiring professional practitioners to engage in a certain amount of formal continuing education to remain license-eligible. Most state licensing boards are at least canvassing licensees to find out what they have been doing to keep abreast of new professional developments.

The simplest and least formal continuing education activities involve reading periodicals, books, and engaging in informal conferences and meetings with colleagues. The prime periodicals for the counselor include the *Journal of Counseling Psychology*, published by the American Psychological Association; the *Counseling Psychologist*, published by Division 17 of APA; and the *Personnel and Guidance Journal*, published by the American Personnel and Guidance Association. Besides these three prime publications are others that counselors should be reading on a regular basis, which include, depending upon the counselor's specialty, periodicals in the career area: *Journal of Vocational Behavior, Journal of Applied Psychology, Personnel Psychology, Vocational Guidance Quarterly;* and publications in other specialty areas, such as *Measurement and Evaluation in Guidance, The American Psychologist, Counselor Education and Supervision;* as well as marriage and family oriented periodicals. It is difficult for most people to regularly read in a detailed manner more than a handful of periodicals, and thus, the practicing counselor must carefully select and make a commitment to some core number of periodicals, which are faithfully read. It is necessary to do so to remain knowledgeable about the research and theory in the field.

The question of what books to read is more difficult because books are not always well publicized to practitioners. One way to keep aware of new important books is to subscribe to *Contemporary Psychology*, a journal that publishes only book reviews. Another way to keep current is using the book review section of the *Personnel and Guidance Journal*. While the advantages of this method will be somewhat delayed, since the book reviews usually do not appear for almost a year after the book is published, it will still allow the practicing counselor to find books that otherwise might have been missed.

Informal (or more formal) professional groups exist for counselors. These groups organize along city, county or regional, and state lines. They sponsor informal luncheons, meetings, conventions, and workshops that counselors can attend in order to interact with their peers and be exposed to the latest developments, get feedback and new ideas, and generally get the kind of support the practitioners need but often do not get to support their work. Sometimes peer supervision groups are available to reduce the isolation of the practitioner.

Formal workshops are usually available to members of professional associations. These workshops are topic specific (e.g., using the MMPI, transactional analysis, career counseling, and the like). They may be as brief as an evening or they may be as long as several weeks. Most of them, however, last a day or two. They are usually technique oriented. In most instances, an expert is available, who teaches the theory and the method associated with the particular technique. Most counselors would find workshops of various types necessary and useful to keep abreast of current developments, and to provide the kind of learning stimulation that one desperately needs when immersed full time in professional practice.

Similar to workshops, but more formal and of a longer duration, are courses that are frequently available at local colleges and universities. Since most counselors are familiar with these offerings, and many of them have gone through the curriculum at their local institution, these actually may not be as helpful as the workshop format might be.

Finally, there are professional conventions that allow one to interact with others from around the country and learn what is going on in one's field on the national scene.

One final item of concern in continuing education for the counselor is retooling for a new specialty. Relatively few counselors retool to go into other specialty areas in the behavioral sciences; but a large number of individuals, trained in basic areas of research in the behavioral sciences, desire to shift into the applied professional areas. Increasingly, because of labor market changes, experimental psychologists, physiological psychologists, and others want to shift from their specialties into various counseling activities. Standards for the preparation of these people are not fully developed, but appear to be moving in the direction that will require systematic and integrated professional training programs—probably lasting a year or more, followed by a full-time internship. Clearly, it will become difficult for individuals to shift their professional emphasis from one specialty within the field to another.

New roles and settings for counselors

Counselors have traditionally worked with school- and college-age individuals in academic settings. More recently, counselors have expanded their roles into the general community, either in the community mental health area or in the private sector. Some counselors have also worked in industry and in personnel work. However, as noted earlier, more and more counselors are moving into new settings and contexts and working with new kinds of clientele. This section briefly describes some of the new kinds of clientele and settings in which counselors are found.

Aging. Perhaps one of the most prominent of the new directions has to do with work with the aging population. Whereas ten years ago there was an adolescent and youth boom, now the birth rate has dropped. As the adolescents and young people of ten years ago grow older, there will be a population bulge that will affect all society until the age group born in the 50s and 60s has passed from the scene. As the mean age of the population gets older, there will be more interest and concern in dealing with problems of aging and the aged. The current growth emphasis on midlife development reflects, to some extent, the anticipation of the bulge in the population moving into middle life. As the group gets older, the emphasis will be increasingly on the aging.

Also, there is simply more interest in the aged population since people are living longer and are healthier because of improvements in medical science. This increased longevity produces many problems of adjustment associated with the changes in social and personal status that accompanies aging. Counselors are finding themselves more and more called upon to work with the aged directly in terms of adjustment to limitations of aging, financial problems, anticipation of death, loss of dear friends and loved ones, and so on. In addition, counselors are being called upon to work with the aging individual's family members, children, in particular. To date, there is relatively little expertise associated with counseling concerning these issues. Counselors would be well advised to keep current regarding skills and concepts associated with counseling an aging population.

The counselor as a consultant

Counselors have increasingly worked in the area of consultation with other professionals. Not only do counselors provide individual face-to-face service for others, but they also work with other professionals, such as teachers, clergy, and lawyers, to help them understand the behavioral implications and behavioral problems of their own clientele. This is an expanding role for which counselors need to develop special skills and expertise.

One aspect of consultation has to do with environmental design. One of the trends in counseling has to do with considering the way the physical environment, as well as the social environment, is designed to eliminate, minimize, or reduce problems that people encounter as a function of artificial systems and devices. For example, high-rise dormitory living on campuses has created certain interpersonal social problems that might have been avoided had behavioral consultants been employed. Similarly, organizational design can increase or decrease interpersonal relationship difficulties in terms of role overload and organizational stress. To an increasing extent, counselors are becoming participants in environmental design.

Career counseling

While this is a venerable specialty for the counselor, it has begun to encompass some new directions. One new direction has to do with career counseling throughout the life span, as opposed to exclusive focusing on the point of entry, so that increasing attention is being paid to career counseling issues that are associated with midlife and beyond. The career development problems of women represent another new specialty area for the career counselor. Career counseling within organizations is still another newly expanding area for the counselor. Finally, the area of occupational mental health has largely been ignored by counselors but offers potential for considerable impact and opportunity for the career counselor (Osipow, 1979).

The counselor in the medical setting

Since counselors have traditionally worked in school settings, they have left medical settings to the clinical psychologists and the psychiatrists. However, to an increasing extent health or medical counseling has become another potential area for the future involvement of the counselor. The counselor's involvement in medical settings can range through pre- and post-abortion counseling, drug abuse counseling, counseling regarding disability and aging, genetic counseling, planning family size, and the holistic health movement. This is, again, another area largely neglected by counselors who have considerable skills to offer.

Counseling in legal settings

While counselors cannot be law practitioners, they can and do participate in situations in which clients are disturbed about potential legal issues. In such settings, counselors may work effectively with legal advisors to help minimize some of the stress and anxiety associated with a variety of legal proceedings. Very few counselors currently function in this kind of role. Moreover, counselors can provide expertise in terms of expert witness testimony which, again, until now has relatively been neglected by counselors.

Counselors' role in social policy development

In a way similar to their functioning as environmental consultants, counselors can legitimately participate in developing social policies. Increasingly, counselors should and probably will become involved in governmental activities associated with the formulation of laws, policies, and programs designed to improve human functioning. Counselors can look to their professional associations to provide leadership in the way that access to these policy-making roles can be obtained.

Family and marriage counseling

Counselors have been doing family and marriage counseling for years, although most marriage and family counseling has been conducted by social workers and clinical psychologists. One related activity in which counselors could function but have not emphasized has to do with the training of people to become better parents. Along those lines, the approach termed *deliberate psychological education* and proposed by Mosher and Sprinthall (1971) is a logical approach to use in teaching good parenting, "spousing," and similar behaviors. Counselors who provide these services effectively are likely to be in demand in the future.

Human resource needs for counselors

The question arises about the demand and the supply of professional counselors. It is difficult to anticipate the need for counseling in the future, because counseling is a need generated by the profession itself to the degree that the services noted earlier are provided and promoted by counselors. This is not an exploitative kind of promotion, but rather one that fulfills significant human needs and enhances the quality of life. To the degree that those services are provided (and paid for), counselors will be in increased demand. It is very difficult, therefore, to indicate the degree to which there is not an oversupply of counselors. What is clear is that at the moment there is an oversupply of counselors desiring employment in particular kinds of institutions, such as schools. However, the private sector counselor appears to be in demand—particularly where skills involving personal counseling, marriage and family counseling, and life-span counseling are offered.

Counselors tend to be concentrated in urban areas, similar to other professionals, but probably are more widely available in small towns and rural settings than many other mental health specialists. Therefore, in some respects, counselors provide services not readily provided by other mental health professionals in certain areas of the country.

One concern about counseling as a profession that needs to be addressed has to do with the problem of counselor "burn out." This is the problem associated with the degree to which one can remain interpersonally sensitive and effective after long-term daily exposure to a wide range of human problems and misery. After a certain number of years, many counselors find that they begin to become less effective in their ability to relate sincerely and supportively to people. This "burn out" is a problem that must be addressed. It probably can be moderated, if not eliminated, by counselor support groups of various types, professional associations, opportunities for temporary (or even permanent) workshifts, clientele changes, and so forth. However, anyone who seriously intends to practice counseling on a long-term basis needs to anticipate and deal with the problem of counselor burn out.

Problems in counseling

Counseling as a profession is subject to some of the same kinds of social concerns and problems as society at large. Three of the most typical problems that need to be addressed by the counseling profession are racism, sexism, and ageism.

Racism. While perhaps to a somewhat lesser extent than some other professions are guilty of racist practices, counseling remains essentially a field dominated by whites. One cannot find an equitable proportion of minority group counselors nor, until recently, at least, has there been any serious attention paid to the development of skills, methods, concepts, and interventions that might be most appropriate in responding to the concerns of minority group members. A literature has begun to develop, which describes the degree to which certain methods may appropriately be used with minority group members. As this literature becomes increasingly well established and defined, better and more effective skills should be available for a wider range of our population. Some of these concepts have been proposed and described in various articles by counselors and psychologists, such as Sue and Sue (1977), Sue (1977), Sue (1975), Pederson (1977), and Ivey (1977).

One of the procedures that can be followed in training programs to enhance our ability to function effectively with minorities is to develop seminars, courses, and practicum opportunities that allow exposure to minority group members and their special problems. Exposure of students to minority group professionals who can teach nonminority group members some of the skills that will improve ability to relate effectively with minority group members is also useful.

What needs to be expunged is the potentially racist attitude in which skills and methods used with minority clients are based on majority white clients without the recognition that there are many cross-cultural nuances and subtleties overlooked by those majority based approaches.

Sexism. Many of the same problems described as concerning racism are equally relevant concerning sex discrimination. While many counselors are females, to a surprising extent the attitudes and methods used by both male and female counselors tend to represent a male-oriented culture. To some extent, then, counselors have inappropriately and all too frequently exerted an inappropriate but subtle influence on their female clients to follow sex-stereotyped occupations—to subordinate their desires to the male-oriented and male-dominated culture, and to engage in stereotypic feminine behaviors. What is important for counselors to recognize in the area of sexism is that, while certain social codes may predominate regarding sex roles, there is sufficient variation in the range of behaviors desired and exhibited by males and females in our culture to warrant a fully open attitude on the part of counselors to the choices and range of behavior alternatives that males and females possess. Sexism not only affects females (although most of the attention has been paid to the impact of sexism on females), but it also effects males because it restricts the range of behaviors open to males in a way analogous to the way sexism restricts female-role alternatives. Sexism has deleterious effects on males in terms of their psychological and physical health, as well as in terms of restricting the family roles, the job roles, and overall behaviors that males can appropriately consider from a sexist perspective.

However, several recent publications have focused on counseling women (e.g., Osipow, 1975; Harway & Astin, 1977; Division 17 of APA, 1978; Harmon, Birk, Fitzgerald & Tanney, 1978).

Ageism.   While ageism is a relatively new notion, it is seen in the work of the counselors largely in the sense that they have neglected the problems of the aged. Counselors have assumed that it would be more productive to work with younger clientele, because when one is effective in altering the behavior of a young client the impact in terms of years of change is significant. With an older client, who has lived most of his or her life, such impact is considerably less. That, to some extent, is probably why little expertise and few methods have been developed in working with the older client.

Ageism has had another, more subtle, impact on counseling, in that young counselors have tended to be perceived as effective while older counselors have sometimes had some difficulty in gaining employment working with young clients. Though this is not a universal problem, it means there is some loss of expertise in wisdom a counselor can obtain throughout a worklife should such age discrimination in employment of counselors continue.

Relations with other professions

As noted before, many individuals in professional specialties work with clients the way counselors do. Clinical psychologists, psychiatrists, and social workers are the most prominent examples. Relations have not always been the best among the mental health professionals because, to some extent, they are competing for clients and social resources. Furthermore, they often have a considerably different conception and viewpoint about human behavior and the proper role of the mental health professional. Counselors usually are among the least powerful politically and socially—at least compared with clinical psychologists and psychiatrists. This has led to considerable conflict in what is viewed as the proper scope of impact, methods that can be used, licensure regulations, sources of reimbursement, areas of authority, and independent practice. In this respect, controversy and conflict among the professions appear to be something that will continue, because each group feels it has a significant and distinctive role to perform that is impinged upon by the other professional groups. In the long-term interest of both the professional groups and the consuming public, however, it is desirable that the controversy and conflict among these professional areas be eliminated, or at least minimized. The most reasonable vehicles to accomplish this, probably, are the various professional societies representing the interests of the various groups.

SUMMARY

This chapter has considered some of the general issues, trends, and ethical considerations associated with counseling as a profession. To that end, we have reviewed a number of the most recent developing trends in the profession, as well as professional organizations, issues concerning licensure and certification, and continuing education. It is clear that counseling as a profession is here to stay. It also is clear that counselors will become increasingly important and have greater impact on a wider range of clientele. It is also clear that, because of this great impact and durability, counseling will become increasingly professionalized and more demanding of its practitioners.

References

Chapter 1

Asa, L. F.   Interview behavior and counselor personality variables. *Counselor Education and Supervision*, 1967, *6*, 324–330.

Bergin, A. E. & Garfield, S. L. (Eds.).   *Handbook of psychotherapy and behavior change: An empirical analysis.* New York: Wiley, 1971.

Beutler, L. E., Johnson, D. T., Neville, C. W., Jr., Elkins, D., & Jobe, A. M.   Attitude similarity and therapist credibility as predictors of attitude change and improvements in psychotherapy. *Journal of Consulting and Clinical Psychology*, 1975, *43*, 90–91.

Carkhuff, R. R.   *Helping and human relations: A primer for lay and professional helpers* (Vols. 1, 2). New York: Holt, Rinehart & Winston, 1969.

Dole, A. A., & Nottingham, J.   Beliefs about human nature held by counseling, clinical, and rehabilitation students. *Journal of Counseling Psychology*, 1969, *16*, 197–202.

Donnan, H. H., & Harlan, G.   Personality of counselors and administrators. *Personnel and Guidance Journal*, 1968, *47*, 228–231.

Dowling, T. H., & Frantz, T. T.   The influence of facilitation relationships on imitative behavior. *Journal of Counseling Psychology*, 1975, *22*, 259–263.

Fromm, E.   *Escape from freedom.* New York: Holt, Rinehart & Winston, 1941.

Henry, W. E., Sims, J. H., & Spray, S. L.   *The fifth profession.* San Francisco: Jossey Bass, 1971.

Heppner, P. P., & Pew, S.   Effects of diplomas, awards, and counselor sex on perceived expertness. *Journal of Counseling Psychology*, 1977, *24*, 147–149.

Ivey, A. E.   *Microcounseling: Innovation in interview training.* Springfield, Ill.: Charles C. Thomas, 1971.

Jordaan, J., Myers, R. A., Layton, W. L., & Morgan, H. H.   *The counseling psychologist.* New York: Teachers College Press, 1968.

Kanfer, F. H., & Saslow, G.   Behavioral analysis: An alternative to diagnostic classification. *Archives of General Psychiatry*, 1965, 1229–38.

Kanfer, F. H., & Saslow, G.   Behavioral diagnosis. In C. Franks (Ed.), *Behavior therapy: appraisal and status.* New York: McGraw-Hill, 1969, 417–444.

Kazienko, L. W., & Neidt, C. O.   Self-description of good and poor counselor trainees. *Counselor Education and Supervision*, 1962, *1*, 106–123.

Krumboltz, J. D., Becker-Haven, J. F., & Burnett, K. F.   Counseling psychology. In M. R. Rosenweig & C. W. Porter (Eds.), *Annual Review of Psychology.* Palo Alto, Calif.: Annual Reviews, Inc., 1979.

LaCrosse, M. B.   Comparative perceptions of counselor behavior: A replication and extension. *Journal of Counseling Psychology*, 1977, *24*, 464–471.

LaCrosse, M. B.   Nonverbal behavior and perceived counselor attractiveness and persuasiveness. *Journal of Counseling Psychology*, 1975, *22*, 563–566.

Milk, D. H., & Abeler, N. Counselor needs for affiliation and nurturance as related to liking for clients and counseling process. *Journal of Clinical Psychology*, 1969, *33*, 317–326.

Osipow, S. H., & Walsh, W. B. *Strategies in counseling for behavior change.* Englewood Cliffs, N.J.: Prentice-Hall, 1970.

Parsons, F. *Choosing a vocation.* Boston: Houghton Mifflin, 1909.

Sanford, F. H. Creative self and the principle of habeus mentum. *American Psychologist*, 1955, *10*, 829–835.

Schmidt, L. D., & Strong, S. R. "Expert" and "inexpert" counselors. *Journal of Counseling Psychology*, 1970, *17*, 115–118.

Strong, S. R. Counseling: An interpersonal influence process. *Journal of Counseling Psychology*, 1968, *15*, 215–224.

Strong, S. R., & Schmidt, L. D. Expertness and influence in counseling. *Journal of Counseling Psychology*, 1970, *17*, 81–87. (a)

Strong, S. R., & Schmidt, L. D. Trustworthiness and influence in counseling. *Journal of Counseling Psychology*, 1970, *17*, 197–204. (b)

Strong, S. R., Taylor, R. G., Bratton, J. C., & Loper, R. G. Nonverbal behavior and perceived counselor characteristics. *Journal of Counseling Psychology*, 1971, *18*, 554–561.

Thompson, A. S., & Super, D. E. (Eds.). *The professional preparation of counseling psychologists report of the Greystone Conference.* New York: Bureau of Publications, Teachers College, 1964.

Tinsley, H. E., & Tinsley, D. J. Different needs, interests, and abilities, of effective and ineffective counselor trainees: Implications for counselor selection. *Journal of Counseling Psychology*, 1977, *24*, 83–86.

Toffler, A. *Future shock.* New York: Random House, 1970.

Truax, C. B. Effective ingredients in psychotherapy: An approach to unravelling the patient-therapist interaction. *Journal of Counseling Psychology*, 1963, *10*, 256–263.

Truax, C. B., & Carkhuff, R. R. *Toward effective counseling and psychotherapy: Training and practice.* Chicago: Aldine, 1967.

Truax, C. B., Carkhuff, R. R., & Kodman, F., Jr. Relationships between therapists-offered conditions and patient change in group psychotherapy. *Journal of Clinical Psychology*, 1965, *21*, 327–329.

Truax, C. B., Wargo, D. B., & Silber, L. Effects of high accurate empathy and non-possession warmth during group psychotherapy upon female institutionalized delinquents. *Journal of Abnormal Psychology*, 1966, *71*, 267–274.

Tyler, L. E. *The work of the counselor.* New York: Appleton-Century-Crofts, 1969.

Urban, H. B., & Ford, D. H. Some historical and conceptual perspectives in psychotherapy and behavior change. In A. E. Bergin & S. L. Garfield (Eds.), *Handbook of psychotherapy and behavior change.* New York: Wiley, 1971.

Whitehorn, J. C., & Betz, B. A study of psychotherapeutic relationships between physicians and schizophrenic patients. *American Journal of Psychiatry*, 1954, *3*, 321–333.

Zarski, J. J., Sweeney, T. J., & Barchihowski, R. S. Counseling effectiveness as a function of counselor social interest. *Journal of Counseling Psychology*, 1977, 24, 1–5.

Chapter 2

Adler, A. *The practice and theory of individual psychology.* New York: Harcourt, Brace & World, 1927.

Alexander, F. *Fundamentals of psychoanalysis.* New York: Norton, 1963.

Bandura, A. *Principles of behavior modification.* New York: Holt, Rinehart & Winston, 1969.

Bergin, A. E. The effect of dissonant persuasive communication upon changes in a self-referring attitude. *Journal of Personality*, 1962, 30, 423–438.

Bergin, A. E. *Toward a theory of human agency.* Provo, Utah: Brigham Young University Press, 1972.

Bordin, E. S. *Psychological counseling.* New York: Appleton-Century-Crofts, 1955.

Bordin, E. S. *Psychological counseling* (2nd ed.). New York: Appleton-Century-Crofts, 1968.

Boss, M. *Psychoanalysis and Daseinsanalysis.* New York: Basic Books, 1963.

Carkhuff, R. R. *Helping and human relations* (Vol. 1). New York: Holt, Rinehart & Winston, 1969a.

Carkhuff, R. R. *Helping and human relations* (Vol. 2). New York: Holt, Rinehart & Winston, 1969b.

Carkhuff, R. R. *Helping and human relationships* (Vols. 1, 2). New York: Holt, Rinehart & Winston, 1970.

Carkhuff, R. R., & Berensen, B. G. *Beyond counseling and psychotherapy.* New York: Holt, Rinehart & Winston, 1967.

Cartwright, R. A. A comparison of the response to psychoanalytic and client-centered psychotherapy. In L. A. Gottschalk & A. H. Auerbach (Eds.), *Methods of research in psychotherapy.* New York: Appleton-Century-Crofts, 1966.

Cash, T. F., Begley, P. J., McCown, D. A., & Weise, B. C. When counselors are heard but not seen: Initial impact of physical attractiveness. *Journal of Counseling Psychology*, 1975, 22, 273–279.

Cheney, T. Attitude similarity, topic importance, and psychotherapeutic attraction. *Journal of Counseling Psychology*, 1975, 22, 2–5.

Cohen, R. The effects of group interaction and progressive hierarchy presentation on desensitization of test anxiety. *Behavior Research and Therapy*, 1969, 7, 15–26.

Colby, K. M. *A primer for psychotherapists.* New York: Ronald Press, 1951.

Cooke, G. Evaluation of the efficacy of the components of reciprocal inhibition psychotherapy. *Journal of Abnormal Psychology*, 1968, 73, 464–467.

Dollard, J., & Miller, N. E. *Personality and psychotherapy.* New York: McGraw-Hill, 1950.

Dua, P. S.   Comparison of the effects of behaviorally oriented action and psychotherapy reeducation on introversion-extraversion, emotionality, and internal-external control. *Journal of Counseling Psychology*, 1970, *17,* 567–572.

Ellis, A.   *Reason and emotion in psychotherapy.* New York: Lyle Stuart, 1962.

Ellis, A.   *Growth through reason.* Palo Alto, Calif.: Science and Behavior Books, 1971.

Ellis, A.   *Humanistic psychotherapy: The rational emotive approach.* New York: Julian Press, 1973a.

Ellis, A.   Rational-emotive therapy. In R. Corsini (Ed.), *Current psychotherapies.* Itasca, Ill.: F. E. Peacock, 1973b.

English, J.   *The effects of reality therapy on elementary age children.* Paper for the California Association of School Psychologists and Psychometrists, Los Angeles, 1970.

Erikson, E.   *Childhood and society.* New York: W. W. Norton, 1950.

Eysenck, H. J.   *The biological basis of personality.* Springfield, Ill.: Charles C Thomas, 1967.

Eysenck, H. J.   *The scientific study of personality.* London: Routledge & Kegan Paul, 1952.

Eysenck, H. J., & Beech, H. R.   *Counter-conditioning and related methods.* In A. E. Bergin & S. L. Garfield (Eds.), *Handbook of psychotherapy and behavior change: An empirical analysis.* New York: Wiley, 1971.

Eysenck, H. J., & Eysenck, S. B.   *The structure and measurement of personality.* San Diego, Calif.: Robert R. Knapp, 1969.

Folkins, C. H.   Temporal factors and the cognitive mediators of stress reaction. *Journal of Personality and Social Psychology*, 1970, *14,* 173–184.

Folkins, C. H., Lawson K. D., Opton, F. M., Jr., & Lazarus, R. S.   Desensitization and the experimental reduction of threat. *Journal of Abnormal Psychology*, 1968, *73,* 100–113.

Frank, J. D.   *Persuasion and healing.* New York: Schocken Books, 1963.

Frankl, V. E.   *Man's search for meaning.* Boston: Beacon Press, 1962.

Garfield, S. L., & Bergin, A. E.   Therapeutic conditions and outcome. *Journal of Abnormal Psychology*, 1971, *77,* 108–114.

Geer, J. H., Davison, G. C., & Gatchel, R. L.   Reduction of stress in humans through non-veridical perceived control of aversion stimulation. *Journal of Personality and Social Psychology*, 1970, *14,* 731–736.

Gendlin, E. T.   Experiential psychotherapy. In R. Corsini (Ed.), *Current psychotherapies.* Itasca, Ill.: F. E. Peacock, 1973.

Gendlin, E. T.   Focusing. *Psychotherapy: Theory, Research, and Practice.* 1969, 6.

Glasser, W.   *Mental health or mental illness?* New York: Harper & Row, 1961.

Glasser, W.   *Reality therapy.* New York: Harper & Row, 1965.

Glasser, W.   *Schools without failure.* New York: Harper & Row, 1969.

Glasser, W., & Zunin, L. M.   Reality therapy. In R. Corsini (Ed.), *Current psychotherapies.* Itasca, Ill.: F. E. Peacock, 1973.

Goldstein, A.   Behavior therapy. In R. Corsini (Ed.), *Current psychotherapies.* Itasca, Ill.: F. E. Peacock, 1973.

Goldstein, A. P.   *Psychotherapeutic attraction.* New York: Pergamon Press, 1971.

Goldstein, A. P., Heller, L., & Sechrest, L. B.   *Psychotherapy and the psychology of behavior change.* New York: Wiley, 1966.

Grinker, R. R., Sr., MacGregor, H., Selan, L., Lein, A., & Kohrman, J.   *Psychiatric social work: A transactional case book.* New York: Basic Books, 1961.

Hawer, R. N.   Reality therapy in the classroom. *Dissertation Abstracts International,* 1971.

Horney, K.   *Neurosis and human growth.* New York: Norton, 1950.

Jung, C. G.   *Collected works, Vol. 16. The practice of psychotherapy.* New York: Pantheon, 1954.

Jordan, B. T., & Kempler, B.   Hysterical personality: An experimental investigation of sex-role conflict. *Journal of Abnormal Psychology,* 1970, *75,* 172–176.

Kaam, A. L. Van.   Counseling and psychotherapy from the viewpoint of existential psychology. In D. S. Arhickle (Ed.), *Counseling and psychotherapy: An overview.* New York: McGraw-Hill, 1967.

Kaul, T. J., & Schmidt, L. D.   Dimensions of interviewer trustworthiness. *Journal of Counseling Psychology,* 1971, *18,* 542–548.

Kelly, G. A.   *The psychology of personal constructs, Vol. I. A theory of personality, Vol. II. Clinical diagnosis and psychotherapy.* New York: W. W. Norton, 1955.

Kilty, K. M.   Some determinants of the strength of the relationship between affect and cognition. *Journal of Social Psychology,* 1970, *1,* 1–24.

Klein, M. H., Mathieu, P. L., Kiesler, D. J., & Gendlin, E. T.   *The experiencing scale manual.* Madison: University of Wisconsin Press, 1970.

Krumboltz, J. P. (Ed.).   *Revolution in counseling.* Boston: Houghton Mifflin, 1966.

Krumboltz, J. P., & Thoresen, C. E. (Eds.).   *Behavioral counseling: Cases and techniques.* New York: Holt, Rinehart & Winston, 1969.

Lazarus, A. A.   Behavior therapy in groups. In G. M. Gazda (Ed.), *Basic approaches to group psychotherapy and group counseling.* Springfield, Ill.: Charles C Thomas, 1968.

Luborsky, L., Chandler, M., Auerbach, A., Cohen, J., & Bachrach, H.   Factors influencing the outcome of psychotherapy: A review of the quantitative research. *Psychological Bulletin,* 1971, *75,* 145–185.

Luborsky, L., & Spence, D. P.   Quantitative research on psychoanalytic therapy. In A. E. Bergin & S. L. Garfield (Eds.), *Handbook of psychotherapy and behavior change: An empirical analysis.* New York: Wiley, 1971.

May, R.   *Psychology and the human dilemma.* Princeton, N.J.: Van Nostrand, 1967.

McCabe, G. E.   When is a good theory practical? *Personnel and Guidance Journal,* 1958, *37,* 47–52.

Meador, B. D., & Rogers, C. R.   Client-centered therapy. In R. Corsini (Ed.), *Current psychotherapies*. Itasca, Ill.: F. E. Peacock, 1973.

Moleski, R., & Tosi, D. J.   Comparative psychotherapy: Rational-emotive therapy versus systematic desensitization in the treatment of stuttering. *Journal of Consulting and Clinical Psychology*, 1976, *44*, 309–311.

Murray, E. J., & Jacobson, L. I.   The nature of learning in traditional and behavioral psychotherapy. In A. E. Bergin & S. L. Garfield (Eds.), *Handbook of psychotherapy and behavior change: An empirical analysis*. New York: Wiley, 1971.

Osipow, S. H., & Walsh, W. B.   *Strategies in counseling for behavior change*. Englewood Cliffs, N.J.: Prentice-Hall, 1970.

Patterson, C. H.   *Theories of counseling and psychotherapy* (2nd ed.). New York: Harper & Row, 1973.

Paul, G. L.   Insight versus desensitization in psychotherapy two years after termination. *Journal of Consulting Psychology*, 1967, *31*, 333–348.

Paul, G. L.   Outcome of systematic desensitization II: Controlled investigation of individual treatment, technique variations and current status. In C. M. Franks (Ed.), *Behavior therapy appraisal and status*. New York: McGraw-Hill, 1969.

Paul, G. L.   Two year follow-up of systematic desensitization in therapy groups. *Journal of Abnormal Psychology*, 1968. *73*, 119–130.

Peoples, V. Y., & Dell, D. M.   Black and white student preferences for counselor roles. *Journal of Counseling Psychology*, 1975, *22*, 529–534.

Pepinsky, H. B., & Pepinsky, P.   *Counseling: Theory and practice*. New York: Ronald Press, 1954.

Pepper, S. W.   *World hypotheses*. Berkeley: University of California Press, 1961.

Perls, F.   *Gestalt therapy verbatim*. Lafayette, Calif.: Real People Press, 1969.

Phillips, E. L., & Wiener, D. N.   *Short-term psychotherapy and structured behavior change*. New York: McGraw-Hill, 1966.

Rachman, S.   Systematic desensitization. *Psychological Bulletin*, 1967, *67*, 93–103.

Rank, O.   *Will therapy and truth and reality*. New York: Knopf, 1947.

Reardon, J. P., & Tosi, D. J.   The effects of rational stage directed therapy on self concept and reduction of psychological stress in adolescent delinquent females. *Journal of Clinical Psychology*, 1977, *33*, 1084–1092.

Rimm, D. C., & Litvak, S. B.   Self-verbalization and emotional arousal. *Journal of Abnormal Psychology*, 1969, *74*, 181–187.

Rogers, C. R.   *Client-centered therapy*. Boston: Houghton Mifflin, 1951.

Rogers, C. R.   *Counseling and psychotherapy*. Boston: Houghton Mifflin, 1942.

Rogers, C. R.   *On becoming a person*. Boston: Houghton Mifflin, 1961.

Rogers, C. R.   Significant trends in the client centered orientation. In D. Bower & L. E. Abt (Eds.), *Progress in clinical psychology* (Vol. 4). New York: Grune & Stratton, 1960.

Rotter, J. B.   *Social learning and clinical psychology*. Englewood Cliffs, N.J.: Prentice-Hall, 1954.

Sartre, J. P. *Being and nothingness.* New York: Philosophical Library, 1956.

Schmidt, L. D., & Strong, S. R. Attractiveness and influence in counseling. *Journal of Counseling Psychology,* 1971, *18,* 348–351.

Shapiro, D. A. Empathy, warmth, and genuineness in psychotherapy. *British Journal of Social and Clinical Psychology,* 1969, *8,* 350–361.

Shlien, J. M., & Zimring, F. M. Research directives and methods in client-centered therapy. In J. T. Hart & T. M. Tomlinson (Eds.), *New directions in client-centered therapy.* Boston: Houghton Mifflin, 1970.

Spiegel, S. B. Expertness, similarity, and perceived counselor competence. *Journal of Counseling Psychology,* 1976, *23,* 436–441.

Stampfl, T. G., & Levis, D. J. Essentials of implosive therapy: A learning theory-based psychodynamic behavioral therapy. *Journal of Abnormal Psychology,* 1967, *72,* 496–503.

Steffy, R. A., Meichenbaum, D., & Best, J. A. Aversive and cognitive factors in the modification of smoking behavior. *Behavior Therapy and Research,* 1970, *8,* 115–125.

Strong, S. R. An interpersonal influence process. *Journal of counseling psychology,* 1968, *15,* 215–224.

Strong, S. R. Causal attribution in counseling and psychotherapy. *Journal of Counseling Psychology,* 1970, *17,* 388–399.

Strong, S. R. Experimental laboratory research in counseling. *Journal of Counseling Psychology,* 1971, *18,* 106–110.

Strong, S. R. Pragmatic causal distortion in counseling. *British Journal of Guidance and Counseling,* 1975, *4,* 59–69.

Strong, S. R. Social psychological approach to psychotherapy research. In A. E. Bergin & S. L. Garfield (Eds.), *Handbook of psychotherapy and behavior change* (2nd ed.). New York: Wiley, 1979.

Strong, S. R. Verbal conditioning and counseling research. *Personnel and Guidance Journal,* 1964, *42,* 660–669.

Strong, S. R., & Dixon, D. N. Expertness, attractiveness, and influence in counseling. *Journal of Counseling Psychology,* 1971, *18,* 562–570.

Strong, S. R., & Schmidt, L. D. Trustworthiness and influence in counseling. *Journal of Counseling Psychology,* 1970, *17,* 197–204.

Strong, S. R., Taylor, R. G., Bratton, J. C., & Loper, R. G. Nonverbal behavior and perceived counselor characteristics. *Journal of Counseling Psychology,* 1971. *18,* 554–561.

Sullivan, H. S. *The interpersonal theory of psychiatry.* New York: W. W. Norton, 1953.

Thorne, F. C. *Personality: A clinical eclectic viewpoint.* Brandon, Vt.: Journal of Clinical Psychology Press, 1961.

Tinsley, H. E., & Harris, D. J. Client expectations for counseling. *Journal of Counseling Psychology,* 1976, *23,* 173–177.

Tosi, D. J. *Youth: Toward personal growth.* Columbus, Ohio: Charles E. Merrill, 1974.

Tosi, D. J., & Carlson, W. A. Dogmatism and perceived counselor attitudes. *Personnel and Guidance Journal,* 1970, *48,* 657–660.

Tosi, D. J., & Eshbaugh, D. M.   The personal beliefs inventory: A factor-analytic study. *Journal of Clinical Psychology*, 1976, *32*, 322–327.

Tosi, D. J., & Reardon, J. P.   The treatment of guilt through rational stage directed therapy. *Rational Living*, 1976, *11*, 8–11.

Truax, C. B., & Carkhuff, R. R.   *Toward effective counseling and psychotherapy*. Chicago: Aldine Press, 1967.

Truax, C. B., & Mitchell, K.   Research on certain therapist interpersonal skills in relation to process and outcome. In A. E. Bergin & S. L. Garfield (Eds.), *Handbook of psychotherapy and behavior change*. New York: Wiley, 1971.

Ullmann, L. P., & Krasner, L. (Eds.), *Case studies in behavior modification*. New York: Holt, Rinehart & Winston, 1965.

Valins, S.   The perception and labelling of bodily changes as determinants of emotional behavior. In P. Black (Ed.), *Physiological correlates of emotion*. New York: Academic Press, 1970.

Velten, E. A.   A laboratory task for induction of mood states. *Behavior Research and Therapy*, 1968, *6*, 473–482.

Williamson, E. G.   *Counseling adolescents*. New York: McGraw-Hill, 1950.

Wolpe, J.   *The practice of behavior therapy*. New York: Pergamon Press, 1969.

Wolpe, J.   *Psychotherapy by reciprocal inhibition*. Stanford, Calif.: Stanford University Press, 1958.

Wolpe, J., & Lazarus, A. A.   *Behavior therapy techniques*. New York: Pergamon Press, 1966.

Wolpin, M., & Rainer, J.   Visual imagery, expected roles and extinction as possible factors in reducing fear and avoidance behavior. *Behavior Research and Therapy*, 1966, *4*, 25–37.

Zeisset, R. M.   Desensitization and relaxation in the modification of psychiatric patients' interview behavior. *Journal of Abnormal Psychology*, 1968, *73*, 18–24.

Chapter 3

Alexander, F., & French, T. M.   *Psychoanalytic therapy: Principles and application*. New York: Ronald Press, 1946.

Alexik, M., & Carkhuff, R.   The effects of manipulation of client depth of self exploration upon high and low functioning counselors. *Journal of Clinical Psychology*, 1967, *23*, 210–212.

Bandura, A.   *Principles of behavior modification*. New York: Holt, Rinehart & Winston, 1969.

Bandura, A.   Behavior therapy and the models of man. *American Psychologist*, 1974, *29*, 859–869.

Barrett-Lennard, G.   Dimensions of therapist response as causal factors in therapeutic change. *Psychological Monographs*, 1962, *76*(562).

Bordin, E.   *Psychological counseling*, 2nd ed. New York: Appleton-Century-Crofts, 1968.

Brammer, L., & Shostrom, E. *Therapeutic psychology*, 3rd ed. Englewood Cliffs, N.J.: Prentice-Hall, 1978.

Ellis, A., & Harper, R. A. *A new guide to rational living*. Englewood Cliffs, N.J.: Prentice-Hall, 1975.

Friel, T. W., Kratochvil, D., & Carkhuff, R. The effects of manipulation of client depth of self exploration upon helpers of different training and experience. *Journal of Clinical Psychology*, 1968, *24*, 247–249.

Gelso, C. J. Effects of recording on counselors and clients. *Counselor Education and Supervision*, 1974, *14*, 5–12.

Grater, H. Client preference for affective or cognitive counselor characteristics and first interview behavior. *Journal of Counseling Psychology*, 1964, *11*, 248–250.

Greenson, R. *The technique and practice of psychoanalysis*. New York: International Universities Press, 1967.

Heine, R. W. A comparison of patient's reports on psychotherapeutic experience with psychoanalytical, non-directive, and Adlerian therapists. Unpublished doctoral dissertation, University of Chicago, 1950.

Kanfer, F. H., & Saslow, G. Behavioral diagnosis. In C. Franks (Ed.), *Behavior therapy: assessment and status*. New York: McGraw-Hill, 1969.

Krasner, L. The operant approach in behavior therapy. In A. Bergin & S. Garfield (Eds.), *Handbook of psychotherapy and behavior change*. New York: Wiley, 1971.

Krasner, L. The therapist as a social reinforcement machine. In H. Strupp & L. Luborsky (Eds.), *Research in psychotherapy* (Vol. 2). Washington, D.C.: American Psychological Association, 1962.

Lazarus, A. *Behavior therapy and beyond*. New York: McGraw-Hill, 1971.

Mahoney, M. *Cognition and behavior modification*. Cambridge, Mass.: Ballinger, 1974.

Mahoney, M., & Thoresen, C. *Self control: Power to the person*. Monterey, Calif.: Brooks/Cole, 1974.

Mullen, J., & Abeles, N. Relationship of liking, empathy and therapist experience to outcome of therapy. In *Psychotherapy*, 1971, an Aldine annual, Chicago: Aldine, 1972, 256–260.

Munroe, R. *Schools of psychoanalytic thought*. New York: Dryden Press, 1955.

Osipow, S. H., & Walsh, W. B. *Strategies in counseling for behavior change*. Englewood Cliffs, N.J.: Prentice-Hall, 1970.

Parloff, M. Some factors affecting the quality of therapeutic relationships. *Journal of Abnormal and Social Psychology*, 1956, *52*, 5–10.

Perls, F. *The Gestalt approach and eye witness to therapy*. Ben Lemond, Calif.: Science and Behavior Books, 1973.

Perls, F., Hefferline, H., & Goodman, P. *Gestalt therapy—excitement and growth in human personality*. New York: Julian Press, 1951.

Piaget, G., Berenson, B., & Carkhuff, R. The differential effects of the manipulation of therapeutic conditions by high and moderate therapists functioning upon high and low functioning clients. *Journal of Consulting Psychology*, 1967, *31*, 481–486.

Rogers, C. R. *On becoming a person.* Boston: Houghton Mifflin, 1961.
Rogers, C. R. *Client-centered therapy.* Boston: Houghton Mifflin, 1951.
Rogers, C. R. *Counseling and psychotherapy.* Boston: Houghton Mifflin, 1942.
Shostrom, E. The measurement of growth in psychotherapy. *Psychotherapy: Theory, Research and Practice,* 1972, *9,* 194–199.
Shostrom, E. *Personal orientation inventory.* San Diego, Calif.: Educational and Industrial Testing Service, 1963.
Skinner, B. F. *Beyond freedom and dignity.* New York: Knopf, 1971.
Sullivan, H. S. *The psychiatric interview.* New York: Norton, 1954.
Thorne, F. *Principles of personality counseling.* Brandon, Vt.: Journal of Clinical Psychology, 1950.
Tosi, D. Dogmatism within the counselor client dyad. *Journal of Counseling Psychology,* 1970, *17,* 284–288.
Tosi, D., & Marzella, J. *Rational stage directed therapy.* Paper delivered at the First Annual Convention on Rational Emotive Psychotherapy, Chicago, 1975.
Tosi, D., Upshaw, K., Lande, A., & Waldron, M. Group counseling with nonverbalizing elementary students: The differential effects of Premack and social reinforcement techniques. *Journal of Counseling Psychology,* 1970, *18,* 437–440.
Truax, C. Variations in levels of accurate empathy offered in the psychotherapy relationship and case outcome. *Brief research reports,* Wisconsin Psychiatric Institute, University of Wisconsin, 1962.
Truax, C. Reinforcement and non-reinforcement in Rogerian psychotherapy. *Journal of Abnormal and Social Psychology,* 1966, *71,* 1–9.
Truax, C., & Carkhuff, R. *Toward effective counseling and psychotherapy training and practice.* Chicago: Aldine, 1967.
Tyler, L. *The work of the counselor,* 3rd ed. New York: Appleton-Century-Crofts, 1968.
Van Deer Veen, F. Client perception of therapist conditions as a factor in psychotherapy. In J. T. Hart & T. M. Tomlinson (Eds.), *New directions in client-centered therapy.* Boston: Houghton Mifflin, 1970.
Vitalo, R. Teaching improved interpersonal functioning as a preferred mode of treatment. *Journal of Clinical Psychology,* 1971, *27,* 166–171.
Wagstaff, A., Rice, L., & Butler, J. *Factors of client verbal participation in therapy.* Counseling Center Discussion Papers, University of Chicago, 1960, *6,* 1–14.
Wolpe, J. *The practice of behavior therapy.* New York: Pergamon Press, 1969.

Chapter 4

American Psychiatric Association, *Diagnostic and statistical manual of psychiatric disorders.* (DSM I), 1952.
American Psychiatric Association, *Diagnostic and statistical manual of psychiatric disorders.* (DSM II), 1968.

American Psychiatric Association, *Diagnostic and statistical manual of psychiatric disorders.* (DSM III), 1979.

Anastasi, A. *Psychological testing* (4th ed.). New York: Macmillan, 1976.

Atkinson, R. *Psychology in progress: Readings from scientific introduction* by R. Atkinson and Study Guides by J. Pinel. San Francisco: W. H. Freeman, 1975.

Beck, A. T. *Cognitive therapy and the emotional disorders.* New York: International Universities Press, 1976.

Brammer, L., & Shostrom, E. *Therapeutic psychology* (3rd ed.) Englewood Cliffs, N.J.: Prentice-Hall, 1977.

Buros, O. K. *The seventh mental measurements yearbook.* Highland Park, N.J.: Gryphon Press, 1972.

Cronbach, L. *Essentials of psychological testing* (3rd ed.). New York: Harper & Row, 1970.

Ellis, A. *Humanistic psychotherapy.* New York: McGraw-Hill, 1973.

Ellis, A. *A new guide to rational living.* Englewood Cliffs, N.J.: Prentice-Hall, 1975.

Erikson, E. *Insight and responsibility.* New York: W. W. Norton, 1964.

Ferster, C. B., & Perrott, M. C. *Behavior principles.* New York: Appleton-Century-Crofts, 1968.

Franks, C. (Ed.). *Behavior therapy: appraisal and status.* New York: McGraw-Hill, 1969.

Goldman, L. *Using tests in counseling* (2nd ed.). Englewood Cliffs, N.J.: Prentice-Hall, 1971.

Kanfer, F., & Phillips, J. *Learning foundations of behavior therapy.* New York: Wiley, 1970.

Kanfer, F., & Saslow, G. Behavioral analysis and associated diagnostic classification. *Archives in General Psychiatry,* 1965, *12,* 529–538.

Lazarus, A. A. *Behavioral therapy and beyond.* New York: McGraw-Hill, 1971.

Lorr, M., Klett, C., & McNair, D. *Syndromes of psychoses.* New York: Pergamon Press, 1963.

Lyman, H. B. *Test scores and what they mean* (2nd ed.). Englewood Cliffs, N.J.: Prentice-Hall, 1971.

Meehl, P. E. *Clinical versus statistical prediction.* Minneapolis: University of Minnesota Press, 1960.

Mischel, W. *Personality assessment.* New York: Wiley, 1968.

Osipow, S., & Walsh, W. B. *Strategies in counseling for behavior change.* Englewood Cliffs, N.J.: Prentice-Hall, 1970.

Skinner, B. F. *The behavior of organisms, an experimental analysis.* New York: Appleton-Century-Crofts, 1938.

Sue, D. W. Eliminating cultural oppression in counseling: Toward a general theory. *Journal of Counseling Psychology,* 1978, *25,* 419–428.

Super, D. E., & Crites, J. O. *Appraising vocational fitness* (2nd ed.). New York: Harper & Row, 1962.

Thoresen, C., & Anton, J. Intensive experimental research in counseling. *Journal of Counseling Psychology,* 1974, *21,* 553–559.

Tosi, D. J. *Youth: Toward personal growth.* Columbus, Ohio: Charles E. Merrill, 1974.

Tosi, D. J., & Marzella, J. N. *Rational stage directed therapy.* Presented at the First Annual Convention of Rational Psychotherapy, Chicago, 1975.

Tyler, L., & Walsh, W. B. *Tests and measurements* (3rd ed.). Englewood Cliffs, N.J.: Prentice-Hall, 1979.

Valins, S., Baum, A., & Harpin, R. E. The role of group phenomena in the experience of crowding. *Environment and Behavior,* 1975, *7,* 185–198.

Webster, D. W., & Fretz, B. R. Asian American, black, and white students' preferences for help giving sources. *Journal of Counseling Psychology,* 1978, *25,* 124–130.

Westbrook, F. D., Miyares, J., & Roberts, J. H. Perceived problem areas by black and white students and hints about comparative counseling needs. *Journal of Counseling Psychology,* 1978, *25,* 119–123.

Williamson, E. G. *How to counsel students.* New York: McGraw-Hill, 1939.

Williamson, E. G. *Vocational counseling: Some historical, philosophical, and theoretical perspectives.* New York: McGraw-Hill, 1965.

Zytowski, D. G. (ed.). *Contemporary approaches to interest measurement.* Minneapolis: University of Minnesota Press, 1973.

Chapter 5

Alexander, F. *Psychosomatic medicine.* New York: W. W. Norton, 1950.

Ashen, B. ,& Donner, L. Covert sensitization with alcoholics: A controlled replication. *Behavior Research and Therapy,* 1968, *6,* 7–12.

Bandura, A. *Principles of behavior modification.* New York: Holt, Rinehart & Winston, 1969.

Barlow, D. H., Leitenberg, H., & Agras, W. Experimental control of sexual deviation through manipulation of the noxious scene in covert sensitization. *Journal of Abnormal Psychology,* 1969, *74,* 596–601.

Beier, E. G. *The silent language of psychotherapy: Social reinforcement of unconscious processes.* Chicago: Aldine, 1966.

Bergin, A. E. Cognitive therapy and behavior therapy: Foci for a multidimensional approach to treatment. *Behavior Therapy,* 1970, *1,* 205–212.

Briggs, R. D., Tosi, D. J., & Morley, R. M. Study habit modification and its effect on academic performance: A behavioral approach. *Journal of Educational Research,* 1971, *64,* 345–350.

Cautela, J. R. Covert sensitization. *Psychological Reports,* 1967, *20,* 459–468.

Cautela, J. R. Treatment of alcoholics by covert sensitization. *Psychotherapy: Theory, Research, and Practice,* 1970, *7,* 86–90. (a)

Cautela, J. R. Covert reinforcement. *Behavior Therapy,* 1970, *1,* 33–50. (b)

Cautela, J. R. Treatment of smoking by covert sensitization. *Psychological Reports,* 1970, *26,* 415–420. (c)

Cautela, J. R. *Rationale and procedures for covert conditioning.* Presentation at the Annual Meeting for the Association for the Advancement of Behavioral Therapy, Miami, 1970. (d)

Cautela, J. R., & Kastenbaum, R.   A reinforcement survey schedule for use in therapy, training, and research. *Psychological Reports*, 1967, *20*, 1115–1130.

Cautela, J. R. & Wisocki, P. A.   The use of imagery in the modification of attitudes toward the elderly. *Journal of Psychology*, 1969, *73*, 193–199.

Deci, E. L.   *Intrinsic motivation.* New York: Plenum, 1975.

Dinsmoor, J.   *Operant conditioning:* An experimental analysis of behavior. Dubuque, Iowa: W. C. Brown, 1971.

Edwards, N.   Case conference: assertive training in a case of homosexual pedophilia. *Journal of Behavior Therapy and Experimental Psychiatry*, 1972, *3*, 55–63.

Eisler, R., Miller, P. M., & Hersen, M.   Components of assertive behavior. *Journal of Clinical Psychology*, 1973, *29*, 295–299.

Ellis, A.   *Growth through reason: Verbatim cases in rational emotive therapy.* Palo Alto, Calif.: Science and Behavior Books, 1971.

Ellis, A.   *Humanistic psychotherapy: A rational emotive approach.* New York: McGraw-Hill, 1973.

Eysenck, H. (Ed.)   *Behavior therapy and the neuroses.* New York: Pergamon Press, 1960.

Flannery, R. B.   A laboratory analogue of two covert reinforcement procedures. *Journal of Behavior Therapy and Experimental Psychiatry*, 1972, *3*, 171–177.

Franks, C. M., & Wilson, T. G.   *Behavior therapy: Theory and practice.* New York: Brunner/Mazel, 1973 (1974) (1975), *1* (2) (4).

Galassi, J. P., Kostka, M. P., & Galassi, D.   Assertive training: A one year follow-up. *Journal of Counseling Psychology*, 1975, *22*, 451–452.

Gellhorn, E.   The neurological basis of anxiety: An hypothesis. *Perspectives of Biological Medicine*, 1965, *8*, 488.

Goldfried, M., & Merbaum, M. A.   Perspective on self control. In M. R. Goldfried & M. Merbaum (Eds.), *Behavior change through self control.* New York: Holt, Rinehart & Winston, 1973.

Gormally, J., Hill, C., Otis, M., & Rainey, L.   A micro-training approach to assertion training. *Journal of Counseling Psychology*, 1975, *22*, 299–303.

Gutride, M., Goldstein, A., & Hunter, G.   The use of modeling and role playing to increase interaction among social psychiatric patients. *Journal of Consulting and Clinical Psychology*, 1973, *40*, 408–415.

Harris, M., & Trujillo, A.   Improving study habits of junior high school students through self management versus group discussion. *Journal of Counseling Psychology*, 1975, *22*, 513–517.

Hedquist, F., & Weinhold, B.   Behavioral group counseling with socially anxious and unassertive college students. *Journal of Counseling Psychology*, 1970, *17*, 237–242.

Ingram, I. M.   The obsessional personality and obsessional illness. *American Journal of Psychiatry*, 1961, *117*, 1016.

Ivey, A.   *Microcounseling.* Springfield, Ill.: Charles C Thomas, 1971.

Ivey, A., & Authier, J. *Microcounseling* (2nd ed.). Springfield, Ill.: Charles C Thomas, 1978.

Jackson, B., & Van Zoost, B. Changing study behaviors through reinforcement contingencies. *Journal of Counseling Psychology,* 1972, *19,* 192–195.

Jacobson, E. *You must relax.* New York: Whittlesey House, 1934.

Jakubowski-Spector, P. Facilitating the growth of women through assertive training. *The Counseling Psychologist,* 1973, *4,* 75–87.

Janda, L. H., & Rimm, D. C. Covert sensitization in the treatment of obesity. *Journal of Abnormal Psychology,* 1972, *80,* 37–42.

Jones, G. Improving study behaviors. In J. P. Krumboltz & E. E. Thoresen (Eds.), *Behavioral counseling.* New York: Holt, Rinehart & Winston, 1969.

Kazdin, A. Self monitoring and behavioral change. In M. J. Mahoney & C. E. Thoresen (Eds.), *Self control: Power to the person.* Monterey, Calif.: Brooks/Cole, 1974.

Kelly, G. *The psychology of personal constructs.* New York: W. W. Norton, 1955.

Kendrick, S., & McCullough, J. Sequential phases of covert reinforcement and covert sensitization in treatment of homosexuality. *Journal of Behavior Therapy and Experimental Psychiatry,* 1972, *3,* 229–231.

Krop, H., Calhoon, B., & Verrier, R. Modification of the self concept of the emotionally disturbed by covert self reinforcement. *Behavior Therapy,* 1971, *2,* 201–204.

Krumboltz, J. D., & Thoresen, C. E. (Eds.). *Behavioral counseling: Cases and techniques.* New York: Holt, Rinehart & Winston, 1969.

Lazarus, A. A. *Behavior therapy and beyond.* New York: McGraw-Hill, 1971.

Luce, G., & Pepper, E. Mind over body, mind over mind. *New York Times Magazine,* Sept. 12, 1971, pp. 34–35, 132–139.

McFall, R. M., & Lillesand, D. B. Behavior rehearsal with modeling and coaching in an assertion training. *Journal of Abnormal Psychology,* 1971, *77,* 313–323.

Mahoney, M. J. *Cognition and behavior modification.* Cambridge, Mass.: Ballinger, 1974.

Manno, B., & Marston, A. Weight reduction as a function of negative covert reinforcement (sensitization) versus positive covert reinforcement. *Behavior Research and Therapy,* 1972 *10,* 201–207.

Maultsby, M. C. *Handbook of rational self counseling.* Lexington: Rational Behavior Training Section, University of Kentucky, 1971.

Meichenbaum, D. *Cognitive factors in behavior modification.* Paper presented at the Fifth Annual Meeting of the Association for the Advancement of Behavior Therapy, Washington, D.C., 1971.

Mikulas, W. *Behavior modification: An overview.* New York: Harper & Row, 1972.

Mikulas, W. (Ed.). *Readings in behavior modification.* New York: MSS Information Corp., 1973.

Norman, R. Affective-cognitive consistency, attitudes, conformity, and behavior. *Journal of Personality and Social Psychology*, 1975, *32*, 83–91.

Osterhouse, R. Desensitization and study skills training as treatment for two types of test anxious students. *Journal of Counseling Psychology*, 1972, *19*, 300–306.

Premack, D. Reinforcement theory. In D. Levine (Ed.), *Nebraska Symposium on Motivation*. Lincoln: University of Nebraska Press, 1965, 123–180.

Payne, B. Uncovering destructive self criticism. *Rational Living*, 1971, *6*, 26–30.

Rathus, S. A. An experimental investigation of assertive training in a group setting. *Journal of Behavior Therapy and Experimental Psychiatry*, 1972, *3*, 81–86.

Reynolds, G. S. *A primer on operant conditioning*. Glenview, Ill.: Scott, Foresman, 1968.

Richards, C. Behavior modification of studying through study skills advice and self control procedures. *Journal of Counseling Psychology*, 1975, *22*, 431–436.

Robinson, F. P. *Effective study* (4th ed.). New York: Harper & Row, 1970.

Rollins, N. A. Soviet study of consciousness and unconsciousness. *Journal of Individual Psychology*, 1975, *30*, 230–238.

Smith, M. J. *When I say no I feel guilty*. New York: Dial Press, 1975.

Stern, R. Treatment of a case of obsessional neurosis using thought stopping techniques. *British Journal of Psychiatry*, 1970, *117*, 441–442.

Stuart, R. Behavioral control of overeating. *Behavior Research and Therapy*, 1967, *5*, 357–365.

Thoresen, C., & Mahoney, M. *Behavioral self control*. New York: Holt, Rinehart & Winston, 1974.

Tosi, D. *Youth: Toward personal growth*. Columbus, Ohio: Charles E. Merrill, 1974.

Tosi, D. J., Upshaw, K., Lande, A., & Waldron, M. Group counseling with nonverbalizing elementary students: Differential effects of Premack and social reinforcement techniques. *Journal of Counseling Psychology*, 1971, *18*, 437–440.

Wisocki, P. A. A covert reinforcement program for the treatment of test anxiety: A brief report. *Behavior Therapy*, 1973, *4*, 264–266.

Wisocki, P. A. The successful treatment of a heroin addict by covert conditioning techniques. *Journal of Behavior Therapy and Experimental Psychiatry*, 1973, *4*, 55–61.

Wisocki, P. A. Treatment of obsessive-compulsive behavior by covert sensitization and covert reinforcement: A case report. *Journal of Behavior Therapy and Experimental Psychiatry*, 1970, *1*, 233–239.

Wolpe, J. *The practice of behavior therapy*. New York: Pergamon Press, 1969.

Wolpe, J., & Lazarus, A. *Behavior therapy techniques: A guide to the treatment of neurosis*. New York: Pergamon Press, 1966.

Chapter 6

Bare, C. E., & Mitchell, R. R. Experimental evaluation of sensitivity training. *Journal of Applied Behavioral Science,* 1972, *8,* 263–276.

Bordin, E. S. *Psychological counseling* (2nd ed.). New York: Appleton-Century-Crofts, 1968.

Cooper, C. L. An attempt to assess the psychologically disturbing effects of T-group training. *British Journal of Social and Clinical Psychology,* 1972, *11,* 342–345.

Diamond, M. J., & Shapiro, J. L. Changes in locus of control as a function of encounter group experiences. A study and replication. *Journal of Abnormal Psychology,* 1973, *82,* 514–518.

Dies, R. R., & Sadowsky, R. A brief encounter group experience and social relationships in a dormitory. *Journal of Counseling Psychology,* 1974, *21,* 112–115.

Gazda, G. M. *Group Counseling: A developmental approach* (2nd ed.). Boston: Allyn & Bacon, 1978.

Goldstein, A., Heller, K., & Sechrest, L. *Psychotherapy and the psychology of behavior change.* New York: Wiley, 1966.

Hare, R. D. *Psychotherapy, theory and research.* New York: Wiley, 1970.

Harrison, R., & Lubin, B. Personal style, group composition and learning. *Journal of Applied Behavioral Science,* 1965, *1,* 286–301.

Jacobs, M., Jacobs, A., Gatz, M., & Schaible, T. Credibility and desirability of positive and negative structured feedback in groups. *Journal of Consulting and Clinical Psychology,* 1973, *40,* 244–252.

Jew, C. C., Clanon, T. L., & Mattocks, A. L. The effectiveness of group psychotherapy in a correctional institution. *American Journal of Psychiatry,* 1972, *129,* 602–605.

Jourard, S. M. *The transparent self.* Princeton, N.J.: Van Nostrand Reinhold, 1971.

Jourard, S. M., & Lasakow, P. Some factors in self disclosure. *Journal of Abnormal and Social Psychology,* 1958, *56,* 91–98.

Kaye, J. D. Group interaction and interpersonal learning. *Small Group Behavior,* 1973, *4,* 424–448.

Locke, N. M. *Group psychoanalysis: Theory and technique.* New York: New York University Press, 1961.

Maultsby, M., Stiefel, L., & Bordsky, L. A theory of rational-behavioral group process. *Rational Living,* 1973, *7,* 28–34.

May, O. P., & Thompson, C. L. Perceived levels of self disclosure, mental health, and helpfulness of group leaders. *Journal of Counseling Psychology,* 1973, *20,* 349–352.

National Training Laboratory. *Feedback and the helping relationship.* NTL Institute: Reading Book (Mimeographed) by the NTL Institute for Applied Behavioral Science, Washington, D.C., 1967, pp. 44–47.

Rotter, J. B. Generalized expectancies for internal vs. external control of reinforcement. *Psychological Monographs,* 1966, *80.* No. 609.

Schaible, T., & Jacobs, A. Feedback III: Sequence effects; enhancement of feedback acceptance and group attractiveness by manipulation of the sequence and valence of feedback. *Small Group Behavior,* 1975, *6,* 151–173.

Shertzer, B., & Stone, S. C. *Fundamentals of guidance* (2nd ed.). Boston: Houghton Mifflin, 1976.

Sprinthall, N. Psychology and teacher education: New directions for school and counseling psychology. *The Counseling Psychologist,* 1977, *6*(4), 53–56.

Stanton, H. E. Change in self-insight during an intensive group experience. *Small Group Behavior,* 1975, *6,* 487–493.

Strassberg, D. S., Gabel, H., & Anchor, K. N. Self disclosure in group therapy with schizophrenics. *Archives of General Psychiatry,* 1975, *32,* 1259–1261.

Tosi, D. J. *Youth: Toward personal growth.* Columbus, Ohio: Charles E. Merrill, 1974.

Tosi, D. J., & Eshbaugh, D. A cognitive experimental approach to the interpersonal and intrapersonal development of counselors and therapists. *Journal of Clinical Psychology,* 1978, *34,* 494–500.

Whitaker, D., & Lieberman, M. *Psychotherapy through the group process.* New York: Atherton, 1964.

Yalom, I. D., Zimerberg, S. M., Hours, P. S., & Rand, K. H. Prediction of improvement in group therapy. *Archives of General Psychiatry,* 1967, *17,* 159–168.

Yalom, I. D. *The theory and practice of group psychotherapy.* New York: Basic Books, 1975.

Chapter 7

Adler, A. *A study of organ inferiority and its psychical compensations.* New York: Nervous and Mental Disease Publishing Co., 1917.

Adler, A. *The practice and theory of individual psychology.* New York: Harcourt, Brace, 1927.

Adler, A. *What life should mean to you.* Boston: Little, Brown, 1931.

Blau, P. M. & Duncan, O. T. *The American occupational structure.* New York: Wiley, 1967.

Blocher, D. *Developmental counseling.* New York: Ronald Press, 1966.

Buehler, C. *Der menschliche Lebenslauf als psychologiches problem.* Leipzig: Hirzel, 1933.

Caplow, T. *The sociology of work.* New York: McGraw-Hill, 1954.

Crites, J. O. *Vocational psychology.* New York: McGraw-Hill, 1969.

Crites, J. O. *Career maturity inventory: Theory and research handbook and administration and use manual.* Del Monte Research Park, Calif.: CTM/McGraw-Hill, 1973.

Crites, J. O. Career counseling: A review of major approaches. *The Counseling Psychologist,* 1974, *4*(3), 3–23.

Crites, J. O. Career counseling: A comprehensive approach. *The Counseling Psychologist,* 1976, *6*(3), 2–12.

Dictionary of occupational titles (4th ed.). Washington, D.C.: U.S. Government Printing Office, 1977.

Erikson, E. H. *Childhood and society* (2nd ed.). New York: W. W. Norton, 1963.

Freud, A. Adolescence. *Psychoanalytic Study of the Child,* 1958, *13,* 255–278.

Freud, A. *Normality and pathology in childhood.* New York: International Universities Press, 1965.

Freud, S. Three essays in the theory of sexuality (1905). *Standard edition of the complete psychological works of Sigmund Freud* (Vol. 7). London: Hogarth, 1953.

Gesell, A., Halverson, H. M., Thompson, H. et al. *The first five years of life.* New York: Harper, 1940.

Gesell, A., & Ilg, F. *The child from five to ten.* New York: Harper, 1946.

Gesell, A., Ilg, F., & Ames, A. B. *Youth: The years from ten to sixteen.* New York: Harper, 1956.

Ginzberg, E., Ginsburg, S. W., Axelrad, S., & Herma, J. L. *Occupational choice: An approach to a general theory.* New York: Columbia University Press, 1951.

Gribbons, W. D., & Lohnes, P. R. *Emerging careers.* New York: Teachers College Press, 1968.

Gross, E. The worker and society. In H. Borow (Ed.), *Man in a world at work.* Boston: Houghton Mifflin, 1964.

Gross, E. A sociological approach to the analysis of preparation for work life. *Personnel and Guidance Journal,* 1967, *45,* 416–423.

Havighurst, R. J. *Human development and education.* New York: Longman Green, 1953.

Havighurst, R. J. Youth in exploration and man emergent. In H. Borow (Ed.), *Man in a world at work.* Boston: Houghton Mifflin, 1964.

Hershenson, D. B. Vocational development theory before 1400. *Journal of the History of the Behavioral Sciences,* 1974, *10,* 170–179.

Holland, J. L. A theory of vocational choice. *Journal of Counseling Psychology,* 1959, *6,* 35–45.

Holland, J. L. *The psychology of vocational choice.* Waltham, Mass.: Blaisdell, 1966.

Holland, J. L. *Making vocational choices: A theory of careers.* Englewood Cliffs, N.J.: Prentice-Hall, 1973.

Horrocks, J. E. *The psychology of adolescence* (3rd ed.). Boston: Houghton Mifflin, 1969.

Krumboltz, J. D., Mitchell, A., & Jones, B. Social learning theory and career development. *The Counseling Psychologist,* 1976, *6*(1), 71–81.

Krumboltz, J. D., & Schroeder, W. W. Promoting career exploration through reinforcement. *Personnel and Guidance Journal,* 1965, *44,* 19–26.

Krumboltz, J. D., & Thoresen, C. E. The effect of behavioral counseling in group and individual settings on information seeking behavior. *Journal of Counseling Psychology,* 1964, *11,* 324–333.

Krumboltz, J. D., Varenhorst, B., & Thoresen, C. E. Non-verbal factors in the effectiveness of models in counseling. *Journal of Counseling Psychology*, 1967, *14*, 412–418.

Osipow, S. H.   What do we really know about career development? In N. Gysbers & D. Pritchard (Eds.), *Proceedings of national conference on vocational education*. Columbia: University of Missouri, 1969.

Osipow, S. H.   *Theories of career development* (2nd ed.). Englewood Cliffs, N.J.: Prentice-Hall, 1973.

Osipow, S. H., Carney, C. G., & Barak, A.   A scale of educational-vocational undecidedness: A typological approach. *Journal of Vocational Behavior*, 1976, *9*, 233–243.

Osipow, S. H., Carney, C. G., Winer, J., Yanico, B., & Koschier, M.   *Career Decision Scale* (3rd rev.). Columbus, Ohio: Authors, 1976.

Osipow, S. H.   *A preliminary manual for the Career Decision Scale*. Columbus, Ohio: Author, 1979.

Parsons, F.   *Choosing a vocation*. Boston: Houghton Mifflin, 1909.

Roe, A.   Early determinants of vocational choice. *Journal of Counseling Psychology*, 1957, *4*, 212–217.

Senesh, L., & Osipow, S. H.   Fundamental ideas of career education. In L. Senesh (Ed.), *New paths in social science curriculum design*. Chicago: Science Research Associates, 1973.

Sullivan, H. S.   *The interpersonal theory of psychiatry*. New York: W. W. Norton, 1953.

Super, D. E.   A theory of vocational development. *American Psychologist*, 1953, *8*, 185–190.

Super, D. E.   Self concepts in vocational development. In D. E. Super et al., *Career development: Self concept theory*. New York: CEEB Research Monograph No. 4, 1963(a).

Super, D. E.   Toward making self concept theory operational. In D. E. Super et al., *Career Development: Self concept theory*. New York: CEEB Research Monograph No. 4, 1963(b).

Super, D. E.   Vocational development in adolescence and early adulthood: Tasks and behaviors. In D. E. Super et al., *Career development: Self concept theory*. New York: CEEB Research Monograph No. 4, 1963(c).

Super, D. E., Starishevsky, R., Matlin, N., & Jordaan, J. P.   *Career development: Self concept theory*. New York: CEEB Research Monograph No. 4, 1963.

Super, D. E., Bohn, M. J., Jr., Forrest, D. J., Jordaan, J. P., Lindeman, R. L., & Thompson, A. S.   *Career questionnaire form IV*. New York: Teachers College, Columbia University, 1971.

Tiedeman, D. V.   Decision and vocational development: A paradigm and its implications. *Personnel and Guidance Journal*, 1951, *40*, 15–21.

Tiedeman, D. V., & O'Hara, R. P.   *Career development: Choice and adjustment*. New York: CEEB Research Monograph No. 3, 1963.

Thoresen, C. E.   Using appropriate models. *American Psychologist*, 1966, *21*, 688.

Thoresen, C. E., Krumboltz, J. D., & Varenhorst, B.   Sex of counselors and models: Effect on client career exploration. *Journal of Counseling Psychology*, 1967, *14*, 503–508.

Toffler, A. *Future shock.* New York: Random House, 1970.

Westbrook, B. W., & Parry-Hill, J. W., Jr. The measure of cognitive vocational maturity. *Journal of Vocational Behavior,* 1973, *3,* 239–252.

Williamson, E. G. *Vocational counseling: Some historical, philosophical, and theoretical perspectives.* New York: McGraw-Hill, 1965.

Zytowski, D. G. Four hundred years before Parsons. *Personnel and Guidance Journal,* 1972, *50,* 443–450.

Chapter 8

Ackerman, N. Family psychotherapy and psychoanalysis: The implications of difference. In N. Ackerman (Ed.), *Family process.* New York: Basic Books, 1970.

Alexander, A. Systematic relaxation and flow rates in asthmatic children: Relationships to emotional precipitants and anxiety. *Journal of Psychosomatic Research,* 1972, *10,* 405–410.

Alexander, F. *Psychosomatic medicine.* New York: W. W. Norton, 1950.

Allen, W. S. *Rehabilitation: A community challenge.* New York: Wiley, 1958.

Anthony, J., & Benedeck, T. *Depression and human existence.* Little, Brown, 1975.

Arieti, S. *Interpretation of schizophrenia.* New York: Robert Brunner, 1955.

Barber, T., Dicara, L., Kamiya, J., Miller, N., Shapiro, D., & Stoyva, J. (Eds.), *Biofeedback and self control.* Chicago: Aldine, 1971.

Beck, A. *Depression—clinical, experimental, and theoretical aspects.* New York: Harper & Row, 1967.

Beck, A. T. *Cognitive therapy and the emotional disorders.* New York: International Universities Press, 1976.

Bell, J. A theoretical position for family group therapy. In N. Ackerman (Ed.), *Family process.* New York: Basic Books, 1970.

Bell, J. Recent advances in family group therapy. In J. G. Howells (Ed.), *Theory and practice of family psychiatry.* New York: Brunner/Mazel, 1971.

Brenner, J., & Kleinman, R. Learned control of decreases in systolic blood pressure. *Nature,* 1970, *226,* 1063.

Boulougouris, J., & Bassiakos, L. Prolonged flooding in cases with obsessive compulsive neurosis. *Behavior Research and Therapy,* 1973, *11,* 227–231.

Budzynski, T., & Stoyva, J. Biofeedback and tension headache: A controlled outcome study. *Psychosomatic Medicine,* 1973, *35,* 489–496.

Cautela, J. R. The treatment of alcoholism by covert sensitization. *Psychotherapy: Theory, Research and Practice,* 1970, *7,* 86–90.

Cooper, A. J. A case of bronchial asthma treated by behavior therapy. *Behavior Research and Therapy,* 1964, *1,* 351–356.

Creer, T. *Psychologic factors in allergic disease.* Invited address at the Twenty-seventh Annual Meeting of the Academy of Allergy, Chicago, 1971.

DeLeon, G., & Sachs, S. Conditioning functional enuresis: A four year follow up. *Journal of Consulting and Clinical Psychology*, 1972, *39*, 299–300.

Eastman, W. F., & Reifler, C. B. Marriage counseling in the student health service. In H. L. Silverman (Ed.), *Marital therapy: Psychological, sociological and moral factors*. Homewood, Ill.: Charles C Thomas, 1972.

Elias, J. E., & Elias, V. D. The sexual world of the adolescent. *The Counseling Psychologist*, 1975, *5*(1), 92–97.

Ellis, A. The treatment of sex and love problems in women. In V. Franks & B. Vasanti (Eds.), *Women in therapy*. New York: Brunner/Mazel, 1974.

Ellis, A. *Humanistic psychotherapy: The rational-emotive approach*. New York: Julian Press, 1973.

Ellis, A. *Growth through reason: Verbatim cases in rational-emotive therapy*. Palo Alto, Calif.: Science and Behavior Books, 1971.

Ellis, A. *Sex without guilt*. N. Hollywood, Calif.: Wilshire Book Co., 1970.

Ellis, A., & Harper, R. *A new guide to rational living*. Hollywood: Wilshire Books, 1975.

Eshbaugh, D., Tosi, D., & Hoyt, C. Female alcoholics: A typological description using the MMPI. Unpublished research paper. The Ohio State University, 1978(a).

Eshbaugh, D., Tosi, D., & Hoyt, C. Some personality patterns and dimensions of alcoholics: A multivariate description. *Journal of Personality Assessment*, 1978(b), *12*, 409–417.

Eysenck, H. *Behavior therapy and the neuroses*. New York: Pergamon Press, 1960.

Fiedler, F. A comparison of therapeutic relationships in psychoanalytic, nondirective, and Adlerian therapy. *Journal of Consulting Psychology*, 1950, *14*, 436–445.

Franks, C. M., & Wilson, T. G. *Behavior therapy: Theory and practice* (Vols. 1, 2, 3). New York: Brunner/Mazel, 1973, 1974, 1975.

Freedman, A., Kaplan, H., & Sadock, B. *Modern synopsis of psychiatry II*. Baltimore: Williams & Wilkins, 1976.

Goldfried, M. R., & Sobocinski, D. Effect of irrational beliefs on emotional arousal. *Journal of Consulting and Clinical Psychology*, 1975, *43*, 504–510.

Kaplan, H. S. *The new sex therapy*. New York: Brunner/Mazel, 1974.

Kaplan, H. S. *The illustrated manual of sex therapy*. New York: Quadrangle/New York Times Book Co., 1975.

Kissin, B. Alcoholism: Is it a treatable disease? *Modern Medicine*, 1973, *14*, 20–33.

Lazarus, A. Multimodal behavior therapy: Treating the basic id. *Journal of Nervous and Mental Disease*, 1973, *156*, 404–411.

Lazarus, A. *Behavior therapy and beyond*. New York: McGraw-Hill, 1971.

Lazarus, A. Desensitization and cognitive restructuring. *Psychotherapy: Theory, Research and Practice*, 1974, *11*, 98–102.

Lazarus, R. *Psychological stress and the coping process*. New York: McGraw-Hill, 1966.

Leitenberg, H.   *Handbook of behavior modification and behavior therapy.*
Englewood Cliffs, N.J.: Prentice-Hall, 1976.

Liberman, R.   Behavioral approaches to family and couple therapy. In C. J.
Sager & H. S. Kaplan (Eds.), *Progress in group and family therapy.* New
York: Brunner/Mazel, 1972.

Lofquist, L. H.   *Vocational counseling with the physically handicapped.* New
York: Appleton-Century-Crofts, 1957.

Lorr, M., Klett, J., & McNair, D.   *Syndromes of psychosis.* New York:
Macmillan, 1963.

Lovibond, S. H.   Critique of Turner, Young, and Rachman's conditioning
treatment of enuresis. *Behavior Research and Therapy*, 1972, *10*, 287–
289.

Luthe, W.   *Autogenic therapy* (Vols. 1–4). New York: Grune & Stratton,
1969–1973.

Mahoney, M. J.   *Cognition and behavior modification.* Cambridge, Mass.:
Ballinger, 1974.

Marks, I. M.   *Fears and phobias.* New York: Academic Press, 1969.

Masters, W., & Johnson, V.   *The pleasure bond.* Boston: Little, Brown,
1974.

Masters, W., & Johnson, V.   *Human sexual inadequacy.* Boston: Little,
Brown, 1970.

Masters, W., & Johnson, V.   *Human sexual response.* Boston: Little, Brown,
1966.

Maultsby, M.   Rational-emotive imagery. *Rational Living*, 1971, *6*(1), 16–
23.

MacGregor, R.   *Multiple impact therapy with families.* New York: Grune &
Stratton, 1964.

Millon, T.   *Modern psychopathology: A bio-social approach to maladaptive
learning and functioning.* Philadelphia: W. B. Saunders, 1969.

Millon, T.   *Theories of psychopathology.* Philadelphia: W. B. Saunders,
1967.

Moleski, D., & Tosi, D.   Comparative psychotherapy: Rational-emotive
therapy vs. systematic desensitization in the treatment of stuttering.
Journal of Consulting and Clinical Psychology, 1976, *44*, 309–311.

Neisworth, J., & Moore, F.   Operant treatment of asthmatic responding
with the parent as therapist. *Behavior Therapy*, 1972, *3*, 95–99.

Paul, G.   Outcome of systematic desensitization II. In Franks, C. M. (Ed.),
Behavior therapy: Appraisal and status. New York: McGraw-Hill,
1969.

Plaut, T.   *Alcohol problems: A report to the nation.* Cooperative Commission on the Study of Alcoholism. New York: University Press, 1967.

Rachman, S., Hodgson, R., & Marks, I.   The treatment of chronic obsessive-
compulsive neurosis behavior. *Research and Therapy*, 1971, *9*, 237–
247.

Reardon, J., Tosi, D., & Gwynne, P. H.   The treatment of depression through
rational stage directed hypnotherapy: A case study. *Psychotherapy: Theory, Research and Practice*, 1977, *14*, 95–103.

Retterstol, N.   *Prognosis in paranoid psychoses.* Springfield, Ill.: Charles C Thomas, 1971.

Rosen, J.   *Direct analysis: Selected papers.* New York: Grune & Stratton, 1953.

Rosenbaum, C., & Beebe, J.   *Psychiatric treatment: Crisis/clinic/consultation.* New York: McGraw-Hill, 1975.

Sargent, J., Walters, E., & Green, E.   Psychosomatic self regulation of migraine and tension headaches. *Psychosomatic Medicine,* 1973, *35,* 129–135.

Satir, V.   *Conjoint family therapy.* Palo Alto, Calif.: Science and Behavior Books, 1964.

Searles, H.   *Collected papers on schizophrenia.* New York: International Universities Press, 1965.

Sergeant, H., & Yorkston, N.   Verbal desensitization in the treatment of bronchial asthma. *Lancet,* 1969, *2,* 1321.

Shapiro, D., Tursky, B., Gerson, E., & Stern, M.   Effect of feedback and reinforcement on the control of human systolic blood pressure. *Science,* 1969, *163,* 588–590.

Silverman, H. L.   *Marital therapy: Psychological, sociological and moral factors.* Springfield, Ill.: Charles C Thomas, 1972.

Sobell, M., & Sobell, L.   Individualized behavior therapy for alcoholics. *Behavior Therapy,* 1973, *4,* 49–72.

Stahmann, R., & Hiebert, W.   *Klemer's counseling in marital and sexual problems.* Baltimore: Williams & Wilkins, 1977.

Stedman, J.   An extension of the Kimmel treatment for enuresis to an adolescent: A case report. *Journal of Behavior Therapy and Experimental Psychiatry,* 1972, *3,* 307–309.

Steinman, A.   Cultural values, female role expectancies and therapeutic goals: Research and interpretation. In V. Franks & B. Vasanti (Eds.), *Women in therapy.* New York: Brunner/Mazel, 1974.

Stern, R.   Treatment of a case of obsessional neurosis using thought stopping techniques. *British Journal of Psychiatry,* 1970, *117,* 441–442.

Sundberg, N., & Tyler, L.   *Clinical psychology.* New York: Appleton-Century-Crofts, 1962.

Sussman, M., & Haug, M.   Rehabilitation counselor recruits. *Journal of Counseling Psychology,* 1968, *15,* 250–256.

Tosi, D.   *Youth: Toward personal growth.* Columbus, Ohio: Charles E. Merrill, 1974.

Tosi, D., & Moleski, R.   Rational emotive crisis intervention therapy. *Rational Living,* 1975, *10,* 32–38.

Tosi, D., Upshaw, K., Lande, A., & Waldron, M.   Group counseling with nonverbalizing elementary students: The differential effects of Premack and social reinforcement techniques. *Journal of Counseling Psychology,* 1971, *18,* 437–440.

Tosi, D., & Eshbaugh, D.   A cognitive experiential approach to the interpersonal and intrapersonal development of counselors and therapists. *Journal of Clinical Psychology,* 1978, *34,* 494–500.

Vandervoort, H., & Blank, J.   A sex counseling program in a university medical center. *The Counseling Psychologist*, 1975, 5(1), 64–67.

Vogler, R., Lunde, S., & Martin D.   Electrical aversion conditioning with chronic alcoholics: Follow up and suggestions for research. *Journal of Consulting and Clinical Psychology*, 1971, 36, 450.

Wisocki, P.   Treatment of obsessive-compulsive behavior by covert sensitization and covert reinforcement: A case report. *Journal of Behavior Therapy and Experimental Psychology*, 1970, 1, 233–239.

Wolman, B. (Ed.).   *The therapist's handbook: Treatment methods of mental disorders*. New York: Van Nostrand Reinhold, 1976.

Wolpe, J., & Lazarus, A.   *Behavior therapy techniques: A guide to treatment of neurosis*. New York: Pergamon Press, 1966.

Yates, A.   *Theory and practice in behavior therapy*. New York: Wiley, 1975.

Zisken, J., & Zisken, M.   Co-marital sex agreements: An emerging issue in sexual counseling. *The Counseling Psychologist*, 1975, 5(1), 81–83.

Zuk, G.   *Family therapy: A triadic-based approach*. New York: Behavioral Publications, 1971.

Chapter 9

American Psychological Association.   *Ethical principles and the conduct of research with human subjects*. Washington, D.C.: APA, 1973.

American Psychological Association.   *Ethical standards of psychologists*. Washington, D.C.: APA, 1972.

American Psychological Association.   *National commission on education and credentialing in psychology*. Washington, D.C.: APA, 1978.

American Psychological Association.   *Standards for professional services*. Washington, D.C.: APA, 1977.

Bergin, A. E.   *The evaluation of therapeutic outcomes*. In A. E. Bergin & S. L. Garfield (Eds.), *Handbook of psychotherapy and behavior change*. New York: Wiley, 1971.

Carkhuff, R. R.   *The art of helping: An introduction to life skills*. Amherst, Mass.: Human Resources Development Press, 1973.

Carkhuff, R. R., & Berenson, B. G.   *Beyond counseling and therapy* (2nd ed.). New York: Holt, Rinehart & Winston, 1977.

Division 17 of the American Psychological Association.   *Principles for counseling/therapy with women*. Adopted at Toronto, Canada, 1978.

Emrick, C. D.   A review of psychologically oriented treatment in alcoholism. *Journal of Studies of Alcohol*, 1975, 36, 88–108.

Eysenck, H. J.   The effects of psychotherapy. In H. J. Eysenck (Ed.), *Handbook of abnormal psychology*. New York: Basic Books, 1961.

Eysenck, H. J.   The effects of psychotherapy. *Journal of psychology*, 1965, 1, 97–118.

Eysenck, H. J.   *The effects of psychotherapy*. New York: International Science Press, 1966.

Eysenck, H. J.   The effects of psychotherapy: An evaluation. *Journal of Consulting Psychology*, 1952, *16*, 319–324.

Harmon, L. W., Birk, J. M., Fitzgerald, L. F., & Tanney, M. F.   *Counseling women.* Monterey, Calif.: Brooks/Cole, 1978.

Harway, M., & Astin, H. S.   *Sex discrimination in career counseling and education.* New York: Praeger, 1977.

Heller, K.   Laboratory interview research as an analogue to treatment. In A. E. Bergin & S. L. Garfield (Eds.), *Handbook of psychotherapy and behavior change.* New York: Wiley, 1971.

Ivey, A. E.   Cultural expertise: Toward systematic outcome criteria in counseling and psychological education. *Personnel and Guidance Journal,* 1977, *55,* 296–301.

Kiesler, D. J.   Experiential designs in psychotherapy research. In A. E. Bergin & S. L. Garfield (Eds.), *Handbook of psychotherapy and behavior change.* New York: Wiley, 1971.

Kiesler, D. J.   A grid model for theory and research in the psychotherapies. In L. D. Eron (Ed.), *The relationship of theory and technique in psychotherapy.* Chicago: Aldine Press, 1968.

Kiesler, D. J.   Some myths of psychotherapy research and the search for a paradigm. *Psychological Bulletin,* 1966, *65,* 110–136.

Lazarus, A. A.   *Multimodal behavior therapy.* New York: Springer Publishing Co., 1976.

Lazarus, A. A., & Wilson, G. T.   Behavior modification: Clinical and experimental perspectives. In B. B. Wolman (Ed.), *The therapist's handbook.* New York: Van Nostrand Reinhold, 1976.

Luborsky, L., Singer, B., & Luborsky, L.   Comparative studies of psychotherapies. *Archives of General Psychiatry,* 1975, *32,* 995–1008.

Mischel, W.   On the future of personality measurement. *American Psychologist,* 1977, *32,* 246–255.

Mosher, R. L., & Sprinthall, N. A.   Psychological education: A means to promote personal development during adolescence. *The Counseling Psychologist,* 1971, *2*(4), 3–85.

Osipow, S. H. (Ed.).   *Emerging woman: Career analysis and outlooks.* Columbus, Ohio: Charles E. Merrill, 1975.

Osipow, S. H.   Occupational mental health: A new role for counseling psychologists. *The Counseling Psychologist,* 1979, *8*(1), 65–70.

Osipow, S. H.   Some ethical dilemmas involved in behavioral and client centered insight counseling. In S. H. Osipow & W. B. Walsh (Eds.), *Behavior change in counseling: Readings and cases.* Englewood Cliffs, N.J.: Prentice-Hall, 1970.

Paul, G. L.   *Effects of insight, desensitization, and attention placebo treatment on anxiety.* Stanford, Calif.: Stanford University Press, 1966.

Paul, G. L.   Insight versus desensitization in psychotherapy. Two years after termination. *Journal of Consulting Psychology,* 1967, *31,* 333–348.

Pederson, P. B.   Triad model of cross cultural counselor training. *Personnel and Guidance Journal,* 1977, *56,* 94–100.

Rogers, C. R., Gendlin, E. T., Kiesler, D. J., & Truax, C. B. *The therapeutic relationship and its impact: A study of psychotherapy with schizophrenics.* Madison: University of Wisconsin Press, 1967.

Smith, M. C., & Glass, G. V. Meta-analysis of psychotherapy outcome studies. *American Psychologist,* 1977, *32,* 752–761.

Strupp, H. H., & Hadley, W. S. A tripartite model of mental health and therapeutic outcome. *American Psychologist,* 1977, *32,* 187–197.

Sue, D. W. Asian-Americans: Social psychological forces affecting lifestyles. In S. Picou & R. Campbell (Eds.), *Career behavior of special groups.* Columbus, Ohio: Charles E. Merrill, 1975.

Sue, D. W. Eliminating cultural oppression in counseling: Toward a general therapy. *Journal of Counseling Psychology,* 1978, *25,* 419–428.

Sue, D. W., & Sue, D. Barriers to effective cross cultural counseling. *Journal of Counseling Psychology,* 1977, *24,* 420–429.

Sue, S. Psychological theory and implications for Asian-Americans. *Personnel and Guidance Journal,* 1977, *55,* 381–390.

Truax, C. B., & Carkhuff, R. R. *Toward effective counseling and psychotherapy: Training and practice.* Chicago: Aldine, 1967.

Truax, C. B., & Mitchell, K. M. Research on certain therapist interpersonal skills in relation to process and outcome. In A. E. Bergin & S. L. Garfield (Eds.), *Handbook of psychotherapy and behavior change.* New York: Wiley, 1971.

Ullmann, L., & Krasner, L. (Eds.). *Case studies in behavior modification.* New York: Holt, Rinehart & Winston, 1965.

Wolpe, J. *The practice of behavior therapy* (2nd ed.). Elmsford, N.Y.: Pergamon Press, 1973.

Wolpe, J. *Theme and variations: A behavior therapy case book.* Elmsford, N.Y.: Pergamon Press, 1973.

Name index

Subject index

255

This book has been set linotype in 10 and 9
point Sabon Antiqua, leaded 2 points. Chapter
numbers are 54 point Korinna Bold and chapter
titles are 18 point Korinna Bold. The size of the
type page is 26 x 45 picas.